KB073367

Because of Winn-Dixie

Kate DiCamillo

BECAUSE OF WINN-DIXIE
Winn-Dixie® is a Federally Registered trademark and service mark owned by
The Winn-Dixie Stores, Inc. This work has not been prepared, manufactured,
approved or licensed by The Winn-Dixie Stores, Inc. Neither the author of this
work nor its publishers are in any way affiliated with The Winn-Dixie Stores, Inc.

ISBN 979-11-91343-97-7 14740

Longtail Books

for Tracey and Beck

because they listened first

Chapter One

My name is India Opal Buloni, and last summer my daddy, the **preacher**, sent me to the store for a box of macaroni-and-cheese,* some white rice and two tomatoes, and I came back with a dog. This is what happened: I walked into the **produce** section* of the Winn-Dixie **grocery store** to **pick out** my two tomatoes and I almost **bump**ed right **into** the store manager. He was standing there all **red-faced**, screaming and **waving** his arms around.

"Who let a dog in here?" he **kept on** shouting. "Who let a dirty dog in here?"

At first, I didn't see a dog. There were just a lot of **vegetable**s rolling around on the floor, tomatoes and

---

★ macaroni-and-cheese 마카로니 치즈. 치즈 소스에 마카로니를 넣은 요리.
⁑ produce section (= produce department) 농산물(produce)을 진열한 코너, 구역(section).

onions and **green peppers**. And there was what seemed like a whole **army** of Winn-Dixie **employees** running around waving their arms just the same way the store manager was waving his.

And then the dog came running around the corner. He was a big dog. And ugly. And he looked like he was having a real good time. His **tongue** was **hang**ing out and he was **wag**ging his **tail**. He **skid**ded to a stop and smiled right at me. I had never before in my life seen a dog smile, but that is what he did. He **pulled back** his lips and showed me all his teeth. Then he wagged his tail so hard that he **knock**ed some oranges **off** a display and they went rolling everywhere, mixing in with the tomatoes and onions and green peppers.

The manager screamed, "Somebody **grab** that dog!"

The dog went running over to the manager, wagging his tail and smiling. He stood up on his **hind** legs. You could tell that all he wanted to do was get **face to face** with the manager and thank him for the good time he was having in the produce department, but somehow he **end**ed **up knock**ing the manager **over**. And the manager must have been having a bad day because, **lying** there on the floor, right in front of everybody, he started to cry. The dog **lean**ed over him, real **concern**ed, and **lick**ed his face.

"Please," said the manager, "somebody call the **pound**."

"Wait a minute!" I **hollere**d. "That's my dog. Don't call the pound."

All the Winn-Dixie employees **turned around** and looked at me, and I knew I had done something big. And maybe stupid, too. But I **couldn't help** it. I couldn't let that dog go to the pound.

"Here, boy," I said.

The dog stopped licking the manager's face and put his ears up in the air and looked at me, like he was trying to remember where he knew me from.

"Here, boy," I said again. And then I **figure**d that the dog was probably just like everybody else in the world, that he would want to get called by a name, only I didn't know what his name was, so I just said the first thing that came into my head. I said, "Here, Winn-Dixie."

And that dog came **trot**ting over to me just like he had been doing it his whole life.

The manager **sat up** and gave me a **hard stare**, like maybe I was **making fun of** him.

"It's his name," I said. "**Honest**."

The manager said, "Don't you know not to bring a dog into a grocery store?"

"Yes sir," I told him. "He got in by mistake. I'm sorry. It won't happen again."

"Come on, Winn-Dixie," I said to the dog.

I started walking and he followed along behind me as I went out of the produce department and down the **cereal aisle** and past all the **cashiers** and out the door.

Once we were safe outside, I checked him over real careful and he didn't look that good. He was big, but **skinny**; you could see his **ribs**. And there were **bald patches** all over him, places where he didn't have any **fur** at all. Mostly, he looked like a big piece of old brown carpet that had been left out in the rain.

"You're a **mess**," I told him. "I **bet** you don't **belong** to anybody."

He smiled at me. He did that thing again, where he pulled back his lips and showed me his teeth. He smiled so big that it made him **sneeze**. It was like he was saying, "I know I'm a mess. Isn't it funny?"

It's hard not to **immediately** fall in love with a dog who has a good sense of **humor**.

"Come on," I told him. "Let's see what the preacher has to say about you."

And the two of us, me and Winn-Dixie, started walking home.

Chapter Two

That summer I found Winn-Dixie was also the summer me and the **preacher** moved to Naomi, Florida, so he could be the new preacher at the Open Arms Baptist Church★ of Naomi. My daddy is a good preacher and a nice man, but sometimes it's hard for me to think about him as my daddy because he spends so much time **preach**ing or thinking about preaching or getting ready to preach. And so, in my mind, I think of him as "the preacher". Before I was born he was a **missionary** in India and that is how I got my first name. But he calls me by my second name, Opal, because that was his mother's name. And he loved her a lot.

★ Baptist Church 침례교회.

Anyway, while me and Winn-Dixie walked home, I told him how I got my name and I told him how I had just moved to Naomi. I also told him about the preacher and how he was a good man, even if he was too **distract**ed with **sermon**s and **prayer**s and **suffer**ing people to go **grocery** shopping.

"But you know what?" I told Winn-Dixie, "you are a suffering dog, so maybe he will take to you right away. Maybe he'll let me keep you."

Winn-Dixie looked up at me and **wagg**ed his **tail**. He was kind of **limp**ing like something was wrong with one of his legs. And I have to **admit**, he **stunk**. Bad. He was an ugly dog, but already I loved him with all my heart.

When we got to the Friendly Corners **Trailer** Park,* I told Winn-Dixie that he had to **behave** right and be quiet, because this was an all adult trailer park and the only reason I got to live in it was because the preacher was a preacher and I was a good, quiet kid. I was what the Friendly Corners Trailer Park manager, Mr. Alfred, called "an **exception**". And I told Winn-Dixie he had to act like an exception, too; **specific**ally, I told him not to **pick** any **fight**s with Mr. Alfred's cats or Mrs. Detweller's little **yappy** Yorkie* dog,

---

★ trailer park 자동차 뒤에 달아 끌고 다니는 이동 주택(trailer)이 모인 주차장·캠프장(park).
✴ Yorkie (=Yorkshire terrier) [동물] 요크셔테리어. 영국 요크셔 지방이 원산인 작은 품종의 애완용 개.

Samuel. Winn-Dixie looked up at me while I was telling him everything, and I **swear** he understood.

"Sit," I told him when we got to my trailer. He sat right down. He had good **manners**. "Stay here," I told him. "I'll be right back."

The preacher was sitting in the living room, working at the little **foldout** table. He had papers **spread** all around him and he was **rub**bing his nose, which always meant he was thinking. Hard.

"Daddy?" I said.

"Hmmm," he said back.

"Daddy, do you know how you always tell me that we should help those less **fortunate** than ourselves?"

"Mmmmmm-hmmm," he said. He rubbed his nose and looked around at his papers.

"Well," I said, "I found a Less Fortunate at the **grocery store**."

"Is that right?" he said.

"Yes sir," I told him. I **stared** at the preacher really hard. Sometimes he **remind**ed me of a **turtle** hiding inside its **shell**, in there thinking about things and not ever **stick**ing his head out into the world. "Daddy, I was **wonder**ing. Could this Less Fortunate, could he stay with us for a while?"

Finally the preacher looked up at me. "Opal," he said,

"what are you talking about?"

"I found a dog," I told him. "And I want to keep him."

"No dogs," the preacher said. "We've talked about this before. You don't need a dog."

"I know it," I said. "I know I don't need a dog. But this dog needs me. Look," I said. I went to the trailer door and I hollered, "Winn-Dixie!" Winn-Dixie's ears shot up in the air and he grinned and sneezed, and then he came limping up the steps and into the trailer and put his head right in the preacher's lap, right on top of a pile of papers.

The preacher looked at Winn-Dixie. He looked at his ribs and his matted-up fur and the places where he was bald. The preacher's nose wrinkled up. Like I said, the dog smelled pretty bad.

Winn-Dixie looked up at the preacher. He pulled back his lips and showed the preacher all of his crooked yellow teeth and wagged his tail and knocked some of the preacher's papers off the table. Then he sneezed and some more papers fluttered to the floor.

"What did you call this dog?" the preacher asked.

"Winn-Dixie," I whispered. I was afraid to say anything too loud. I could see that Winn-Dixie was having a good effect on the preacher. He was making him poke his head out of his shell.

"Well," said the preacher, "he's a stray if ever I've seen

one." He put down his pencil and scratched Winn-Dixie behind the ears. "And a Less Fortunate, too. That's for sure. Are you looking for a home?" the preacher asked, real soft, to Winn-Dixie.

Winn-Dixie wagged his tail.

"Well," the preacher said, "I guess you've found one."

Chapter Three

I started in on Winn-Dixie right away, trying to clean him up. First I gave him a bath. I used the garden hose and some baby shampoo. He stood still for it, but I could tell he didn't like it. He looked insulted and the whole time he didn't show me his teeth or wag his tail once. After he was all washed and dried, I brushed him good. I used my own hairbrush and worked real hard at all the knots and patches of fur stuck together. He didn't mind being brushed. He wiggled his back, like it felt pretty good.

The whole time I was working on him, I was talking to him. And he listened. I told him how we were alike. "See," I said, "you don't have any family and neither do I. I've got the preacher, of course. But I don't have a mama. I mean, I have one, but I don't know where she is. She left when I was three years old. I can't **hardly** remember her. And I **bet** you don't remember your mama much either. So we're almost like **orphans**."

Winn-Dixie looked straight at me when I said that to him, like he was feeling **relieved** to finally have somebody understand his **situation**. I **nod**ded my head at him and **went on** talking.

"I don't even have any friends, because I had to leave them all behind when we moved here from Watley. Watley's up in north Florida. Have you ever been to north Florida?"

Winn-Dixie looked down at the ground, like he was trying to remember if he had.

"You know what?" I said. "Ever since we moved here, I've been thinking about my mama **extra**-extra hard, more than I ever did when I was in Watley."

Winn-Dixie **twitch**ed his ears and raised his **eyebrows**.

"I think the preacher thinks about my mama all the time, too. He's still in love with her; I know that because I heard the ladies at the church in Watley talking about him. They said he's still hoping she'll come back. But he doesn't tell me that. He won't talk to me about her at all. I want to know more about her. But I'm afraid to ask the preacher; I'm afraid he'll get mad at me."

Winn-Dixie looked at me hard, like he was trying to say something.

"What?" I said.

He stared at me.

"You think I should make the preacher tell me about her?"

Winn-Dixie looked at me so hard he sneezed.

"I'll think about it," I said.

When I was done working on him, Winn-Dixie looked a whole lot better. He still had his bald spots, but the fur that he did have had cleaned up nice. It was all shiny and soft. You could still see his ribs, but I intended to feed him good and that would take care of that. I couldn't do anything about his crooked yellow teeth because he got into a sneezing fit every time I started brushing them with my toothbrush, and I finally had to give up. But for the most part he looked a whole lot better, and so I took him into the trailer and showed him to the preacher.

"Daddy," I said.

"Hmmm," he said. He was working on a sermon and kind of muttering to himself.

"Daddy, I wanted to show you the new Winn-Dixie."

The preacher put down his pencil and rubbed his nose, and finally he looked up.

"Well," he said, smiling real big at Winn-Dixie, "well, now. Don't you look handsome."

Winn-Dixie smiled back at the preacher. He went over

and put his head in the preacher's **lap**.

"He smells nice, too," said the preacher. He rubbed Winn-Dixie's head and looked into his eyes.

"Daddy," I said, real quick before I **lost** all **my nerve**, "I've been talking to Winn-Dixie."

"Is that right?" the preacher said; he scratched Winn-Dixie's head.

"I've been talking to him and he agreed with me that, since I'm ten years old, you should tell me ten things about my mama. Just ten things, that's all."

The preacher stopped rubbing Winn-Dixie's head and held real **still**. I could see him thinking about pulling his head back into his **shell**.

"One thing for each year I've been alive," I told him. "Please."

Winn-Dixie looked up at the preacher and kind of gave him a **nudge** with his nose.

The preacher **sigh**ed. He said to Winn-Dixie, "I should have guessed you were going to be trouble." Then he looked at me. "Come on, Opal," he said. "Sit down. And I will tell you ten things about your mama."

Chapter Four

"One," said the **preacher**. We were sitting on the **couch** and Winn-Dixie was sitting between us. Winn-Dixie had already decided that he liked the couch a lot. "One," said the preacher again. Winn-Dixie looked at him kind of hard. "Your mama was funny. She could make just about anybody laugh.

"Two," he said. "She had red hair and **freckles**."

"Just like me," I said.

"Just like you." The preacher **nod**ded.

"Three. She liked to plant things. She had a **talent** for it. She could stick a tire in the ground and grow a car."

Winn-Dixie started **chew**ing on his **paw**, and I **tap**ped him on the head to make him stop.

"Four," said the preacher. "She could run fast. If you

were racing her, you couldn't ever let her **get a head start**, because she would **beat** you for sure."

"I'm that way, too," I said. "Back home, in Watley, I raced Liam Fullerton, and beat him, and he said it wasn't fair, because boys and girls shouldn't race each other to begin with. I told him he was just a **sore loser**."

The preacher nodded. He was quiet for a minute.

"I'm ready for number five," I told him.

"Five," he said. "She couldn't cook. She burned everything, including water. She had a hard time opening a can of beans. She **couldn't make head nor tail of** a piece of meat. Six." The preacher rubbed his nose and looked up at the **ceiling**. Winn-Dixie looked up, too. "Number six is that your mama loved a story. She would sit and listen to stories all day long. She loved to be told a story. She **especially** liked funny ones, stories that made her laugh." The preacher nodded his head like he was agreeing with himself.

"What's number seven?" I asked.

"Let's see," he said. "She knew all the **constellation**s, every **planet** in the nighttime sky. Every last one of them. She could **name** them. And **point** them **out**. And she never **got tired of** looking up at them.

"Number eight," said the preacher, with his eyes closed, "was that she hated being a preacher's wife. She said she just couldn't **stand** having the ladies at church **judge** what she was wearing and what she was cooking and how she was singing. She said it made her feel like a bug under a **microscope**."

Winn-Dixie **lay** down on the couch. He put his nose in the preacher's lap and his tail in mine.

"Ten," said the preacher.

"Nine," I told him.

"Nine," said the preacher. "She drank. She drank beer. And whiskey. And wine. Sometimes she couldn't stop drinking. And that made me and your mama fight quite a bit. Number ten," he said with a long **sigh**, "number ten is that your mama loved you. She loved you very much."

"But she left me," I told him.

"She left us," said the preacher softly. I could see him pulling his old **turtle** head back into his stupid turtle shell. "She packed her bags and left us, and she didn't leave one thing behind."

"Okay," I said. I got up off the couch. Winn-Dixie **hop**ped off, too. "Thank you for telling me," I said.

I went right back to my room and wrote down all ten things that the preacher had told me. I wrote them down just the way he said them to me so that I wouldn't forget them, and then I read them out loud to Winn-Dixie until I had them **memorized**. I wanted to know those ten things

inside and out. That way, if my mama ever came back, I could **recognize** her, and I would be able to **grab** her and **hold on to** her **tight** and not let her **get away** from me again.

Chapter Five

Winn-Dixie couldn't **stand** to be left alone; we found that out real quick. If me and the preacher **went off** and left him **by himself** in the trailer, he **pull**ed all the cushions **off** the **couch** and all the toilet paper* off the roll. So we started **tying** him **up** outside with a rope when we left. That didn't work either. Winn-Dixie **howl**ed until Samuel, Mrs. Detweller's dog, started howling, too. It was exactly the kind of noise that people in an all adult trailer park do not like to hear.

"He just doesn't want to be left alone," I told the preacher. "That's all. Let's take him with us." I could understand the way Winn-Dixie felt. Getting left behind

---

★ toilet paper 화장실(toilet)용 휴지(paper).

probably made his heart feel **empty**.

After a while the preacher **gave in**. And everywhere we went, we took Winn-Dixie. Even to church.

The Open Arms Baptist Church of Naomi isn't a regular-looking church. The building **used to** be a Pick-It-Quick store, and when you walk in the front door, the first thing you see is the Pick-It-Quick **motto**. It's written on the floor in little **tiny** red tiles that make great big letters that say "PICK PICK PICK QUICK QUICK QUICK". The preacher tried painting over those tiles but the letters won't stay **cover**ed **up**, and so the preacher has just **given up** and let them be.

The other thing about the Open Arms that is different from other churches is there aren't any **pews**. People bring in their own **foldup** chairs and **lawn** chairs,* and so sometimes it looks more like the **congregation** is watching a parade or sitting at a barbecue instead of being at church. It's kind of a strange church and I thought Winn-Dixie would **fit** right **in**.

But the first time we brought Winn-Dixie to the Open Arms, the preacher tied him outside the front door.

"Why did we bring him **all the way** here just to tie him up?" I asked the preacher.

★ lawn chair 잔디밭(lawn) 등 야외에서 쓰는 접이식 의자(chair).

"Because dogs don't **belong** in church, Opal," the preacher said. "That's why."

He tied Winn-Dixie to a tree and said how there was lots of **shade** for him and that it ought to work out real good.

Well, it didn't. The **service** started and there was some singing and some sharing and some **pray**ing, and then the preacher started **preach**ing. And he wasn't but two or three words into his **sermon** when there was a **terrible** howl outside.

The preacher tried to **ignore** it.

"Today," he said.

"*Aaaaaarrooo,*" said Winn-Dixie.

"Please," said the preacher.

"*Arrrrooooowwww,*" said Winn-Dixie back.

"Friends," said the preacher.

"*Arrruiiiipppp,*" **wail**ed Winn-Dixie.

Everyone turned in their lawn chairs and foldup chairs and looked at **one another**.

"Opal," said the preacher.

"*Owwwwww,*" said Winn-Dixie.

"Yes sir?" I said.

"Go get that dog!" he **yell**ed.

"Yes sir!" I yelled back.

I went outside and **untie**d Winn-Dixie and brought

24

him inside, and he sat down beside me and smiled up at the preacher, and the preacher **couldn't help** it; he smiled back. Winn-Dixie had that **effect** on him.

And so the preacher **start**ed **in** preaching again. Winn-Dixie sat there listening to it, **wiggling** his ears this way and that, trying to catch all the words. And everything would have been all right, **except** that a mouse ran across the floor.

The Open Arms had mice. They were there from when it was a Pick-It-Quick and there were lots of good things to eat in the building, and when the Pick-It-Quick became the Open Arms Baptist Church of Naomi, the mice stayed around to eat all the **leftover crumb**s from the potluck★ **supper**s. The preacher **kept on** saying he was going to have to do something about them, but he never did. Because the truth is, he couldn't stand the thought of hurting anything, even a mouse.

Well, Winn-Dixie saw that mouse, and he was **up** and after him. One minute everything was quiet and serious and the preacher was going on and **on and on**; the next minute Winn-Dixie looked like a **furry bullet** shooting across the building, **chasing** that mouse. He was **bark**ing and his feet were **skid**ding all over the **polish**ed Pick-It-Quick floor, and

★ potluck 주최자는 장소와 간단한 음식만 준비하고, 참석자들이 자신의 취향에 맞는 요리나 술을 가지고 오는 파티.

people were **clap**ping and **holler**ing and pointing. They really **went wild** when Winn-Dixie actually caught the mouse.

"I have never in my life seen a dog catch a mouse," said Mrs. Nordley. She was sitting next to me.

"He's a special dog," I told her.

"I **imagine** so," she said back.

Winn-Dixie stood up there in front of the whole church, **wag**ging his **tail** and holding the mouse real careful in his mouth, **hold**ing **on to** him **tight** but not **squish**ing him.

"I believe that mutt* has got some **retriever** in him," said somebody behind me. "That's a hunting dog."

Winn-Dixie took the mouse over to the preacher and dropped it at his feet. And when the mouse tried to **get away**, Winn-Dixie put his **paw** right on the mouse's tail. Then he smiled up at the preacher. He showed him all his teeth. The preacher looked down at the mouse. He looked at Winn-Dixie. He looked at me. He **rub**bed his nose. It got real quiet in the Pick-It-Quick.

"Let us pray," the preacher finally said, "for this mouse."

And everybody started laughing and clapping. The preacher **pick**ed **up** the mouse by the tail and walked and threw it out the front door of the Pick-It-Quick, and

---

★ mutt 잡종인 개를 뜻하는 비속어.

26

everybody **applaud**ed again.

Then he came back and we all prayed together. I prayed for my mama. I told God how much she would have enjoyed hearing the story of Winn-Dixie catching that mouse. It would have made her laugh. I asked God if maybe I could be the one to tell her that story some day.

And then I talked to God about how I was lonely in Naomi because I didn't know that many kids, only the ones from church. And there weren't that many kids at the Open Arms, just Dunlap and Stevie Dewberry, two brothers who weren't twins but looked like they were. And Amanda Wilkinson, whose face was always **pinch**ed up like she was smelling something real bad; and Sweetie Pie Thomas, who was only five years old and still mostly a baby. And none of them wanted to be my friend anyway because they probably thought I'd **tell on** them to the preacher for every little thing they did wrong; and then they would get in trouble with God and their parents. So I told God that I was lonely, even having Winn-Dixie.

And finally I prayed for the mouse, like the preacher suggested. I prayed that he didn't get hurt when he went flying out the door of the Open Arms Baptist Church of Naomi. I prayed that he **land**ed on a nice soft **patch** of grass.

Chapter Six

I spent a lot of time that summer at the Herman W. Block **Memorial** Library. The Herman W. Block Memorial Library sounds like it would be a big **fancy** place, but it's not. It's just a little old house full of books, and Miss Franny Block is **in charge of** them all. She is a very small, very old woman with short gray hair, and she was the first friend I made in Naomi.

It all started with Winn-Dixie not liking it when I went into the library, because he couldn't go inside, too. But I showed him how he could stand up on his **hind** legs and look in the window and see me in there, **select**ing my books; and he was okay, as long as he could see me. But the thing was, the first time Miss Franny Block saw Winn-Dixie standing up on his hind legs like that, looking in the window, she didn't think he was a dog. She thought he was a bear.

This is what happened: I was **pick**ing **out** my books and kind of **hum**ming to myself, and all of a sudden there was this loud and **scary** scream. I went running up to the front of the library, and there was Miss Franny Block, sitting on the floor behind her desk.

"Miss Franny?" I said. "Are you all right?"

"A bear," she said.

"A bear?" I asked.

"He has come back," she said.

"He has?" I asked. "Where is he?"

"Out there," she said and raised a finger and pointed at Winn-Dixie standing up on his hind legs, looking through the window for me.

"Miss Franny Block," I said, "that's not a bear. That's a dog. That's my dog. Winn-Dixie."

"Are you **positive**?" she asked.

"Yes ma'am," I told her. "I'm positive. He's my dog. I would know him anywhere."

Miss Franny sat there **trembling** and shaking.

"Come on," I said. "Let me help you up. It's okay." I **stuck** out my hand and Miss Franny took hold of it, and I **pull**ed her **up** off the floor. She didn't **weigh hardly** anything at all. Once she was standing on her feet, she started acting all **embarrass**ed, saying how I must think she was a **silly** old lady, mistaking a dog for a bear, but that she had a bad experience with a bear coming into the Herman W. Block Memorial Library a long time ago and she never had quite **gotten over** it.

"When did that happen?" I asked her.

"Well," said Miss Franny, "it is a very long story."

"That's okay," I told her. "I am like my mama in that I like to be told stories. But before you start telling it, can Winn-Dixie come in and listen, too? He gets lonely without me."

"Well, I don't know," said Miss Franny. "Dogs are not **allow**ed in the Herman W. Block Memorial Library."

"He'll be good," I told her. "He's a dog who goes to church." And before she could say yes or no, I went outside and got Winn-Dixie, and he came in and lay down with a "*huummmppff*" and a sigh, right at Miss Franny's feet.

She looked down at him and said, "He most certainly is a large dog."

"Yes ma'am," I told her. "He has a large heart, too."

"Well," Miss Franny said. She **bent** over and gave Winn-Dixie a **pat** on the head, and Winn-Dixie wagged his tail **back and forth** and **snuffle**d his nose on her little old-lady feet. "Let me get a chair and sit down so I can tell this story properly."

Chapter Seven

"Back when Florida was wild, when it **consist**ed of nothing but palmetto trees* and **mosquito**es so big they could fly away with you," Miss Franny Block **start**ed **in**, "and I was just a little girl no bigger than you, my father, Herman W. Block, told me that I could have anything I wanted for my birthday. Anything at all."

Miss Franny looked around the library. She **lean**ed in close to me. "I don't want to appear **pride**ful," she said, "but my daddy was a very rich man. A very rich man." She **nod**ded and leaned back and said, "And I was a little girl who loved to read. So I told him, I said, 'Daddy, I would most certainly love to have a library for my birthday; a

---

★ palmetto tree [식물] 팔메토 야자나무. 종려나무 모양의 잎을 가진 나무.

small little library would be wonderful.' "

"You asked for a whole library?"

"A small one." Miss Franny nodded. "I wanted a little house full of nothing but books and I wanted to **share** them, too. And I got my wish. My father built me this house, the very one we are sitting in now. And at a very young age I became a **librarian**. Yes ma'am."

"What about the bear?" I said.

"Did I **mention** that Florida was wild in those days?" Miss Franny Block said.

"Uh-huh, you did."

"It was wild. There were wild men and wild women and wild animals."

"Like bears!"

"Yes ma'am. That's right. Now, I have to tell you, I was a little-miss-know-it-all. I was a miss-smarty-pants★ with my library full of books. Oh, yes ma'am, I thought I knew the answers to everything. Well, one hot Thursday I was sitting in my library with all the doors and windows open and my nose stuck in a book, when a **shadow** crossed the desk. And without looking up, yes ma'am, without even looking up, I said, 'Is there a book I can help you find?'

"Well, there was no answer. And I thought it might

★ smarty-pants 자부심이 강한 사람, 잘난 척 하는 사람.

32

have been a wild man or a wild woman, scared of all these books and afraid to speak up. But then I became **aware** of a very **peculiar** smell, a very strong smell. I raised my eyes slowly. And standing right in front of me was a bear. Yes ma'am. A very large bear."

"How big?" I asked.

"Oh, well," said Miss Franny, "perhaps three times the size of your dog."

"Then what happened?" I asked her.

"Well," said Miss Franny, "I looked at him and he looked at me. He put his big nose up in the air and **sniff**ed and sniffed as if he was trying to decide if a little-miss-know-it-all librarian was what he was **in the mood** to eat. And I sat there. And then I thought, well, if this bear **intend**s to eat me, I am not going to let it happen without a fight. No ma'am. So very slowly and very carefully I raised up the book I was reading."

"What book was that?" I asked.

"Why, it was *War and Peace*,★ a very large book. I raised it up slowly and then I **aim**ed it carefully and I threw it right at that bear and screamed, 'Be gone!' And do you know what?"

"No ma'am," I said.

★ War and Peace 톨스토이가 쓴 소설 『전쟁과 평화』. 세계 문학에서 가장 중요한 작품 중 하나로 손꼽힌다.

"He went. But this is what I will never forget. He took the book with him."

"Nuh-uh," I said.

"Yes ma'am," said Miss Franny. "He **snatch**ed it up and ran."

"Did he come back?" I asked.

"No, I never saw him again. Well, the men in town used to **tease** me about it. They **used to** say, 'Miss Franny, we saw that bear of yours out in the woods today. He was reading that book and he said it sure was good and would it be all right if he kept it for just another week.' Yes ma'am. They did tease me about it." She **sigh**ed. "I **imagine** I'm the only one left from those days. I imagine I'm the only one who even **recalls** that bear. All my friends, everyone I knew when I was young, they are all dead and gone."

She sighed again. She looked sad and old and **wrinkle**d. It was the same way I felt sometimes, being **friendless** in a new town and not having a mama to **comfort** me. I sighed, too.

Winn-Dixie raised his head off his **paw**s and looked **back and forth** between me and Miss Franny. He **sat up** then and showed Miss Franny his teeth.

"Well now, look at that," she said. "That dog is smiling at me."

"It's a **talent** of his," I told her.

"It is a fine talent," Miss Franny said. "A very fine talent." And she smiled back at Winn-Dixie.

"We could be friends," I said to Miss Franny. "I mean, you and me and Winn-Dixie, we could all be friends."

Miss Franny smiled even bigger. "Why, that would be **grand**," she said, "just grand."

And right at that minute, right when the three of us had decided to be friends, who should come **march**ing into the Herman W. Block **Memorial** Library but old **pinch**-faced Amanda Wilkinson. She walked right up to Miss Franny's desk and said, "I finished *Johnny Tremain*★ and I enjoyed it very much. I would like something even more difficult to read now, because I am an **advanced** reader."

"Yes dear, I know," said Miss Franny. She got up out of her chair.

Amanda **pretend**ed like I wasn't there. She **stared** right past me. "Are dogs **allow**ed in the library?" she asked Miss Franny as they walked away.

"Certain ones," said Miss Franny, "a **select** few." And then she **turn**ed **around** and winked at me. I smiled back. I had just made my first friend in Naomi, and nobody was going to **mess** that **up** for me, not even old pinch-faced Amanda Wilkinson.

★ Johnny Tremain 에스더 포브스가 쓴 아동 소설. 1944년 뉴베리 메달을 수상했다.

Chapter Eight

Winn-Dixie's **bald spot**s started growing **fur**, and the fur that he had to begin with started looking **shiny** and healthy; and he didn't **limp** any more. And you could tell that he was proud of looking so good, proud of not looking like a **stray**. I thought what he needed most was a **collar** and a **leash**, so I went into Gertrude's Pets, where there were fish and snakes and mice and **lizard**s and gerbils★ and pet **supplies**, and I found a real handsome red **leather** collar with a matching leash.

Winn-Dixie was not **allow**ed to come inside the store (there was a big sign on the door that said NO DOGS ALLOWED), so I held the collar and the leash up to the

★ gerbil 애완용으로 기르는 게르빌루스쥐.

window. And Winn-Dixie, who was standing on the other side of the window, **pull**ed **up** his lip and showed me his teeth and **sneezed** and **wagg**ed his **tail** something **furious**; so I knew he **absolute**ly loved that leash and collar **combination**. But it was very **expensive**.

I decided to **explain** my **situation** to the man behind the counter. I said, "I don't get a big enough **allowance** to **afford** something this **fancy**. But I love this collar and leash, and so does my dog, and I was thinking that maybe you could **set** me **up** on an **installment** plan."

"Installment plan?" said the man.

"Gertrude!" somebody screamed in a real **irritating** voice.

I looked around. It was a **parrot**. She was sitting on top of one of the **fish tank**s, looking right at me.

"An installment plan," I said, **ignoring** the parrot, "you know, where I **promise** to give you my allowance every week and you give me the leash and the collar now."

"I don't think I can do that," said the man. He shook his head. "No, the **owner**, she wouldn't like that." He looked down at the counter. He wouldn't look at me. He had thick black hair, and it was **slick**ed **back** like Elvis Presley's.* He had on a name tag that said OTIS.

★ **Elvis Presley** 엘비스 프레슬리. 미국의 가수 겸 영화배우로 '로큰롤의 제왕'이라 불리며 전세계적인 명성을 날렸다.

"Or I could work for you," I said. "I could come in and **sweep** the floors and **dust** the **shelves** and **take out** the trash. I could do that."

I looked around Gertrude's Pets. There was sand and sunflower seed **shell**s and big dust bunnies* all over the floor. I could tell that it needed to be swept.

"Uh," said Otis. He looked down at the counter some more.

"Gertrude!" the parrot screamed again.

"I'm real **trustworthy**," I said. "I'm new in town but my daddy is a **preacher**. He's the preacher at the Open Arms Baptist Church of Naomi, so I'm real **honest**. But the only thing is, Winn-Dixie, my dog, he would have to come inside with me, because if we get **separate**d for too long, he starts to **howl** something **terrible**."

"Gertrude doesn't like dogs," said Otis.

"Is she the owner?" I asked.

"Yes, I mean, no, I mean . . ." He finally looked up. He pointed at the fish tank. "*That* Gertrude. The parrot. I **name**d her after the owner."

"Gertrude's a pretty bird!" screamed Gertrude.

"She might like Winn-Dixie," I told Otis. "Almost everybody does. Maybe he could come inside and meet

---

★ **dust bunny** 먼지(dust)가 뭉쳐진 덩어리. 덩어리 진 모습이 마치 토끼(bunny) 같아서 생긴 단어이다. 'dust mouse'라고 부르기도 한다.

38

her, and if the two of them **get along**, then could I have the job?"

"Maybe," Otis **mumbl**ed. He looked down at the counter again.

So I went and opened the door, and Winn-Dixie came **trot**ting on inside the store.

"Dog!" screamed Gertrude.

"I know it," Otis told her.

And then Gertrude got real quiet. She sat on the top of the fish tank and **cock**ed her head from one side to the other, looking at Winn-Dixie. And Winn-Dixie stood and stared back at her. He didn't hardly move. He didn't wag his tail. He didn't smile. He didn't sneeze. He just stared at Gertrude and she stared at him. And then she **spread** her wings out real far and flew and **land**ed on top of Winn-Dixie's head.

"Dog," she **croak**ed.

Winn-Dixie wagged his tail just a little **tiny** bit.

And Otis said, "You can start on Monday."

"Thank you," I told him. "You won't be sorry."

On the way out of Gertrude's Pets, I said to Winn-Dixie, "You are better at making friends than anybody I have ever known. I bet if my mama knew you, she would think you were the best dog ever."

Winn-Dixie was smiling up at me and I was smiling

down at him, and so **neither** one of us was looking where we were going and we almost **bump**ed right **into** Sweetie Pie Thomas. She was standing there, **suck**ing on the **knuckle** of her third finger, staring in the window of Gertrude's Pets.

She took her finger out of her mouth and looked at me. Her eyes were all big and round. "Was that bird sitting on that dog's head?" she asked. She had her hair tied up in a **ponytail** with a pink ribbon. But it wasn't much of a ponytail, it was mostly ribbon and a few **strand**s of hair.

"Yes," I told her.

"I seen it," she said. She nodded her head and put her knuckle back in her mouth. Then she took it out again real quick. "I seen that dog in church, too. He was catching a mouse. I want a dog just like it, but my mama won't let me get no dog. She says if I'm real good, I might get to buy me a **goldfish** or one of them gerbils. That's what she says. Can I **pet** your dog?"

"Sure," I told her.

Sweetie Pie **strok**ed Winn-Dixie's head so long and serious that his eyes **droop**ed half closed and **drool** came out of the side of his mouth. "I'm going to be six years old in September. I got to stop sucking on my knuckle once I'm six," said Sweetie Pie. "I'm having a party. Do you want to come to my party? The **theme** is pink."

"Sure," I told her.

"Can this dog come?" she asked.

"You **bet**," I told her.

And all of a sudden I felt happy. I had a dog. I had a job. I had Miss Franny Block for a friend. And I had my first **invitation** to a party in Naomi. It didn't matter that it came from a five-year-old and the party wasn't until September. I didn't feel so lonely any more.

Chapter Nine

Just about everything that happened to me that summer happened because of Winn-Dixie. **For instance**, without him I would never have met Gloria Dump. He was the one who introduced us.

What happened was this: I was riding my bike home from Gertrude's Pets and Winn-Dixie was running along beside me. We went past Dunlap and Stevie Dewberry's house, and when Dunlap and Stevie saw me, they got on their bikes and started following me. They wouldn't ride with me; they just rode behind me and **whisper**ed things that I couldn't hear. **Neither** one of them had any hair on his head, because their mama **shaved** their heads every week during the summer because of the one time Dunlap got **flea**s in his hair from their cat, Sadie. And now they looked like two **identical** bald-headed babies, even though they weren't twins. Dunlap was ten years old, like me, and Stevie was nine and tall for his age.

"I can hear you," I **holler**ed back at them. "I can hear what you're saying." But I couldn't.

Winn-Dixie started to race way ahead of me.

"You better **watch out**," Dunlap hollered. "That dog is **head**ed right for the **witch**'s house."

"Winn-Dixie," I called. But he **kept on** going faster and **hop**ped over a gate and went into the most **overgrown** jungle of a yard that I had ever seen.

"You better go get your dog out of there," Dunlap said.

"The witch will eat that dog," Stevie said.

"Shut up," I told them.

I **got off** my bike and went up to the gate and hollered, "Winn-Dixie, you better come on out of there."

But he didn't.

"She's probably eating him right now," Stevie said. He and Dunlap were standing behind me. "She eats dogs all the time."

"Get lost,★ you bald-headed babies," I said.

"Hey," said Dunlap, "that ain't✳ a very nice way for a preacher's daughter to talk." He and Stevie **back**ed **off** a

---

★ get lost 썩 꺼져 버려!
✳ ain't 'am/are/is not'의 구어체.

little.

I stood there and thought for a minute. I finally decided that I was more afraid of losing Winn-Dixie than I was of having to **deal** with a dog-eating witch, so I went through the gate and into the yard.

"That witch is going to eat the dog for dinner and you for **dessert**," Stevie said.

"We'll tell the preacher what happened to you," Dunlap shouted after me.

By then, I was deep in the jungle. There was every kind of thing growing everywhere. There were flowers and **vegetable**s and trees and **vine**s.

"Winn-Dixie?" I said.

"Heh-heh-heh." I heard: "This dog sure likes to eat."

I went around a really big tree all covered in **moss**, and there was Winn-Dixie. He was eating something right out of the witch's hand. She looked up at me. "This dog sure likes peanut butter,★" she said. "You can always trust a dog that likes peanut butter."

She was old with **crinkly** brown skin. She had on a big **floppy** hat with flowers all over it, and she didn't have any teeth, but she didn't look like a witch. She looked nice. And Winn-Dixie liked her, I could tell.

★ peanut butter 땅콩 버터.

44

"I'm sorry he got in your garden," I said.

"You ain't got to be sorry," she said. "I enjoy a little **company.**"

"My name's Opal," I told her.

"My name's Gloria Dump," she said. "Ain't that a **terrible** last name? Dump?"

"My last name is Buloni," I said. "Sometimes the kids at school back home in Watley called me 'Lunch Meat'★."

"Hah!" Gloria Dump laughed. "What about this dog? What you call him?"

"Winn-Dixie," I said.

Winn-Dixie **thump**ed his tail on the ground. He tried smiling, but it was hard with his mouth all full of peanut butter.

"Winn-Dixie?" Gloria Dump said. "You mean like the **grocery store?**"

"Yes ma'am," I said.

"Whoooeee," she said. "That takes the strange name **prize**, don't it?"

"Yes ma'am," I said.

"I was just **fix**ing to make myself a peanut-butter sandwich," she said. "You want one, too?"

"All right," I said. "Yes, please."

★ Lunch Meat (= luncheon meat) 런천 미트. 다진 고기를 양념하여 뭉친 다음 통조림으로 만든 것으로, 우리가 흔히 말하는 스팸(Spam)은 런천 미트의 특정 상표명이다.

"**Go on** and sit down," she said, pointing at a **lawn** chair with the back all **bust**ed out of it. "But sit down careful."

I sat down careful and Gloria Dump made me a peanut butter sandwich on white bread.

Then she made one for herself and put her false teeth* in, to eat it; when she was done, she said to me, "You know, my eyes ain't too good at all. I can't see nothing but the **general shape** of things, so I got to **rely on** my heart. Why don't you go on and tell me everything about yourself, so as I can see you with my heart."

And because Winn-Dixie was looking up at her like she was the best thing he had ever seen, and because the peanut-butter sandwich had been so good, and because I had been waiting for a long time to tell some person everything about me, I did.

★ false teeth 틀니, 의치.

Chapter Ten

I told Gloria Dump everything. I told her how me and the **preacher** had just moved to Naomi and how I had to leave all my friends behind. I told her about my mama leaving, and I listed the ten things that I knew about her; I **explain**ed that here, in Naomi, I missed Mama more than I ever had in Watley. I told her about the preacher being like a **turtle**, hiding all the time inside his **shell**. I told her about finding Winn-Dixie in the **produce** department and how, because of him, I became friends with Miss Franny Block and got a job working for a man **named** Otis at Gertrude's Pets and got **invite**d to Sweetie Pie Thomas's birthday party. I even told Gloria Dump how Dunlap and Stevie Dewberry called her a **witch**. But I told her they were stupid, **mean**, bald-headed boys and I didn't believe them, not for long **anyhow**.

And the whole time I was talking, Gloria Dump was listening. She was **nod**ding her head and smiling and **frown**ing and saying, "Hmmm," and "Is that right?"

I could feel her listening with all her heart, and it felt good.

"You know what?" she said when I was all done.

"What?"

"Could be that you got more of your mama in you than just red hair and **freckle**s and running fast."

"Really?" I said. "Like what?"

"Like maybe you got her green **thumb**.★ The two of us could plant something and see how it grows; test your thumb out."

"OK," I said.

What Gloria Dump picked for me to grow was a tree. Or she said it was a tree. To me, it looked more like a plant. She had me **dig** a hole for it and put it in the ground and **pat** the **dirt** around it **tight**, like it was a baby and I was **tuck**ing it into bed.

"What kind of tree is it?" I asked Gloria Dump.

"It's a wait-and-see tree," she said.

"What's that mean?"

★ green thumb 식물을 잘 재배하는 재능.

"It means you got to wait for it to grow up before you know what it is."

"Can I come back and see it tomorrow?" I asked.

"Child," she said, "as long as this is my garden, you're welcome in it. But that tree ain't going to have changed much by tomorrow."

"But I want to see you, too," I said.

"Hmmmph," said Gloria Dump. "I ain't going nowhere. I be right here."

I woke Winn-Dixie up then. He had peanut butter in his **whiskers**, and he kept **yawn**ing and **stretch**ing. He **lick**ed Gloria Dump's hand before we left, and I thanked her.

That night when the preacher was tucking me into bed, I told him how I got a job at Gertrude's Pets, and I told him all about making friends with Miss Franny Block and getting invited to Sweetie Pie's party, and I told him about meeting Gloria Dump. Winn-Dixie **lay** on the floor, waiting for the preacher to leave so he could **hop** up on the bed like he always did. When I was done talking, the preacher kissed me good night, and then he **lean**ed way over and gave Winn-Dixie a kiss, too, right on top of his head.

"You can go ahead and get up there now," he said to Winn-Dixie.

Winn-Dixie looked at the preacher. He didn't smile at him, but he opened his mouth wide like he was laughing, like the preacher had just told him the funniest joke in the world, and this is what **amaze**d me the most: the preacher laughed back. Winn-Dixie hopped up on the bed, and the preacher got up and **turn**ed **out** the light. I leaned over and kissed Winn-Dixie, too, right on the nose, but he didn't **notice**. He was already **asleep** and **snoring**.

Chapter Eleven

That night there was a real bad **thunderstorm**. But what woke me up wasn't the **thunder** and **lightning**. It was Winn-Dixie, **whining** and **butt**ing his head against my bedroom door.

"Winn-Dixie," I said. "What are you doing?"

He didn't **pay** any **attention** to me. He just kept **beat**ing his head against the door and whining and **whimper**ing. When I got out of bed and went over and put my hand on his head, he was shaking and **trembling** so hard that it scared me. I **knelt** down and **wrap**ped my arms around him, but he didn't turn and look at me or smile or **sneeze** or **wag** his **tail**, or do any **normal** kind of Winn-Dixie thing; he just kept beating his head against the door and crying and shaking.

"You want the door open?" I said. "Huh? Is that what you want?" I stood up and opened the door and Winn-Dixie flew through it like something big and ugly and **mean** was **chasing** him.

"Winn-Dixie," I **hiss**ed, "come back here." I didn't want him going and waking the preacher up.

But it was too late. Winn-Dixie was already at the other end of the **trailer**, in the preacher's room. I could tell because there was a *sproi-i-ing* sound that must have come from Winn-Dixie jumping up on the bed, and then there was a sound from the preacher like he was real surprised. But none of it **last**ed long, because Winn-Dixie came **tear**ing back out of the preacher's room, **pant**ing and running like crazy. I tried to **grab** him, but he was going too fast.

"Opal?" said the preacher. He was standing at the door to his bedroom, and his hair was all kind of wild on top of his head, and he was looking around like he wasn't sure where he was. "Opal, what's going on?"

"I don't know," I told him. But just then there was a huge **crack** of thunder, one so loud that it shook the whole trailer, and Winn-Dixie came shooting back out of my room and went running right past me and I screamed, "Daddy, **watch out**!"

But the preacher was still **confused**. He just stood

52

there, and Winn-Dixie came **barrel**ing right toward him like he was a bowling ball and the preacher was the only pin left standing, and *wham*, they both fell to the ground.

"Uh-oh," I said.

"Opal?" said the preacher. He was lying on his **stomach**, and Winn-Dixie was sitting on top of him, panting and whining.

"Yes sir," I said.

"Opal," the preacher said again.

"Yes sir," I said louder.

"Do you know what a **pathological** fear is?"

"No sir," I told him.

The preacher raised a hand. He **rub**bed his nose. "Well," he said, after a minute, "it's a fear that goes way beyond normal fears. It's a fear you can't be talked out of or **reason**ed **out** of."

Just then there was another crack of thunder and Winn-Dixie rose straight up in the air like somebody had **poke**d him with something hot. When he hit the floor, he started running. He ran back to my bedroom and I didn't even try to catch him; I just got out of his way.

The preacher lay there on the ground, rubbing his nose. Finally he **sat up**. He said, "Opal, I believe Winn-Dixie has a pathological fear of thunderstorms." And just when he finished his **sentence**, here came Winn-Dixie again, running to save his life. I got the preacher up off the floor and out of the way just **in time**.

There didn't seem to be a thing we could do for Winn-Dixie to make him feel better, so we just sat there and watched him run **back and forth**, all **terrorized** and panting. And every time there was another crack of thunder, Winn-Dixie acted all over again like it was surely the end of the world.

"The **storm** won't last long," the preacher told me. "And when it's over, the real Winn-Dixie will come back."

After a while the storm did end. The rain stopped. And there wasn't any more lightning, and finally the last **rumble** of thunder **went away** and Winn-Dixie **quit** running back and forth and came over to where me and the preacher were sitting and **cock**ed his head, like he was saying, "What in the world are you two doing out of bed in the middle of the night?"

And then he **crept** up on the **couch** with us in this funny way he has, where he gets on the couch an inch* at a time, kind of **sliding** himself onto it, looking off in a different direction, like it's all happening **by accident**, like he doesn't **intend** to get on the couch, but all of a sudden, there he is.

★ inch 길이의 단위 인치. 1인치는 약 2.54센티미터이다.

And so the three of us sat there. I rubbed Winn-Dixie's head and scratched him behind the ears the way he liked. And the preacher said, "There are an **awful** lot of thunderstorms in Florida in the summertime."

"Yes sir," I said. I was afraid that maybe he would say we couldn't keep a dog who went crazy with pathological fear every time there was a crack of thunder.

"We'll have to **keep an eye on** him," the preacher said. He put his arm around Winn-Dixie. "We'll have to make sure he doesn't get out during a storm. He might **run away**. We have to make sure we keep him safe."

"Yes sir," I said again. All of a sudden it was hard for me to talk. I loved the preacher so much. I loved him because he loved Winn-Dixie. I loved him because he was going to **forgive** Winn-Dixie for being afraid. But most of all I loved him for putting his arm around Winn-Dixie like that, like he was already trying to keep him safe.

Chapter Twelve

Me and Winn-Dixie got to Gertrude's Pets so early for my first day of work that the CLOSED sign was still in the window. But when I pushed on the door it swung open, and so we went on inside. I was about to call out to Otis that we were there, but then I heard music. It was the prettiest music I have ever heard in my life. I looked around to see where it was coming from, and that's when I noticed that all the animals were out of their cages. There were rabbits and hamsters and gerbils and mice and birds and lizards and snakes, and they were all just sitting there on the floor like they had turned to stone, and Otis was standing in the middle of them. He was playing a guitar and he had on skinny pointy-toed cowboy boots and he was tapping them while he was playing the music. His eyes were closed and he was smiling.

Winn-Dixie got a **dreamy** kind of look on his face. He smiled really hard at Otis and then he sneezed and then his **whisker**s went all **fuzzy**, and then he **sigh**ed and kind of dropped to the floor with all the other animals. Just then, Gertrude **caught sight of** Winn-Dixie. "Dog," she **croak**ed, and flew over and **land**ed on his head. Otis looked up at me. He stopped playing his guitar and the **spell** was broken. The rabbits started **hop**ping and the birds started flying and the lizards started **leap**ing and the snakes started **slither**ing and Winn-Dixie started **barking** and **chasing** everything that was moving, and Otis shouted, "Help me!"

For what seemed like a long time, me and Otis ran around trying to catch mice and gerbils and hamsters and snakes and lizards. We **kept on bump**ing **into** each other and **trip**ping over the animals, and Gertrude kept screaming, "Dog! Dog!"

Every time I caught something, I put it back in the first cage I saw; I didn't care if it was the right cage or not. I just put it in and **slam**med the door. And the whole time I was chasing things, I was thinking that Otis must be some kind of snake charmer,★ the way he could play his guitar and make all the animals turn to stone. And then I

★ snake charmer 악기를 연주하여 뱀에게 최면을 걸어 춤추게 하는 사람.

thought, this is **silly**. I shouted over Winn-Dixie's barking and Gertrude's **yell**ing. I said, "Play some more music, Otis."

He looked at me for a minute. Then he started playing his guitar, and in just a few seconds everything was quiet. Winn-Dixie was lying on the floor, **blink**ing his eyes and smiling to himself and sneezing every now and then, and the mice and the gerbils and the rabbits and the lizards and the snakes that we hadn't caught yet got quiet and sat **still**, and I **pick**ed them **up** one by one and put them back in their cages.

When I was all done, Otis stopped playing. He looked down at his boots. "I was just playing them some music. It makes them happy."

"Yes sir," I said. "Did they **escape** from their cages?"

"No," Otis said. "I **take** them **out**. I feel sorry for them being **lock**ed **up** all the time. I know what it's like, being locked up."

"You do?" I said.

"I have been in **jail**," Otis said. He looked up at me real quick and then looked back down at his boots.

"You have?" I said.

"**Never mind**," said Otis. "Aren't you here to **sweep** the floor?"

"Yes sir," I told him.

58

He walked over to the counter and started **dig**ging through a **pile** of things, and finally he came up with a **broom**.

"Here," he said. "You should start sweeping." Only he must have gotten **confused**. He was holding out his guitar to me, instead of the broom.

"With your guitar?" I asked.

He **blush**ed and **hand**ed me the broom and I started to work. I am a good **sweeper**. I swept the whole store and then **dust**ed some of the **shelves**. The whole time I worked, Winn-Dixie followed me, and Gertrude followed him, flying behind him and sitting on his head and his back and croaking real quiet to herself, "Dog, dog."

When I was done, Otis thanked me. I left Gertrude's Pets thinking about how the **preacher** probably wouldn't like it very much that I was working for a **criminal**.

Sweetie Pie Thomas was waiting for me right out front. "I seen that," she said. She stood there and **suck**ed on her **knuckle** and **stare**d at me.

"Seen what?" I said.

"I seen all them animals out of their cages and keeping real still. Is that man magic?" she asked.

"Kind of," I told her.

She hugged Winn-Dixie around the neck. "Just like this **grocery-store** dog, right?"

"Right," I said.

I started walking, and Sweetie Pie took her knuckle out of her mouth and put her hand in mine.

"Are you coming to my birthday party?" she asked.

"I surely am," I told her.

"The **theme** is pink," she said.

"I know it," I told her.

"I gotta* go," she said all of a sudden. "I gotta go home and tell my mama about what I seen. I live right down there. In that yellow house. That's my mama on the **porch**. You see her? She's **waving** at you."

I waved at the woman on the porch and she waved back, and I watched Sweetie Pie **run off** to tell her mama about Otis being a magic man. It made me think about my mama and how I wanted to tell her the story about Otis **charm**ing all the animals. I was collecting stories for her. I would also tell her about Miss Franny and the bear, and about meeting Gloria Dump and believing for just a minute that she was a witch. I had a feeling that these were the kind of stories my mama would like, the kind that would make her laugh out loud, the way the preacher said she liked to laugh.

★ gotta 'got a/got to'의 구어체.

Chapter Thirteen

Me and Winn-Dixie got into a **daily routine** where we would leave the **trailer** early in the morning and get down to Gertrude's Pets **in time** to hear Otis play his guitar music for the animals. Sometimes Sweetie Pie **snuck** in for the concert, too. She sat on the floor and **wrap**ped her arms around Winn-Dixie and **rock**ed him back and forth like he was a big old teddy bear. And then when the music was over, she would walk around trying to **pick out** which pet she wanted; but she always **gave up** and went home, because the only thing she really wanted was a dog like Winn-Dixie. After she was gone, I would sweep and clean up and even **arrange** some of Otis's **shelves**, because he did not have an eye for arranging things and I did. And when I was done, Otis would write down my time in a notebook that he had **mark**ed on the outside, "One red **leather collar,** one red leather **leash**". And the whole time, he did not in any way ever act like a **criminal.**

After working at Gertrude's Pets, me and Winn-Dixie would go over to the Herman W. Block **Memorial** Library and talk to Miss Franny Block and listen to her tell us a story. But my favorite place to be that summer was in Gloria Dump's yard. And I **figure**d it was Winn-Dixie's favorite place to be, too, because when we got up to the last block before her house, Winn-Dixie would **break away** from my bike and start to run **for all he was worth,** heading for Gloria Dump's backyard and his **spoonful** of peanut butter.

Sometimes Dunlap and Stevie Dewberry would follow me. They would **holler,** "There goes the preacher's daughter, visiting the **witch.**"

"She's not a witch," I told them. It made me mad the way they wouldn't listen to me and kept on believing whatever they wanted to believe about Gloria Dump.

One time Stevie said to me, "My mama says you shouldn't be spending all your time **coop**ed up in that pet shop and at that library, sitting around talking with old ladies. She says you should get out in the fresh air and play with kids your own age. That's what my mama says."

"Oh, **lay off** her," Dunlap said to Stevie. Then he

turned to me. "He don't mean it," he said.

But I was already mad. I shouted at Stevie. I said, "I don't care what your mama says. She's not my mama, so she can't tell me what to do."

"I'm going to tell my mama you said that," shouted Stevie, "and she'll tell your daddy and he'll **shame** you in front of the whole church. And that pet shop man is **retarded** and he was in **jail** and I **wonder** if your daddy knows that."

"Otis is not retarded," I said. "And my daddy knows that he was in jail." That was a **lie**. But I didn't care. "And you can go ahead and **tell on** me if you want, you big **bald**-headed baby."

I **swear**, it about **wore** me **out yell**ing at Dunlap and Stevie Dewberry every day; by the time I got to Gloria Dump's yard I felt like a **soldier** who had been fighting a hard **battle**. Gloria would make me a peanut-butter sandwich **straight off** and then she would **pour** me a cup of coffee with half coffee and half milk and that would **refresh** me.

"Why don't you play with them boys?" Gloria asked me.

"Because they're **ignorant**," I told her. "They still think you're a witch. It doesn't matter how many times I tell them you're not."

"I think they are just trying to make friends with you in a **roundabout** way," Gloria said.

"I don't want to be their friend," I said.

"It might be fun having them two boys for friends."

"I'd rather talk with you," I said. "They're stupid. And mean. And they're boys."

Gloria would shake her head and sigh, and then she would ask me what was going on in the world and did I have any stories to tell her. And I always did.

Chapter Fourteen

Sometimes I told Gloria the story Miss Franny Block had just told me. Or I **imitate**d Otis **tap**ping his **pointy-toed** boots and playing for all the animals, and that always made her laugh. And sometimes I made up a story and Gloria Dump would listen to it **all the way** through from beginning to end. She told me she **used to** love to read stories, but she couldn't any more because her eyes were so bad.

"Can't you get some really strong glasses?" I asked her.

"Child," she said, "they don't make glasses strong enough for these eyes."

One day, when the **storytelling** was done, I decided to tell Gloria that Otis was a **criminal**. I thought maybe I should tell an adult about it, and Gloria was the best adult I knew.

"Gloria?" I said.

"Mmmm-hmmm," she said back.

"You know Otis?"

"I don't know him. But I know what you tell me 'bout him."

"Well, he's a criminal. He's been in **jail**. Do you think I should be afraid of him?"

"What for?"

"I don't know. For doing bad things, I guess. For being in jail."

"Child," said Gloria, "let me show you something." She got up out of her chair real slow and took hold of my arm. "Let's the two of us walk all the way to the back of this yard."

"OK," I said.

We walked and Winn-Dixie followed right behind us. It was a huge yard and I had never been all the way back in it. When we got to a big old tree, we stopped.

"Look at this tree," Gloria said.

I looked up. There were bottles **hang**ing from just about every **branch**. There were whiskey bottles and beer bottles and wine bottles all tied on with **string**, and some of them were **clank**ing against each other and making a **spooky** kind of noise. Me and Winn-Dixie stood and stared at the tree, and the hair on top of his head rose up a little bit and he **growl**ed deep in his **throat**.

Gloria Dump pointed her **cane** at the tree.

"What you think about this tree?"

I said, "I don't know. Why are all those bottles on it?"

"To **keep** the ghosts **away**," Gloria said.

"What ghosts?"

"The ghosts of all the things I done wrong."

I looked at all the bottles on the tree. "You did that many things wrong?" I asked her.

"Mmmm-hmmm," said Gloria. "More than that."

"But you're the nicest person I know," I told her.

"Don't mean I haven't done bad things," she said.

"There's whiskey bottles on there," I told her. "And beer bottles."

"Child," said Gloria Dump, "I know that. I'm the one who put 'em there. I'm the one who drank what was in 'em."

"My mama drank," I **whisper**ed.

"I know it," Gloria Dump said.

"The **preacher** says that sometimes she couldn't stop drinking."

"Mmmm-hmmm," said Gloria again. "That's the way it is for some **folks**. We get started and we can't get stopped."

"Are you one of those people?"

"Yes ma'am. I am. But these days I don't drink nothing stronger than coffee."

"Did the whiskey and beer and wine, did they make you do the bad things that are ghosts now?"

"Some of them," said Gloria Dump. "Some of them I would've done anyway, with **alcohol** or without it. Before I learned."

"Learned what?"

"Learned what is the most important thing."

"What's that?" I asked her.

"It's different for everyone," she said. "You find out on your own. But **in the meantime**, you got to remember, you can't always **judge** people by the things they done. You got to judge them by what they are doing now. You judge Otis by the pretty music he plays and how kind he is to them animals, because that's all you know about him right now. All right?"

"Yes ma'am," I said.

"And them Dewberry boys, you try not to judge them too **harsh** either, all right?"

"All right," I said.

"All right then," said Gloria Dump, and she turned and started walking away. Winn-Dixie **nudge**d me with his **wet** nose and **wag**ged his **tail**; when he saw I wasn't going, he **trot**ted after Gloria. I stayed where I was and studied the tree. I wondered if my mama, wherever she was, had a tree full of bottles; and I wondered if I was a ghost to her, the same way she sometimes seemed like a ghost to me.

Chapter Fifteen

The Herman W. Block Memorial Library's **air-conditioning unit** didn't work very good, and there was only one **fan**; and from the minute me and Winn-Dixie got in the library, he **hog**ged it all. He lay right in front of it and wagged his tail and let it blow his **fur** all around. Some of his fur was **pretty** loose and blew right off him like a dandelion* **puff**. I worried about him hogging the fan, and I worried about the fan blowing him bald; but Miss Franny said not to worry about either thing, that Winn-Dixie could hog the fan if he wanted and she had never in her life seen a dog made bald by a fan.

Sometimes, when Miss Franny was telling a story, she

★ dandelion [식물] 민들레.

would have a **fit**. They were small fits and they didn't **last** long. But what happened was she would forget what she was saying. She would just stop and start to shake like a little **leaf**. And when that happened, Winn-Dixie would get up from the fan and sit right at Miss Franny Block's side. He would **sit up** tall, **protect**ing her, with his ears standing up straight on his head, like **soldier**s. And when Miss Franny stopped shaking and started talking again, Winn-Dixie would **lick** her hand and lie back down in front of the fan.

Whenever Miss Franny had one of her fits, it **remind**ed me of Winn-Dixie in a **thunderstorm**. There were a lot of thunderstorms that summer. And I got real good at **hold**ing **on to** Winn-Dixie whenever they came. I held on to him and **comfort**ed him and whispered to him and **rock**ed him, just the same way he tried to comfort Miss Franny when she had her fits. Only I held on to Winn-Dixie for another reason, too. I held on to him **tight** so he wouldn't **run away**.

It all made me think about Gloria Dump. I wondered who comforted her when she heard those bottles **knock**ing together, those ghosts **chatter**ing about the things she had done wrong. I wanted to comfort Gloria Dump. And I decided that the best way to do that would be to read her a book, read it to her loud enough to keep the ghosts away.

And so I asked Miss Franny. I said, "Miss Franny, I've got a **grown-up** friend whose eyes are going on her, and I would like to read her a book out loud. Do you have any **suggestion**s?"

"Suggestions?" Miss Franny said. "Yes ma'am, I have suggestions. Of course I have suggestions. How about *Gone with the Wind*?★"

"What's that about?" I asked her.

"Why," said Miss Franny, "it's a wonderful story about the Civil War.✷"

"The Civil War?" I said.

"Do not tell me you have never heard of the Civil War?" Miss Franny Block looked like she was going to **faint**. She **wave**d her hands in front of her face.

"I know about the Civil War," I told her. "That was the war between the South and the North over **slavery**."

"Slavery, yes," said Miss Franny. "It was also about states' **right**s and money. It was a **terrible** war. My great-grandfather fought in that war. He was just a boy."

"Your great-grandfather?"

"Yes ma'am, Littmus W. Block. Now *there's* a story."

★ Gone with the Wind 마거릿 미첼이 쓴 소설 「바람과 함께 사라지다」. 1,000페이지가 넘는 대작으로 집필에만 10년이 걸렸다. 1936년에 출판되어, 1937년 퓰리처상(賞)을 받았다.
✷ the Civil War (= American Civil War) 남북전쟁. 1861년 노예제를 지지하던 미국의 남부주들이 모여 남부연합을 형성하며 미합중국으로부터의 분리를 선언한 뒤 섬터 요새를 포격하는 것으로 시작되어, 1865년까지 4년 동안 벌어진 전쟁이다. 전쟁 결과, 남군이 패했고, 미국 전역에서 노예제가 폐지되는 중요한 계기가 되었다.

Winn-Dixie **yawn**ed real big and lay down on his side with a **thump** and a **sigh**. I **swear** he knew that **phrase**: "Now *there's* a story." And he knew it meant we weren't going anywhere real soon.

"Go ahead and tell it to me, Miss Franny," I said. And I sat down **cross-legged** next to Winn-Dixie. I pushed him and tried to get him to **share** the fan. But he **pretend**ed he was **asleep**. And he wouldn't move.

I was all **settled** in and ready for a good story when the door **bang**ed and **pinch**-faced Amanda Wilkinson came in. Winn-Dixie sat up and **stared** at her. He tried out a smile on her, but she didn't smile back and so he lay down again.

"I'm ready for another book," Amanda said, **slam**ming her book down on Miss Franny's desk.

"Well," said Miss Franny, "maybe you wouldn't **mind** waiting. I am telling India Opal a story about my great-grandfather. You are, of course, more than welcome to listen. It will be just one minute."

Amanda sighed a real big **dramatic** sigh and stared past me. She pretended like she wasn't interested, but she was, I could tell.

"Come sit over here," said Miss Franny.

"I'll stand, thank you," said Amanda.

"**Suit yourself.**" Miss Franny **shrug**ged. "Now where was I? Oh, yes. Littmus. Littmus W. Block."

Chapter Sixteen

"Littmus W. Block was just a boy when the **firing** on Fort Sumter* **occur**red," Miss Franny Block said as she **start**ed **in** on her story.

"Fort Sumter?" I said.

"It was the firing on Fort Sumter that started the war," said Amanda.

"OK," I said. I **shrug**ged.

"Well, Littmus was fourteen years old. He was strong and big, but he was still just a boy. His daddy, Artley W. Block, had already **enlist**ed, and Littmus told his mama that he could not **stand by** and let the South get **beat**, and so he went to fight, too." Miss Franny looked around the

---

* Fort Sumter 미국 사우스캐롤라이나주 중부에 있는 섬터 요새. 1861년 남북 전쟁 발발지이다.

library and then she whispered, "Men and boys always want to fight. They are always looking for a reason to go to war. It is the saddest thing. They have this **abiding notion** that war is fun. And no history lesson will **convince** them differently.

"Anyway, Littmus went and enlisted. He **lied** about his age. Yes ma'am. Like I said, he was a big boy. And the **army** took him, and Littmus **went off** to war, just like that. Left behind his mother and three sisters. He went off to be a hero. But he soon found out the truth." Miss Franny closed her eyes and shook her head.

"What truth?" I asked her.

"Why, that war is **hell**," Miss Franny said with her eyes still closed. "**Pure** hell."

"*Hell* is a cuss word,★" said Amanda. I **stole a look** at her. Her face was pinched up even more than usual.

"*War*," said Miss Franny with her eyes still closed, "should be a cuss word, too." She shook her head and opened her eyes. She pointed at me and then she pointed at Amanda. "You, **neither** of you, can **imagine**."

"No ma'am!" Amanda and me said at exactly the same time. We looked real quick at each other and then back at Miss Franny.

★ cuss word 저주(cuss)하는 말(word). 악담.

"You cannot imagine. Littmus was hungry all the time. And he was covered with **all manner of** vermin:* **fleas** and lice.* And in the winter, he was so cold he thought for sure he would **freeze** to death. And in the summer, why there's nothing worse than war in the summertime. It **stink**s so. And the only thing that made Littmus forget that he was hungry and **itchy** and hot or cold was that he was getting shot at. And he got shot at quite a bit. And he was nothing more than a child."

"Did he get killed?" I asked Miss Franny.

"Good **grief**,*" said Amanda. She rolled her eyes.

"Now, Opal," Miss Franny said, "I wouldn't be standing in this room telling this story if he was killed. I wouldn't **exist**. No ma'am. He had to live. But he was a changed man. Yes ma'am. A changed man. He walked back home when the war was over. He walked from Virginia all the way back to Georgia. He didn't have a horse. Nobody had a horse **except** for the Yankees.* He walked. And when he got home, there was no home there."

"Where was it?" I asked her. I didn't care if Amanda thought I was stupid. I wanted to know.

"Why," Miss Franny shouted so loud that Winn-Dixie

★ vermin 해충, 기생충.

✴ lice (louse의 복수형) 기생충. 이.

✳ good grief [감탄사] 어머나! 맙소사! 앗!

✶ Yankee 미국 남북전쟁 당시의 북군 병사.

76

and Amanda Wilkinson and me all jumped, "the Yankees burned it! Yes ma'am. Burned it to the ground."

"What about his sisters?" Amanda asked. She moved around the desk and came and sat on the floor. She looked up at Miss Franny. "What happened to them?"

"Dead. Dead of typhoid **fever**.*"

"Oh no," Amanda said in a real soft voice.

"And his mama?" I whispered.

"Dead, too."

"And his father?" Amanda asked. "What happened to him?"

"He died on the **battlefield**."

"Littmus was an **orphan**?" I asked.

"Yes ma'am," said Miss Franny Block. "Littmus was an orphan."

"This is a sad story," I told Miss Franny.

"It sure is," said Amanda. I was **amaze**d that she was agreeing with me about something.

"I am not done yet," Miss Franny said.

Winn-Dixie started to **snore**, and I **nudge**d him with my foot to try to make him **quit**. I wanted to hear the **rest** of the story. It was important to me to hear how Littmus **survive**d after losing everything he loved.

★ typhoid fever 장티푸스. 고열이 계속되고, 전신이 쇠약해지는 질환.

Chapter Seventeen

"Well, Littmus came home from the war," said Miss Franny as she **went on** with her story, "and found himself alone. And he sat down on what **used to** be the front step of his house, and he cried and cried. He cried just like a baby. He missed his mama and he missed his daddy and he missed his sisters and he missed the boy he used to be. When he finally finished crying, he had the strangest **sensation**. He felt like he wanted something sweet. He wanted a piece of candy. He hadn't had a piece of candy in years. And it was right then that he made a **decision**. Yes ma'am. Littmus W. Block **figure**d the world was a sorry affair* and that it had enough ugly things in it and what

---

* sorry affair 애석한(sorry) 일(affair).

he was going to do was **concentrate** on putting something sweet in it. He got up and started walking. He walked **all the way** to Florida. And the whole time he was walking, he was planning."

"Planning what?" I asked.

"Why, planning the candy **factory**."

"Did he build it?" I asked.

"Of course he did. It's still **standing out** on Fairville Road."

"That old building?" said Amanda. "That big **spooky** one?"

"It is not spooky," said Miss Franny. "It was the **birthplace** of the family **fortune**. It was there that my great-grandfather **manufacture**d the Littmus Lozenge, a candy that was famous the world over."

"I've never heard of it," said Amanda.

"Me neither," I said.

"Well," said Miss Franny, "they aren't made any more. The world, it seems, lost its **appetite** for Littmus Lozenges. But I still **happen to** have a few." She opened the top **drawer** of her desk. It was full of candy. She opened the drawer below that. It was full of candy, too. Miss Franny Block's whole desk was full of candy.

"**Would you care for** a Littmus Lozenge?" she asked Amanda and me.

"Yes, please," said Amanda.

"Sure," I said. "Can Winn-Dixie have one, too?"

"I have never known a dog that cared for hard candy," said Miss Franny, "but he is welcome to try one."

Miss Franny gave Amanda one Littmus Lozenge and me two. I **unwrap**ped one and **held** it **out** to Winn-Dixie. He sat up and **sniff**ed it and **wag**ged his tail and took the candy from between my fingers real gentle. He tried to **chew** on it, and when that didn't work, he just **swallow**ed the whole thing in one big **gulp**. Then he wagged his tail at me and lay back down.

I ate my Littmus Lozenge slow. It tasted good. It tasted like root beer* and strawberry and something else I didn't have a name for, something that made me feel kind of sad. I looked over at Amanda. She was **suck**ing on her candy and thinking hard.

"Do you like it?" Miss Franny asked me.

"Yes ma'am," I told her.

"What about you, Amanda? Do you like the Littmus Lozenge?"

"Yes ma'am," she said. "But it makes me think of things I feel sad about."

I **wonder**ed what in the world Amanda Wilkinson had

★ root beer 루트비어. 생강과 여러 식물 뿌리로 만든 탄산음료.

to feel sad about. She wasn't new to town. She had a mama and a daddy. I had seen her with them in church.

"There's a secret **ingredient** in there," Miss Franny said.

"I know it," I told her. "I can taste it. What is it?"

"**Sorrow**," Miss Franny said. "Not everybody can taste it. Children, **especially**, seem to have a hard time knowing it's there."

"I taste it," I said.

"Me, too," said Amanda.

"Well, then," Miss Franny said, "you've probably both had your **share** of **sadness**."

"I had to move away from Watley and leave all my friends," I said. "That is one sadness I have had. And Dunlap and Stevie Dewberry are always **pick**ing **on** me. That's another sadness. And the biggest one, my biggest sadness, is that my mama left me when I was still small. And I can **hardly** remember her; I keep hoping I'll get to meet her and tell her some stories."

"It makes me miss Carson," said Amanda. She sounded like she was going to cry. "I have to go." And she got up and almost ran out of the Herman W. Block **Memorial** Library.

"Who's Carson?" I asked Miss Franny.

She shook her head. "Sorrow," she said. "It is a sorrow-filled world."

"But how do you put that in a piece of candy?" I asked

her. "How do you get that taste in there?"

"That's the secret," she said. "That's why Littmus made a fortune. He manufactured a piece of candy that tasted sweet and sad at the same time."

"Can I have a piece to take to my friend Gloria Dump? And another one to take to Otis down at Gertrude's Pets? And one for the **preacher**? And one for Sweetie Pie, too?"

"You may have as many as you want," said Miss Franny.

So I **stuff**ed my pockets full of Littmus Lozenges and I thanked Miss Franny for her story and I **check**ed **out** *Gone with the Wind* (which was a very big book) and I told Winn-Dixie to get up, and the two of us left and went over to Gloria Dump's. I rode right past the Dewberrys' house. Dunlap and Stevie were playing football in the front yard and I was just getting ready to **stick** my **tongue** out at them; but then I thought about what Miss Franny said, about war being **hell**, and I thought about what Gloria Dump said, about not **judging** them too hard. And so I just **wave**d instead. They stood and **stare**d at me; but when I was almost all the way past, I saw Dunlap put his hand up in the air and wave back.

"Hey," he **holler**ed. "Hey, Opal."

I waved harder and I thought about Amanda Wilkinson and how it was **neat** that she liked a good story the same as I did. And I wondered again . . . who was Carson?

Chapter Eighteen

When we got to Gloria Dump's, I told her I had two surprises for her and asked which one did she want first, the small one or the big one.

"The small one," said Gloria.

I **hand**ed her the Littmus Lozenge and she moved it around in her hands, feeling it.

"Candy?" she said.

"Yes ma'am," I told her. "It's called a Littmus Lozenge."

"Oh Lord,★ yes. I remember these candies. My daddy **used to** eat them." She **unwrap**ped the Littmus Lozenge and put it in her mouth and **nod**ded her head.

"Do you like it?" I asked her.

★ Oh Lord [감탄사] (놀람 · 만족 · 기쁨을 나타내어) 아무렴, 그렇다마다.

"Mmmm-hmmm." She nodded her head slowly. "It taste sweet. But it also taste like people leaving."

"You mean sad?" I asked. "Does it taste like **sorrow** to you?"

"That's right," she said. "It taste **sorrowful** but sweet. Now. What's surprise number two?"

"A book," I said.

"A book?"

"Uh-huh," I said. "I'm going to read it out loud to you. It's called *Gone with the Wind*. Miss Franny says it's a great book. It's about the Civil War. Do you know all about the Civil War?"

"I have heard it **mention**ed a time or two," said Gloria, nodding her head and **suck**ing on her Littmus Lozenge.

"It's going to take us a long time to read this book," I told her. "There are one thousand and thirty-seven pages."

"Whoooeee," said Gloria. She **lean**ed back in her chair and crossed her hands on her **stomach**. "We best get started then."

And so I read the first chapter of *Gone with the Wind* out loud to Gloria Dump. I read it loud enough to keep her ghosts away. And Gloria listened to it good. And when I was done, she said it was the best surprise she had ever had and she couldn't wait to hear chapter two.

That night I gave the preacher his Littmus Lozenge

right before he kissed me good night.

"What's this?" he said.

"It's some candy that Miss Franny's great-grandfather invented. It's called a Littmus Lozenge."

The preacher unwrapped it and put it in his mouth, and after a minute he started rubbing his nose and nodding his head.

"Do you like it?" I asked him.

"It has a peculiar flavor . . ."

"Root beer?" I said.

"Something else."

"Strawberry?"

"That, too. But there's still something else. It's odd."

I could see the preacher getting further and further away. He was hunching up his shoulders and lowering his chin and getting ready to pull his head inside his shell.

"It almost tastes a little melancholy," he said.

"*Melancholy?* What's that?"

"Sad," said the preacher. He rubbed his nose some more. "It makes me think of your mother."

Winn-Dixie sniffed at the candy wrapper in the preacher's hand.

"It tastes sad," he said, and sighed. "It must be a bad batch."

"No," I told him. I sat up in bed. "That's the way it's

supposed to taste. Littmus came back from the war and his whole family was dead. His daddy died fighting. And his mama and his sisters died from a **disease** and the Yankees burned his house down. And Littmus was sad, very sad, and what he wanted more than anything in the whole world was something sweet. So he built a candy **factory** and made Littmus Lozenges, and he put all the sad he was feeling into the candy."

"My goodness,*" said the preacher.

Winn-Dixie **snuffle**d the candy wrapper out of the preacher's hand and started **chew**ing on it.

"Give me that," I said to Winn-Dixie. But he wouldn't **give** it **up**. I had to **reach** inside his mouth and pull it out. "You can't eat candy wrappers," I told him.

The preacher cleared his **throat**. I thought he was going to say something important, maybe tell me another thing that he remembered about my mama; but what he said was, "Opal, I had a talk with Mrs. Dewberry the other day. She said that Stevie says that you called him a **bald**-headed baby."

"It's true," I said. "I did. But he calls Gloria Dump a **witch** all the time, and he calls Otis **retarded**. And once he even said that his mama said I shouldn't spend all my time

---

★ **My goodness** [감탄사] 저런! 어머나!

with old ladies. That's what he said."

"I think you should **apologize**," said the preacher.

"Me?" I said.

"Yes," he said. "You. You tell Stevie you're sorry if you said anything that hurt his feelings. I'm sure he just wants to be your friend."

"I don't think so," I told him. "I don't think he wants to be my friend."

"Some people have a strange way of going about making friends," he said. "You apologize."

"Yes sir," I said. Then I remembered Carson. "Daddy," I said, "do you know anything about Amanda Wilkinson?"

"What kind of thing?"

"Do you know something about her and somebody **named** Carson?"

"Carson was her brother. He **drowned** last year."

"He's dead?"

"Yes," said the preacher. "His family is still **suffering** a **great deal.**"

"How old was he?"

"Five," said the preacher. "He was only five years old."

"Daddy," I said, "how could you not tell me about something like that?"

"Other people's **tragedies** should not be the **subject** of **idle conversation.** There was no reason for me to tell you."

"It's just that I needed to know," I said. "Because it helps **explain** Amanda. No **wonder** she's so **pinch**-faced."

"What's that?" said the preacher.

"Nothing," I said.

"Good night, India Opal," the preacher said. He leaned over and kissed me, and I smelled the root beer and the strawberry and the **sadness** all mixed together on his **breath**. He **pat**ted Winn-Dixie on the head and got up and turned off the light and closed the door.

I didn't go to sleep right away. I **lay** there and thought how life was like a Littmus Lozenge, how the sweet and the sad were all mixed up together and how hard it was to **separate** them out. It was **confusing**.

"Daddy!" I shouted.

After a minute, he opened the door and raised his **eyebrow**s at me.

"What was that word you said? The word that meant sad?"

"*Melancholy*," he said.

"*Melancholy*," I **repeat**ed. I liked the way it sounded, like there was music **hidden** somewhere inside it.

"Good night now," the preacher said.

"Good night," I told him back.

I got up out of bed and unwrapped a Littmus Lozenge and sucked on it hard and thought about my mama leaving me. That was a melancholy feeling. And then I thought about Amanda and Carson. And that made me feel melancholy, too. Poor Amanda. And poor Carson. He was the same age as Sweetie Pie. But he would never get to have his sixth birthday party.

Chapter Nineteen

In the morning, me and Winn-Dixie went down to **sweep** the pet store, and I took a Littmus Lozenge for Otis.

"Is it Halloween?" Otis asked when I handed him the candy.

"No," I said. "Why?"

"Well, you're giving me candy."

"It's just a gift," I told him. "For today."

"Oh," said Otis. He **unwrap**ped the Littmus Lozenge and put it in his mouth. And after a minute tears started rolling down his face.

"Thank you," he said.

"Do you like it?" I asked him.

He nodded his head. "It tastes good, but it also tastes a little bit like being in **jail**."

"Gertrude," Gertrude **squawk**ed. She **picked up** the Littmus Lozenge **wrapper** in her **beak** and then dropped it and looked around. "Gertrude!" she screamed again.

"You can't have any," I told her. "It's not for birds." Then, real quick, before I **lost my nerve**, I said, "Otis, what were you in jail for? Are you a **murder**er?"

"No ma'am," he said.

"Are you a **burglar**?"

"No ma'am," Otis said again. He **sucked** on his candy and **stared** down at his **pointy-toed** boots.

"You don't have to tell me," I said. "I was just **wonder**ing."

"I ain't a dangerous man," Otis said, "if that's what you're thinking. I'm lonely. But I ain't dangerous."

"OK," I said. And I went into the back room to get my **broom**. When I came back out, Otis was standing where I left him, still staring down at his feet.

"It was **on account of** the music," he said.

"What was?" I asked.

"Why I went to jail. It was on account of the music."

"What happened?"

"I wouldn't stop playing my guitar. **Used to** be I played it on the street and sometimes people would give me money. I didn't do it for the money. I did it because the music is better if someone is listening to it. Anyway, the police came. And they told me to stop it. They said how I was **breaking the law,** and the whole time they were talking to me, I went right on playing my music. And that made them mad. They tried to put **handcuffs** on me." He sighed. "I didn't like that. I wouldn't have been able to play my guitar with them things on."

"And then what happened?" I asked him.

"I hit them," he **whispered.**

"You hit the police?"

"Uh-huh. One of them. I **knocked** him **out.** Then I went to jail. And they **locked** me **up** and wouldn't let me have my guitar. And when they finally let me out, they made me **promise** I wouldn't never play my guitar on the street again." He looked up at me real quick and then back down at his boots. "And I don't. I only play it in here. For the animals. Gertrude, the human Gertrude, she owns this shop, and she gave me this job when she read about me in the paper and she said it's all right for me to play music for the animals."

"You play your music for me and Winn-Dixie and Sweetie Pie," I said.

"Yeah," he agreed. "But you ain't on the street."

"Thank you for telling me about it, Otis," I said.

"It's all right," he said. "I don't **mind.**"

Sweetie Pie came in and I gave her a Littmus Lozenge,

and she **spit** it right out; she said that it tasted bad. She said that it tasted like not having a dog.

I swept the floor real slow that day. I wanted to **keep** Otis **company**. I didn't want him to be lonely. Sometimes it seemed like everybody in the world was lonely. I thought about my mama. Thinking about her was the same as the hole you **keep on** feeling with your **tongue** after you lose a **tooth**. Time after time my mind kept going to that **empty spot**, the spot where I felt like she should be.

Chapter Twenty

When I told Gloria Dump about Otis and how he got arrested, she laughed so hard she had to grab hold of her false teeth so they wouldn't fall out of her mouth.

"Whoooeee," she said when she was finally done laughing. "That sure is some dangerous criminal."

"He's a lonely man," I told her. "He just wants to play his music for somebody."

Gloria wiped her eyes with the hem of her dress. "I know it, sugar," she said. "But sometimes things are so sad they get to be funny."

"You know what else?" I said, still thinking about sad things. "That girl I told you about, the pinch-faced one? Amanda? Well, her brother drowned last year. He was only five years old, the same age as Sweetie Pie Thomas."

Gloria stopped smiling. She nodded her head. "I remember hearing about that," she said. "I remember hearing about a little drowned boy."

"That's why Amanda is so pinch-faced," I said. "She misses her brother."

"Most likely," Gloria agreed.

"Do you think everybody misses somebody? Like I miss my mama?"

"Mmmm-hmmm," said Gloria. She closed her eyes. "I believe, sometimes, that the whole world has an **aching** heart."

I couldn't stand to think about sad things that couldn't be helped any more, so I said, "Do you want to hear some more *Gone with the Wind*?"

"Yes **indeed**," Gloria said. "I been **looking forward to** it all day. Let's see what Miss Scarlett is up to now."

I opened up *Gone with the Wind* and started to read, but the whole time I was thinking about Otis, worrying about him not being **allow**ed to play his guitar for people. In the book, Scarlett was looking forward to going to a big barbecue where there was going to be music and food. That's how I got the idea.

"That's what we need to do," I said. I **slam**med the book shut. Winn-Dixie's head **shot up** from **underneath** Gloria's chair. He looked around all **nervous**like.

"Huh?" said Gloria Dump.

"Have a party," I told her. "We need to have a party and **invite** Miss Franny Block and the **preacher** and Otis, and Otis can play his guitar for everybody. Sweetie Pie can come, too. She listens to his music good."

" 'We' who?" Gloria asked.

" 'We' me and you. We can make some food and have the party right here in your yard."

"Hmmm," said Gloria Dump.

"We could make peanut-butter sandwiches and cut them up in **triangle**s to make them look **fancy**."

"Lord," said Gloria Dump, "I don't know if the whole world likes peanut butter as much as you and me and this dog."

"Okay then," I said, "we could make egg-salad sandwiches. Adults like those."

"You know how to make egg salad?"

"No ma'am," I said. "I don't have a mama around to teach me things like that. But I **bet** you know. I bet you could teach me. Please."

"Maybe," said Gloria Dump. She put her hand on Winn-Dixie's head. She smiled at me. I knew she was telling me yes.

"Thank you," I said. I went over and hugged her. I **squeeze**d her hard. Winn-Dixie **wag**ged his **tail** and tried to get in between the two of us. He couldn't **stand** being left out of anything.

"It's going to be the best party ever," I told Gloria.

"You got to make me one promise, though," Gloria said.

"All right," I told her.

"You got to invite them Dewberry boys."

"Dunlap and Stevie?"

"Hmmm-mmm, ain't gonna be no party unless you invite them."

"I have to?"

"Yes," said Gloria Dump. "You promise me."

"I promise," I said. I didn't like the idea. But I promised.

I started inviting people right away. I asked the preacher first.

"Daddy," I said.

"Opal?" the preacher said back.

"Daddy, me and Winn-Dixie and Gloria Dump are having a party."

"Well," said the preacher, "that's nice. You have a good time."

"Daddy," I said, "I'm telling you because you're invited."

"Oh," said the preacher. He **rub**bed his nose. "I see."

"Can you come?" I asked him.

He **sigh**ed. "I don't see why not," he said.

Miss Franny Block took to the idea right away. "A party!" she said, and **clap**ped her hands together.

"Yes ma'am," I told her. "It will be kind of like the barbecue at Twelve Oaks in *Gone with the Wind*. Only it's not going to be as many people, and we're going to serve egg-salad sandwiches instead of barbecue."

"That sounds lovely," Miss Franny said. And then she pointed at the back of the library and whispered, "Maybe you should ask Amanda, too."

"She probably won't want to come," I said. "She doesn't like me very much."

"Ask her and see what she says," Miss Franny whispered.

So I walked to the back of the library and I asked Amanda Wilkinson in my best-manners voice to please come to my party. She looked around all nervous and **stuff**.

"A party?" she said.

"Yes," I said. "I sure would like it if you could come."

She stared at me with her mouth open. "OK," she said after a minute. "I mean, yes. Thank you. I would love to."

And just like I promised Gloria, I asked the Dewberry boys.

"I ain't going to no party at a witch's house," Stevie said.

Dunlap **knock**ed Stevie with his **elbow**. "We'll come," he said.

"We will not," said Stevie. "That witch might cook us up in her big old witch's **pot**."

"I don't care if you come or not," I told them. "I'm just asking because I promised I would."

"We'll be there," said Dunlap. And he nodded at me and smiled.

Sweetie Pie was very excited when I invited her.

"What's the **theme**?" she asked.

"Well, there isn't one," I said.

"You got to think of a theme," she told me. She **stuck** her **knuckle** in her mouth and then pulled it back out. "It ain't a party without a theme. Is this dog coming?" she asked. She **wrap**ped her arms around Winn-Dixie and squeezed him so hard that his eyes almost **pop**ped out of his head.

"Yes," I told her.

"Good," she said. "You could make that the theme. It could be a dog party."

"I'll think about it," I told her.

The last person I asked was Otis. I told him all about the party and that he was invited and he said, "No, thank you."

"Why not?" I asked.

"I don't like parties," said Otis.

"Please," I **beg**ged. "It won't be a party **unless** you come. I'll give you a whole free week of **sweep**ing and **arranging** and **dust**ing. If you come to the party, that's what I'll do."

"A whole week for free?" Otis said, looking up at me.

"Yes sir," I told him.

"But I don't have to talk to people, right?"

"No sir," I said. "You don't. But bring your guitar. Maybe you could play us some music."

"Maybe," said Otis. He looked down at his boots again real quick, trying to hide his smile.

"Thank you," I told him. "Thank you for deciding to come."

Chapter Twenty-One

After I got Otis **convinced** to come, the **rest** of getting ready for the party was easy and fun. Me and Gloria decided to have the party at night, when it would be cooler. And the afternoon before, we worked in Gloria's kitchen and made egg-salad sandwiches. We cut them up in **triangle**s and cut off the **crusts** and put little **toothpicks** with **frilly** tops in them. Winn-Dixie sat in the kitchen and looked at us the whole time. He **kept on wagging** his **tail**.

"That dog thinks we making these sandwiches for him," said Gloria Dump.

Winn-Dixie showed Gloria all his teeth.

"These ain't for you," she told him.

But when she thought I wasn't looking, she gave Winn-Dixie an egg-salad sandwich, without the toothpick.

We also made punch.* We mixed together orange juice and grapefruit* juice and **soda** in a big **bowl**. Gloria called it Dump Punch. She said she was world famous for it. But I had never heard of it before.

The last thing we did was **decorate** the yard all up. I **strung** pink and orange and yellow crêpe paper* in the trees to make it look **fancy**. We also **filled up** paper bags with sand and put **candle**s in them, and right before it was time for the party to start, I went around and **lit** all the candles. It turned Gloria Dump's yard into a **fairyland**.

"Mmmm-hmmm," said Gloria Dump, looking around. "Even somebody with bad eyes can tell it looks good."

It did look pretty. It looked so pretty that it made my heart feel funny, all **swollen** and full, and I wished **desperate**ly that I knew where my mama was so she could come to the party, too.

Miss Franny Block was the first person to arrive. She was wearing a pretty green dress that was all **shiny** and **shimmer**y. And she had on **high-heeled** shoes that made her **wobble back and forth** when she walked. Even when she was standing still, she still kind of **sway**ed, like she was standing on a boat. She was carrying a big glass bowl full

---

★ punch 펀치. 술, 설탕, 레몬 등으로 만드는 음료.
✹ grapefruit [식물] 자몽.
✳ crêpe paper 주름 종이.

of Littmus Lozenges. "I brought a little after-dinner **treat**," she said, **hand**ing the bowl to me.

"Thank you," I said. I put the bowl on the table next to the egg-salad sandwiches and the punch. Then I introduced Miss Franny to Gloria, and they **shook hands** and said **polite** things to each other.

And then Sweetie Pie's mother came by with Sweetie Pie. Sweetie Pie had a whole **handful** of pictures of dogs that she had cut out of magazines. "It's to help you with your **theme**," she said. "You can use them to decorate. I brung* tape, too." And she started going around taping the pictures of the dogs to the trees and the chairs and the table.

"She ain't talked about nothing but this party all day long," said her mother. "Can you walk her home when it's over?"

I **promise**d that I would, and then I introduced Sweetie Pie to Miss Franny and to Gloria, and right after that the preacher **show**ed **up**. He was wearing a coat and tie and looked real serious. He shook Gloria Dump's hand and Miss Franny Block's hand and said how pleased he was to meet them both and how he had heard nothing but good things about both of them. He **pat**ted Sweetie Pie on the head

---

★ brung bring의 과거·과거분사인 'brought'의 사투리.

and said it was good to see her outside of church. And the whole time Winn-Dixie was standing right in the middle of everybody, wagging his tail so hard that I thought for sure he would **knock** Miss Franny right **off** her high heels.

Amanda Wilkinson came and she had her **blond** hair all **curl**ed up and she looked shy and not as **mean** as usual, and I stood real close to her and introduced her to Gloria Dump. I was surprised at how glad I was to see Amanda. And I wanted to tell her I knew about Carson. I wanted to tell her I understood about losing people, but I didn't say anything. I was just **extra** nice.

We were all standing around smiling at **one another** and acting kind of **nervous**, when a real **screech**y voice said, "Gertrude is a pretty bird."

Winn-Dixie's ears went straight up on his head, and he **bark**ed once and looked around. I looked, too, but I didn't see Gertrude. Or Otis.

"I'll be right back," I said to everybody. Me and Winn-Dixie went running around to the front of the house. And sure enough, standing there on the **sidewalk** was Otis. He had his guitar on his back and Gertrude on his shoulder, and in his hands he was holding the biggest **jar** of pickles I had ever seen in my life.

"Otis," I said to him, "come on around the back, that's where the party is."

"Oh," he said. But he didn't move. He just stood there, holding on to his jar of pickles.

"Dog," screeched Gertrude. She flew off Otis's shoulder and **land**ed on Winn-Dixie's head.

"It's all right, Otis," I told him. "It's just a few people, **hardly** any people at all."

"Oh," said Otis again. He looked around like he was **lost**. Then he held up the jar of pickles. "I brought pickles," he said.

"I saw them," I said. "It's just exactly what we needed. They will go perfect with the egg-salad sandwiches." I talked to him real soft and gentle and low, like he was a wild animal that I was trying to get to take food out of my hand.

He took one **tiny** step forward.

"Come on," I whispered. I started walking and Winn-Dixie followed me. And when I **turned around**, I saw Otis was following me, too.

Chapter Twenty-Two

Otis followed me **all the way** into the backyard, where the party was. Before he could **run away**, I introduced him to the preacher.

"Daddy," I said, "this is Otis. He's the one who **runs** Gertrude's Pets. He's the one who plays the guitar so good."

"How do you do?" said the preacher. He **stuck** his hand out to Otis. And Otis stood there and **shuffled** his big **jar** of pickles **back and forth**, trying to **free up** a hand to **offer** back to the preacher. Finally he **ended up bend**ing over and setting the jar down on the ground. But when he did that, his guitar **slid** forward and hit him in the head with a little *boing* sound; Sweetie Pie laughed and pointed at him like he was doing the whole thing **on purpose** just to **amuse** her.

"Ouch," said Otis. He stood back up and took the guitar off his shoulder and put it down on the ground next to the jar of pickles, and then he **wiped** his hand on his pants and stuck it out to the preacher, who took it and said, "It sure is a **pleasure** to **shake** your **hand**."

"Thank you," said Otis. "I brought pickles."

"I **noticed**," said the preacher.

After the preacher and Otis were done shaking hands, I introduced Otis to Miss Franny Block and to Amanda.

And then I introduced him to Gloria Dump. Gloria took his hand and smiled at him. And Otis looked right in her eyes and smiled back. He smiled big.

"I brought pickles for your party," Otis told her.

"And I am so glad," she said. "It just ain't a party without pickles."

Otis looked down at his big jar of pickles. His face was all red.

"Opal," said Gloria, "when are them boys getting here?"

"I don't know," I said. I **shrug**ged. "I told them what time we were starting." What I didn't tell her was that they probably weren't coming, because they were afraid to go to a party at a **witch**'s house.

"Well," said Gloria. "We got egg-salad sandwiches. We got Dump Punch. We got pickles. We got dog pictures. We got Littmus Lozenges. And we got a preacher, who can

bless this party for us."

Gloria Dump looked over at the preacher.

He **nod**ded his head at Gloria and cleared his **throat** and said, "Dear God, thank you for warm summer nights and **candlelight** and good food. But thank you most of all for friends. We **appreciate** the **complicated** and wonderful gifts you give us in each other. And we appreciate the **task** you put down before us, of loving each other the best we can, even as you love us. We **pray** in Christ's name. Amen."

"Amen," said Gloria Dump.

"Amen," I **whisper**ed.

"Gertrude," **croak**ed Gertrude.

"Are we **fix**ing to eat now?" Sweetie Pie asked.

"Shhh," said Amanda.

Winn-Dixie **sneeze**d.

There was a **far-off rumble** of **thunder**. I thought at first that it was Winn-Dixie's **stomach growl**ing.

"It ain't supposed to rain," said Gloria Dump. "They didn't **predict** no rain."

"This dress is silk," said Miss Franny Block. "I cannot get it **wet**."

"Maybe we should go inside," said Amanda.

The preacher looked up at the sky.

And just then, the rain came **pour**ing down.

Chapter Twenty-Three

"Save the sandwiches," Gloria Dump yelled to me. "Save the punch."

"I got my dog pictures," screamed Sweetie Pie. She went running around, tearing them off the trees and the chairs. "Don't worry," she kept shouting. "I got 'em."

I grabbed the platter of egg-salad sandwiches and the preacher grabbed the punch, and we ran into the kitchen with them; and when I ran back outside, I saw that Amanda had hold of Miss Franny Block and was helping her into the house. Miss Franny was so teetery in her high heels that the rain would have knocked her right over if Amanda hadn't held on to her.

I grabbed Gloria Dump's arm.

"I'm all right," she said. But she put her hand on my arm

and held on to me **tight**.

I looked around the garden before we left. All the crêpe paper was **melt**ed and the **candle**s were out, and then I saw Otis. He was standing there by his **jar** of pickles, looking down at his feet.

"Otis," I **holler**ed at him over the rain, "come on, we're going inside."

When we got in the kitchen, Amanda and Miss Franny were laughing and shaking themselves like dogs.

"What a **downpour**," said Miss Franny. "Wasn't that something?"

"That came right out of nowhere," said the **preacher**.

"Whoooeee," said Gloria.

"Dog," **squawk**ed Gertrude. I looked at her. She was sitting on the kitchen table. The **thunder** was really **boom**ing and **crack**ing.

"Oh no," I said. I looked around the kitchen.

"Don't worry," said Sweetie Pie. "I saved them dog pictures. I got 'em right here." She **wave**d around her **wad** of magazine pages.

"Where's Winn-Dixie?" I shouted. "I forgot about him. I was just thinking about the party and I forgot about Winn-Dixie. I forgot about **protect**ing him from the thunder."

"Now, Opal," the preacher said, "he's probably right out

in the yard, hiding **underneath** a chair. Come on, you and I will go look."

"Hold on," said Gloria Dump, "let me get you a **flashlight** and some umbrellas."

But I didn't want to wait. I went running out into the yard. I looked under all the chairs and around all the **bush**es and trees. I called his name real loud. I felt like crying. It was my **fault**. I was supposed to hold on to him. And I forgot.

"Opal," I heard the preacher call.

I looked up. He was standing on the **porch** with Gloria. And Dunlap and Stevie Dewberry were standing there, too.

"Your guests are here," the preacher said.

"I don't care," I hollered.

"Come on up here," Gloria Dump said, her voice all hard and serious. She **shone** her flashlight out at me.

I walked up to the porch and she **hand**ed me the flashlight. "Tell these boys, 'hey'," she said. "Tell them you are glad they came and that you will be right back just as soon as you find your dog."

"Hey," I said. "Thank you for coming. I just got to find Winn-Dixie and then I'll be right back."

Stevie **stared** at me with his mouth wide open.

"You want me to help?" Dunlap asked.

I shook my head. I tried not to cry.

"Come here, child," Gloria Dump said. She reached for me and pulled me close to her and whispered in my ear, "There ain't no way you can hold on to something that wants to go, you understand? You can only love what you got while you got it."

She squeezed me hard.

"Good luck now," she called, as me and the preacher stepped off the porch and out into the rain.

"Good luck," Miss Franny called from the kitchen.

"That dog ain't lost," I heard Sweetie Pie holler to somebody inside. "That dog's too smart to get lost."

I turned around and looked back, and the last thing I saw was the porch light shining on Dunlap Dewberry's bald head. It made me sad, him standing on Gloria's porch, his bald head glowing. Dunlap saw me looking, and he raised up his hand and waved to me. I didn't wave back.

Chapter Twenty-Four

Me and the **preacher** started walking and calling Winn-Dixie's name. I was glad it was raining so hard, because it made it easy to cry. I cried and cried and cried, and the whole time I was calling for Winn-Dixie.

"Winn-Dixie," I screamed.

"Winn-Dixie," the preacher shouted. And then he **whistle**d loud and long. But Winn-Dixie didn't **show up**.

We walked all through town. We walked past the Dewberrys' house and the Herman W. Block **Memorial** Library and Sweetie Pie's yellow house and Gertrude's Pets. We walked out to the Friendly Corners Trailer Park and looked underneath our **trailer**. We walked **all the way** out to the Open Arms Baptist Church of Naomi. We walked past the **railroad track**s and right on down Highway 50.

Cars were rushing past us and their tail lights* glowed red, like mean eyes staring at us.

"Daddy," I said. "Daddy, what if he got run over?"

"Opal," the preacher said. "We can't worry about what might have happened. All we can do is keep looking."

We walked and walked. And in my head I started on a list of ten things that I knew about Winn-Dixie, things I could write on big old posters and put up around the neighborhood, things that would help people look for him.

Number one was that he had a pathological fear of thunderstorms.

Number two was he liked to smile, using all his teeth.

Number three was he could run fast.

Number four was that he snored.

Number five was that he could catch mice without squishing them to death.

Number six was he liked to meet people.

Number seven was he liked to eat peanut butter.

Number eight was he couldn't stand to be left alone.

Number nine was he liked to sit on couches and sleep in beds.

Number ten was he didn't mind going to church.

I kept on going over and over the list in my head. I

★ tail light 자동차나 자전거 뒤에 붙은 꼬리(tail)등(light).

114

memorized it the same way I had memorized the list of ten things about my mama. I memorized it so if I didn't find him, I would have some part of him to **hold on to**. But at the same time I thought of something I had never thought of before, and that was that a list of things couldn't even begin to show somebody the real Winn-Dixie, just like a list of ten things couldn't ever get me to know my mama. And thinking about that made me cry even more.

Me and the preacher looked for a long time; and finally he said we had to **quit**.

"But Daddy," I said, "Winn-Dixie's out there somewhere. We can't leave him."

"Opal," the preacher said, "we have looked and looked, and there's only so much looking we can do."

"I can't believe you're going to **give up**," I told him.

"India Opal," the preacher said, **rub**bing his nose, "don't **argue** with me."

I stood and stared at him. The rain had **let up** some. It was mostly a **drizzle** now.

"It's time to **head** back," the preacher said.

"No," I told him. "You go ahead and go, but I'm going to keep on looking."

"Opal," the preacher said in a real soft voice, "it's time to give up."

"You always give up!" I shouted. "You're always pulling

your head inside your stupid old **turtle shell**. I **bet** you didn't even go out looking for my mama when she left. I bet you just let her **run off**, too."

"Baby," the preacher said. "I couldn't stop her. I tried. Don't you think I wanted her to stay, too? Don't you think I miss her every day?" He **spread** his arms out wide and then dropped them to his sides. "I tried," he said. "I tried." Then he did something I couldn't believe.

He started to cry. The preacher was crying. His shoulders were moving up and down. And he was making **snuffly** noises. "And don't believe that losing Winn-Dixie doesn't upset me as much as it does you," he said. "I love that dog. I love him, too."

"Daddy," I said. I went and **wrap**ped my arms around his **waist**. He was crying so hard he was shaking. "It's all right," I told him. "It's okay. Shhhhh," I said to him like he was a scared little kid. "Everything will be okay."

We stood there hugging and **rocking back and forth**, and after a while the preacher stopped shaking and I still held on to him; and I finally got the **nerve** to ask the question I wanted to ask.

"Do you think she's ever going to come back?" I **whisper**ed.

"No," the preacher said. "No, I do not. I've hoped and **pray**ed and dreamed about it for years. But I don't think

116

she'll ever come back."

"Gloria says that you can't hold on to anything. That you can only love what you've got while you've got it."

"She's right," the preacher said. "Gloria Dump is right."

"I'm not ready to let Winn-Dixie go," I said. I had forgotten about him for a minute, what with thinking about my mama.

"We'll keep looking," said the preacher. "The two of us will keep looking for him. But do you know what? I just **realize**d something, India Opal. When I told you your mama took everything with her, I forgot one thing, one very important thing that she left behind."

"What?" I asked.

"You," he said. "Thank God your mama left me you." And he hugged me **tight**er.

"I'm glad I've got you, too," I told him. And I meant it. I took hold of his hand, and we started walking back into town, calling and whistling for Winn-Dixie the whole way.

Chapter Twenty-Five

We heard the music before we even got to Gloria Dump's house. We heard it almost a block★ away. It was guitar-playing and singing and **clap**ping.

"I **wonder** what's going on?" my father said.

We walked up Gloria's **sidewalk** and around the back, through her yard and into her kitchen, and what we saw was Otis playing his guitar, and Miss Franny and Gloria sitting there smiling and singing, and Gloria holding Sweetie Pie in her **lap**. Amanda and Dunlap and Stevie were sitting on the kitchen floor, clapping along and having the best possible time. Even Amanda was smiling. I couldn't believe they were so happy when Winn-Dixie was

---

★ block 블록. 시가지나 주거 지대의 작은 단위들을 몇 개 합친 일정한 구획.

missing.

"We didn't find him," I shouted at them.

The music stopped and Gloria Dump looked at me and said, "Child, we know you didn't find him. You didn't find him because he was right here all along."

She took her **cane** and **poke**d at something under her chair. "Come on out of there," she said.

There was a **snuffle** and a **sigh**.

"He's asleep," she said. "He's **plumb wore out**."

She poked around with her cane again. And Winn-Dixie stood up from **underneath** her chair and **yawn**ed.

"Winn-Dixie!" I **holler**ed.

"Dog," Gertrude **squawk**ed.

Winn-Dixie **wag**ged his **tail** and showed me all his teeth and **sneeze**d. I went pushing past everybody. I dropped to the floor and **wrap**ped my arms around him.

"Where have you been?" I asked him.

He yawned again.

"How did you find him?" I asked.

"Now there's a story," said Miss Franny. "Gloria, why don't you tell it?"

"Well," said Gloria Dump, "we was all just sitting around waiting on you two. And after I **convince**d these Dewberry boys that I ain't no **scary witch** all full of **spells** and **potion**s—"

"She ain't no witch," Stevie said. He shook his **bald** head. He looked kind of disappointed.

"Naw," said Dunlap. "She ain't. If she was, she would've **turned** us **into toad**s by now." He **grin**ned.

"I could have told you that she wasn't a witch. Witches don't **exist**," said Amanda. "They are just **myth**s."

"All right now," said Gloria. "What happened was we got through all them **witchy** things and then Franny said, why don't we have a little music while we wait for those two to get back. And so Otis played his guitar. And whoooeee, there ain't a song he don't know. And if he don't know it, he can **pick** it **up** right quick if you **hum** it to him. He has a **gift**."

Gloria stopped and smiled over at Otis, and he smiled back. He looked all **lit** up from the inside.

"Tell what happened," Sweetie Pie said. "Tell about that dog."

"So," said Gloria. "Franny and me, we started thinking about all these songs we knew from when we was girls. We got Otis to play them and we started singing them, teaching the words to these children."

"And then somebody sneezed," Sweetie Pie shouted.

"That's right," said Gloria. "Somebody sneezed and it wasn't none of us. So we looked around, wondering who did, thinking that maybe we got us a **burglar** in the house.

120

We looked around and we didn't see nothing, so we started into singing again. And sure enough, there was another big *achoo*. Sounded like it was coming from my bedroom. So I sent Otis in there. I said, 'Otis, **go on** in there and see who is sneezing.' So Otis went. And do you know what he found?"

I shook my head.

"Winn-Dixie!" shouted Sweetie Pie.

"That dog of yours was all hid underneath my bed, **squeeze**d under there like the world was about to end. But he was smiling like a fool every time he heard Otis play the guitar, smiling so hard he sneezed."

My daddy laughed.

"It is true," Miss Franny said.

"It's the truth," said Stevie.

Dunlap **nod**ded and smiled right at me.

"So," Gloria Dump said, "Otis played his guitar right to that dog, and, a little bit at a time, Winn-Dixie came **creep**ing out from underneath the bed."

"He was covered in **dust**," said Amanda.

"He looked like a ghost," said Dunlap.

"Yeah," said Sweetie Pie, "just like a ghost."

"Mmmm-hmmm," said Gloria. "Looked just like a ghost. Anyway, the **storm** stopped after a while. And your dog **settle**d in under my chair. And **fell asleep**. And that's where he's been ever since, just waiting on you to come back and find him."

"Winn-Dixie," I said. I hugged him so **tight** he **wheezed**. "We were out there **whistling** and calling for you and you were right here all along. Thank you," I said to everybody.

"Well," said Gloria Dump. "We didn't do nothin'. We just sat here and waited and sang some songs. We all got to be good friends. Now. The punch ain't nothin' but water and the egg-salad sandwiches got **tore** up by the rain. You got to eat them with a spoon if you want egg salad. But we got pickles to eat. And Littmus Lozenges. And we still got a party going on."

My daddy pulled out a kitchen chair and sat down.

"Otis," he said, "do you know any **hymns**?"

"I know some," said Otis.

"You hum it," said Miss Franny, nodding her head, "and he can play it."

So my daddy started humming something and Otis started picking it out on his guitar, and Winn-Dixie wagged his tail and **lay** back down underneath Gloria's chair. I looked around the room at all the different faces, and I felt my heart **swell** up inside me with **pure** happiness.

"I'll be back in a minute," I said.

But they were all singing now and laughing, and Winn-Dixie was **snoring**, so no one heard me.

Chapter Twenty-Six

Outside, the rain had stopped and the clouds had gone away and the sky was so clear it seemed like I could see every star ever made. I walked all the way to the back of Gloria Dump's yard. I walked back there and looked at her mistake tree. The bottles were quiet; there wasn't a **breeze**, so they were just **hang**ing there. I looked at the tree and then I looked up at the sky.

"Mama," I said, just like she was standing right beside me, "I know ten things about you, and that's not enough, that's not near enough. But Daddy is going to tell me more; I know he will, now that he knows you're not coming back. He misses you and I miss you, but my heart doesn't feel **empty** any more. It's full **all the way** up. I'll still think about you, I **promise**. But probably not as much as I did this summer."

That's what I said that night **underneath** Gloria Dump's mistake tree. And after I was done saying it, I stood just **staring** up at the sky, looking at the **constellations** and **planets**. And then I remembered my own tree, the one Gloria had helped me plant. I hadn't looked at it for a long time. I went **crawl**ing around on my hands and knees, searching for it. And when I found it, I was surprised at how much it had grown. It was still small. It still looked more like a plant than a tree. But the **leaves** and the **branch**es felt real strong and good and right. I was down there on my knees when I heard a voice say, "Are you **pray**ing?"

I looked up. It was Dunlap.

"No," I said. "I'm not praying. I'm thinking."

He crossed his arms and looked down at me. "What about?" he asked.

"All kinds of different things," I said. "I'm sorry that I called you and Stevie **bald**-headed babies."

"That's all right," he said. "Gloria told me to come out here and get you."

"I told you she wasn't a **witch**."

"I know it," he said. "I knew it all along. I was just **teasing** you."

"Oh," I said. I looked at him close. It was hard to see

him good in the dark yard.

"Ain't you ever gonna stand up?" he asked.

"Yeah," I said.

And then he surprised me. He did something I never in a million years thought a Dewberry boy would do. He **held out** his hand to help me up. And I took it. I let him pull me to my feet.

"I'll **race** you back to the house," Dunlap said. And he started to run.

"OK," I shouted. "But I'm **warn**ing you, I'm fast."

We ran, and I **beat** him. I touched the corner of Gloria Dump's house right before he did.

"You shouldn't be running around in the dark," said Amanda. She was standing on the **porch**, looking at us. "You could **trip** over something."

"Aw, Amanda," said Dunlap, and he shook his head.

"Aw, Amanda," I said, too. And then I remembered Carson and I felt bad for her. I went up on the porch and took hold of her hand and pulled on her. "Come on," I said, "let's go inside."

"India Opal," Daddy said when me and Amanda and Dunlap walked in. "Are you here to sing some songs with us?"

"Yes sir," I said. "Only I don't know that many songs."

"We'll teach you," he said. He smiled at me real big. It was a good thing to see.

"That's right," said Gloria Dump. "We will." Sweetie Pie was still sitting in her **lap**, but her eyes were closed.

"**Care for** a Littmus Lozenge?" Miss Franny asked, **pass**ing me the **bowl**.

"Thank you," I told her. I took a Littmus Lozenge and **unwrap**ped it and put it in my mouth.

"Do you want a pickle?" Otis asked, holding up his big **jar** of pickles.

"No, thank you," I said. "Not right now."

Winn-Dixie came out from underneath Gloria Dump's chair. He sat down next to me and **lean**ed into me the same as I was leaning into my daddy. And Amanda stood right there beside me, and when I looked over at her, she didn't look **pinch**-faced at all to me.

Dunlap **crack**ed his **knuckle**s and said, "Well, are we gonna sing or what?"

"Yeah," Stevie **echo**ed, "Are we gonna sing or what?"

"Let's sing," said Sweetie Pie, opening her eyes and **sit**ting **up** straight. "Let's sing for the dog."

Otis laughed and **strum**med his guitar, and the **flavor** of the Littmus Lozenge opened in my mouth like a flower **bloom**ing, all sweet and sad. And then Otis and Gloria and Stevie and Miss Franny and Dunlap and Amanda and Sweetie Pie and my daddy all started to sing a song. And I listened careful, so I could learn it right.

Because of Winn-Dixie

Because of Winn-Dixie

Kate DiCamillo

Contents

뉴베리 상이란?

'아동 도서계의 노벨상!' 미국 최고 권위의 아동 문학상

뉴베리 상(Newbery Award)은 미국 도서관 협회에서 해마다 미국 아동 문학 발전에 가장 크게 이바지한 작가에게 수여하는 아동 문학상입니다. 1922년에 시작된 이 상은 미국에서 가장 오랜 역사를 지닌 아동 문학상일 뿐 아니라, '아동 도서계의 노벨상'이라 불릴 만큼 최고의 권위를 자랑하고 있습니다.

뉴베리 상은 그 역사와 권위만큼이나 심사기준이 까다롭기로 유명한데, 심사단은 책의 주제의식은 물론 정보의 깊이와 스토리의 정교함, 캐릭터와 문체의 적정성 등을 꼼꼼히 평가하여 수상작을 결정합니다.

그해 최고의 작품으로 선정되면 금색 메달을 수여하기 때문에 '뉴베리 메달 (Newbery Medal)'이라고 부르며, 후보에 올랐던 주목할 만한 작품들은 '뉴베리 아너(Newbery Honor)'라고 하여 은색 마크를 수여합니다.

뉴베리 상을 받게 되면 미국의 모든 도서관에 비치되어 더 많은 독자들을 만나게 되며, 대부분 수십에서 수백만 부가 판매되는 베스트셀러가 됩니다. 뿐만 아니라 뉴베리 상을 수상한 작가는 그만큼 필력과 작품성을 인정받게 되어, 수상작이 아닌 작품들도 수상작 못지않게 커다란 주목과 사랑을 받습니다.

왜 뉴베리 수상작인가?
쉬운 어휘로 쓰인 '검증된' 영어원서!

'뉴베리 수상작'들은 '검증된 원서'로 국내 영어 학습자들에게 큰 사랑을 받고 있습니다. '뉴베리 수상작'이 원서 읽기에 좋은 교재인 이유는 무엇일까요?

1. 아동 문학인 만큼 어휘가 어렵지 않습니다.
2. 어렵지 않은 어휘를 사용하면서도 '문학상'을 수상한 만큼 문장의 깊이가 상당합니다.
3. 적당한 난이도의 어휘와 깊이 있는 문장으로 구성되어 있기 때문에 초등 고학년부터 성인까지, 영어 초보자부터 실력자까지 모든 영어 학습자들이 읽기에 좋습니다.

실제로 뉴베리 수상작은 국제중·특목고에서는 입시 필독서로, 대학교에서는 영어 강독 교재로 다양하고 폭넓게 활용되고 있습니다. 이런 이유로 뉴베리 수상작은 한국어 번역서보다 오히려 원서가 훨씬 많이 판매되는 기현상을 보이고 있습니다.

'베스트 오브 베스트'만을 엄선한 「뉴베리 컬렉션」

「뉴베리 컬렉션」은 뉴베리 메달 및 아너 수상작, 그리고 뉴베리 수상 작가의 유명 작품들을 엄선하여 한국 영어 학습자들을 위한 최적의 교재로 재탄생시킨 영어 원서 시리즈입니다.

  1. 어휘 수준과 문장의 난이도, 분량 등 국내 영어 학습자들에게 적합한 정도를 종합적으로 검토하여 선정하였습니다.
  2. 기존 원서 독자층 사이의 인기도까지 감안하여 최적의 작품들을 선별하였습니다.
  3. 판형이 좁고 글씨가 작아 읽기 힘들었던 원서 디자인을 대폭 수정하여, 판형을 시원하게 키우고 읽기에 최적화된 영문 서체를 사용하여 가독성을 극대화하였습니다.
  4. 함께 제공되는 워크북은 어려운 어휘를 완벽하게 정리하고 이해력을 점검하는 퀴즈를 덧붙여 독자들이 원서를 보다 쉽고 재미있게 읽을 수 있도록 구성하였습니다.
  5. 기존에 높은 가격에 판매되어 구입이 부담스러웠던 오디오북을 부록으로 제공하여 리스닝과 소리 내어 읽기에까지 원서를 두루 활용할 수 있도록 했습니다.

케이트 디카밀로(Kate DiCamillo)는 화려한 수상 경력을 가지고 있는, 미국의 대표적인 아동 문학 작가입니다. 그녀는 『Because of Winn-Dixie』로 뉴베리 아너를 수상하며 이름을 알리기 시작했고, 『The Tiger Rising』으로 전미도서상(National Book Award)의 최종 후보에 올랐습니다. 그리고 판타지 문학 작품인 『The Tale of Despereaux』는 "미국 아동 문학에 가장 크게 기여한" 작품이라는 평과 함께 뉴베리 메달을 수상하여 큰 인기몰이를 하였습니다. 또한 『The Miraculous Journey of Edward Tulane』으로 우수한 아동 문학에 수여하는 보스턴 글로브-혼 도서상(Boston Globe-Horn Book Award)을 받는 등 문학성을 여러 차례 검증 받고 있습니다.

『Because of Winn-Dixie』는 주인공 인디아 오팔(India Opal)과 목사인 그녀의 아버지가 플로리다(Florida)주 나오미(Naomi)로 이주한 후 일어난 일들을 그리고 있습니다. 어느 여름 날, 오팔은 Winn-Dixie 슈퍼마켓에서 우연히 주인 잃은 개와 마주치고, 그 개를 윈딕시(Winn-Dixie)라고 이름을 부르며 함께 생활하기 시작합니다. 온화하고 상냥하며 사람들에게 친근한 윈딕시 덕분에 오팔은 목사에게서 그녀 곁을 떠난 엄마에 대한 이야기를 듣게 되고, 또 상처와 아픔을 가진 마을 사람들을 만나 그것에 대한 이야기를 듣게 됩니다. 그리고 그 모두에게서 오팔은 우정과 용서를 배우게 됩니다.
이 작품은 2000년 출간된 직후 뉴베리 상 후보에 올라 뉴베리 아너를 수상하였고, "긍정적이고 현실적인 방식으로 어려움을 극복하고 성장해가는 아동 및 청소년의 모습을 그린, 문학적 가치"를 지닌 작품에 수여하는 조세트 프랭크상(Josette Frank Award)도 수상하였습니다. 또한 두 차례나 "교사들이 선정한 아동 문학 100선"에 오르기도 했으며, 영화로도 제작되어 큰 인기를 얻었습니다.

이 책의 구성

원서 본문

내용이 담긴 원서 본문입니다.
원어민이 읽는 일반 원서와 같은 텍스트지만,
암기해야 할 중요 어휘들은 볼드체로 표시되
어 있습니다. 이 어휘들은 지금 들고 계신 워
크북에 챕터별로 정리되어 있습니다.

학습 심리학 연구 결과에 따르면, 한 단어씩
따로 외우는 단어 암기는 거의 효과가 없다고
합니다. 단어를 제대로 외우기 위해서는 문맥
(context) 속에서 단어를 암기해야 하며, 한 단
어당 문맥 속에서 15번 이상 마주칠 때 완벽하
게 암기할 수 있다고 합니다.

이 책의 본문에서는 중요 어휘를 볼드체로 강조하여, 문맥 속의 단어들을 더 확
실히 인지(word cognition in context)하도록 돕고 있습니다. 또한 대부분의 중요 단
어들은 다른 챕터에서도 반복해서 등장하기 때문에 이 책을 읽는 것만으로도 자
연스럽게 어휘력을 향상시킬 수 있습니다.

또한 본문 하단에는 내용 이해를 돕기 위한
'각주'가 첨가되어 있습니다. 각주는 군이 암기
할 필요는 없지만, 알아 두면 도움이 될 만한
정보를 설명하고 있습니다. 각주를 참고하면
스토리를 더 깊이 있게 이해할 수 있어 원서를
읽는 재미가 배가됩니다.

워크북(Workbook)

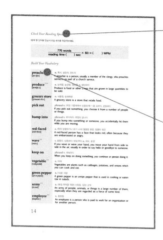

Check Your Reading Speed

해당 챕터의 단어 수가 기록되어 있어, 리딩 속도를 측정할 수 있습니다. 특히 리딩 속도를 중시하는 독자들이 유용하게 사용할 수 있습니다.

Build Your Vocabulary

본문에 볼드 표시되어 있던 단어들이 정리되어 있습니다. 리딩 전, 후에 반복해서 보면 원서를 더욱 쉽게 읽을 수 있고, 어휘력도 빠르게 향상될 것입니다.

단어는 〈스펠링 – 빈도 – 발음기호 – 품사 – 한글 뜻 – 영문 뜻〉 순서로 표기되어 있으며 빈도 표시(★)가 많을수록 필수 어휘입니다. 반복해서 등장하는 단어는 빈도 대신 '복습'으로 표기되어 있습니다. 품사는 아래와 같이 표기했습니다.

n. 명사 | a. 형용사 | ad. 부사 | v. 동사
conj. 접속사 | prep. 전치사 | int. 감탄사 | idiom 숙어 및 관용구

Comprehension Quiz

간단한 퀴즈를 통해 읽은 내용에 대한 이해력을 점검해 볼 수 있습니다.

이 책의 활용법

「뉴베리 컬렉션」 이렇게 읽어 보세요!

아래와 같이 프리뷰(Preview) → 리딩(Reading) → 리뷰(Review) 세 단계를 거치면서 읽으면, 더욱 효과적으로 영어 실력을 향상할 수 있습니다!

1. 프리뷰(Preview) : 오늘 읽을 내용을 먼저 점검하자!

- 워크북을 통해 오늘 읽을 챕터에 나와 있는 단어들을 쭉 훑어봅니다. 어떤 단어들이 나오는지, 내가 아는 단어와 모르는 단어가 어떤 것들이 있는지 가벼운 마음으로 살펴봅니다.
- 평소처럼 하나하나 쓰면서 암기하려고 하지는 마세요! 익숙하지 않은 단어들을 주의 깊게 보되, 어차피 리딩을 하면서 점차 익숙해질 단어라는 것을 기억하며 빠르게 훑어봅니다.
- 뒤 챕터로 갈수록 '복습'이라고 표시된 단어들이 늘어나는 것을 알 수 있습니다. '복습' 단어인데도 여전히 익숙하지 않다면 더욱 신경을 써서 봐야겠죠? 매일매일 꾸준히 읽는다면, 익숙한 단어들이 점점 많아진다는 것을 몸으로 느낄 수 있습니다.

2. 리딩(Reading) : 내용에 집중하며 빠르게 읽어 나가자!

- 프리뷰를 마친 후 바로 리딩을 시작합니다. 방금 살펴봤던 어휘들을 문장 속에서 다시 만나게 되는데 이 과정에서 단어의 쓰임새와 어감을 자연스럽게 익히게 됩니다.
- 모르는 단어나 이해되지 않는 문장이 나오더라도 멈추지 말고 전체적인 맥락을 잡아가면서 속도감 있게 읽어 나가세요. 이해되지 않는 문장들은 따로 표시를 하되, 일단 넘어가고 계속 읽는 것이 좋습니다. 뒷부분을 읽다 보면 자연히 이해가 되는 경우도 있고, 정 이해가 되지 않는 부분은 리딩을 마친 이후에 따로 리뷰하는 시간을 가지면 됩니다. 문제집을 풀듯이 모든 문장을 분석하면서 원서를 읽는 것이 아니라, 리딩을 할 때는 리딩에만, 리뷰를 할 때는 리뷰에만 집중하는 것이 필요합니다.
- 볼드 처리된 단어의 의미가 궁금하더라도 워크북을 바로 펼치지 마세요. 정 궁금하다면 한 번씩 참고하는 것도 나쁘진 않지만, 워크북과 원서를 번갈아 보면서 읽는 것은 리딩의 흐름을 끊고 단어 하나하나에 집착하는 좋지 않은 리딩 습관을 심어 줄 수 있습니다.
- 같은 맥락에서 번역서를 구해 원서와 동시에 번갈아 보는 것도 좋은 방법이 아닙니다. 한글 번역을 가지고 있다고 해도 일단 영어로 읽을 때는 영어에만 집중하고 어느 정도 분량을 읽은 후에 번역서와 비교하도록 하세요. 모든 문장을 일일이 번역해서 완벽하게 이해하려는 것은 오히려 좋지 않은 리딩 습관을 심

10

어 주어 장기적으로는 바람직하지 않은 결과를 얻을 수 있습니다. 처음부터 완벽하게 이해하려고 하는 것보다는 빠른 속도로 2~3회 반복해서 읽는 방식이 실력 향상에 더 도움이 됩니다. 만일 반복해서 읽어도 내용이 전혀 이해되지 않아 곤란하다면 책 선정에 문제가 있다고 할 수 있습니다. 그럴 때는 좀 더 쉬운 책을 골라 실력을 다진 뒤 다시 도전하는 것이 좋습니다.

- 초보자라면 분당 150단어의 리딩 속도를 목표로 잡고 리딩을 합니다. 분당 150단어는 원어민이 말하는 속도로, 영어 학습자들이 리스닝과 스피킹으로 넘어가기 위해 가장 기초적으로 달성해야 하는 단계입니다. 분당 50~80단어 정도의 낮은 리딩 속도를 가지고 있는 경우는 대부분 영어 실력이 부족해서라기보다 '잘못된 리딩 습관'을 가지고 있어서 그렇습니다. 이해력이 조금 떨어진다고 하더라도 분당 150단어까지는 속도에 대한 긴장감을 놓치지 말고 속도감 있게 읽어 나가도록 하세요.

3. 리뷰(Review) : 이해력을 점검하고 꼼꼼하게 다시 살펴보자!

- 해당 챕터의 Comprehension Quiz를 통해 이해력을 점검해 봅니다.
- 오늘 만난 어휘들을 다시 한번 복습합니다. 이때는 읽으면서 중요하다고 생각했던 단어를 연습장에 써 보면서 꼼꼼하게 외우는 것도 좋습니다.
- 이해가 되지 않는다고 표시해 두었던 부분도 주의 깊게 분석해 봅니다. 다시 한번 문장을 꼼꼼히 읽고, 어떤 이유에서 이해가 되지 않았는지 생각해 봅니다. 따로 메모를 남기거나 노트를 작성하는 것도 좋은 방법입니다.
- 사실 꼼꼼히 리뷰하는 것은 매우 고된 과정입니다. 원서를 읽고 리뷰하는 시간을 가지는 것이 영어 실력 향상에 많은 도움이 되기는 하지만, 이 과정을 철저히 지키려다가 원서 읽기의 재미를 반감시키는 것은 바람직하지 않습니다. 그럴 때는 차라리 리뷰를 가볍게 하는 것이 좋을 수 있습니다. '내용에 빠져서 재미있게', 문제집에서는 상상도 못할 '많은 양'을 읽으면서, 매일매일 조금씩 꾸준히 실력을 키워가는 것이 원서를 활용하는 기본적인 방법이며, 영어 공부의 왕도입니다. 문제집 풀듯이 원서 읽기를 시도하고 접근해서는 실패할 수밖에 없습니다.
- 이런 방식으로 원서를 끝까지 다 읽었다면, 다시 반복해서 읽거나 오디오북을 활용하는 등 다양한 방식으로 원서 읽기를 확장해 나갈 수 있습니다. 이에 대한 자세한 안내가 워크북 말미에 실려 있습니다.

1. Where did Opal find the dog?
   A. A restaurant
   B. A grocery store
   C. A farmer's market
   D. The library

2. What did the dog do when he skidded to a stop?
   A He smiled at Opal.
   B. He growled at the employees.
   C. He barked at customers.
   D. He whined from pain.

3. What was NOT true about the dog?
   A. He was big.
   B. He was skinny.
   C. He had black spots.
   D. He had bald patches.

4. Why did Opal's father call her "Opal"?
   A. She was born in a town called Opal.
   B. Her grandmother's name was Opal.
   C. Opal was her favorite gem.
   D. Opal was named after her mother.

5. Opal's father is a _____.
   A. lawyer
   B. doctor
   C. businessman
   D. preacher

6. Why was Opal allowed to live at the Friendly Corners Trailer Park?
   A. She was good and quiet.
   B. Her dad was the park manager.
   C. She took care of the park's animals.
   D. Any child could live at the park.

7. Opal's father sometimes looked like a _____.
   A. dog
   B. squirrel
   C. cat
   D. turtle

Check Your Reading Speed

1분에 몇 단어를 읽는지 리딩 속도를 측정해보세요.

$$\frac{776 \text{ words}}{\text{reading time ( ) sec}} \times 60 = (\quad) \text{ WPM}$$

Build Your Vocabulary

preacher
[príːtʃər]

n. 목사, 설교자, 전도자
A preacher is a person, usually a member of the clergy, who preaches sermons as part of a church service.

produce***
[prədjúːs]

n. 농작물, 농산물, 생산품; v. 생산하다
Produce is food or other things that are grown in large quantities to be sold.

grocery store
[gróusəri stɔːr]

n. 식품점, 슈퍼마켓
A grocery store is a store that retails food.

pick out

phrasal v. (여럿 가운데에서 신중하게) ~을 고르다, 선발하다
If you pick out something, you choose it from a number of people or things.

bump into

phrasal v. 부닥치다; 우연히 만나다
If you bump into something or someone, you accidentally hit them while you are moving.

red-faced
[réd-féist]

a. (특히 당황하거나 화가 나서) 얼굴을 붉힌, 얼굴이 벌건
A red-faced person has a face that looks red, often because they are embarrassed or angry.

wave**
[wéiv]

v. 흔들다, 신호하다; 파도치다; n. 파도, 물결
If you wave or wave your hand, you move your hand from side to side in the air, usually in order to say hello or goodbye to someone.

keep on

phrasal v. 계속하다
When you keep on doing something, you continue or persist doing it.

vegetable**
[védʒətəbl]

n. 야채
Vegetables are plants such as cabbages, potatoes, and onions which you can cook and eat.

green pepper
[griːn pépər]

n. [식물] 피망
A green pepper is an unripe pepper that is used in cooking or eaten raw in salads.

army**
[áːrmi]

n. (특정 목적을 위한) 사람들, 집단; 군대
An army of people, animals, or things is a large number of them, especially when they are regarded as a force of some kind.

employee**
[implɔ́iiː]

n. 종업원
An employee is a person who is paid to work for an organization or for another person.

14

tongue**
[tʌŋ]

n. 혀; 말, 말씨
Your tongue is the soft movable part inside your mouth which you use for tasting, eating, and speaking.

hang***
[hæŋ]

v. 매달리다; 걸다, 달아매다; 교수형에 처하다 (hang out **phrasal v.** 내밀다)
If something hangs in a high place or position, or if you hang it there, it is attached there so it does not touch the ground.

wag*
[wæg]

v. (꼬리 등을) 흔들다, 흔들리다; **n.** 흔들기
When a dog wags its tail, it repeatedly waves its tail from side to side.

tail*
[teil]

n. (동물의) 꼬리
The tail of an animal, bird, or fish is the part extending beyond the end of its body.

skid
[skid]

v. 미끄러지다; **n.** 미끄럼, 옆으로 미끄러짐
If a vehicle skids, it slides sideways or forward while moving, for example when you are trying to stop it suddenly on a wet road.

pull back

phrasal v. 뒤로 끌어당기다; 후퇴하다
If you pull back something, you move it back from a place.

knock off

phrasal v. 넘어뜨리다, 바닥에 떨어뜨리다; 때려눕히다
If you knock something off, you remove it and usually make it fall to the ground, by hitting it.

grab*
[græb]

v. 부여잡다, 움켜쥐다; **n.** 부여잡기
If you grab something, you take it or pick it up suddenly and roughly.

hind*
[haind]

a. 뒤쪽의, 후방의
An animal's hind legs are at the back of its body.

**face to face
(with)**

idiom (~과) 마주 대하여
When you get face to face with someone, you are close enough to meet, talk, or see them.

end up

phrasal v. (구어) 마침내는 (~으로) 되다; 끝나다
If you end up doing something or end up in a particular state, you do that thing or get into that state even though you did not originally intend to.

knock over

phrasal v. 뒤집어엎다; 때려눕히다
If you knock something over, you push or hit it and making it fall or turn on its side.

lie***
[lai]

vi. 눕다, 누워 있다; 놓여 있다, 위치하다; 거짓말하다; **n.** 거짓말
If you are lying somewhere, you are in a horizontal position and are not standing or sitting.

lean**
[liːn]

① **v.** 몸을 구부리다, 기울다; 기대다, 의지하다 ② **a.** 야윈, 마른
When you lean in a particular direction, you bend your body in that direction.

concern**
[kənsə́ːrn]

vt. 염려하다; ~에 관계하다; 관심을 갖다; **n.** 염려; 관심
If something concerns you, it worries you.

lick*
[lik]

vt. 핥다; (불길이 혀처럼) 날름거리다, 넘실거리다; n. 핥기
When people or animals lick something, they move their tongue across its surface.

pound
[paund]

① n. 동물보호소 ② v. 마구 치다, 세게 두드리다; 쿵쿵 울리다; n. 타격
③ n. 파운드(무게의 단위)
A pound is a place where dogs and cats found wandering in the street are taken and kept until they are claimed by their owners.

holler
[hálər]

v. 고함지르다; 큰 소리로 부르다; n. 외침, 큰 소리
If you holler, you shout loudly.

turn around

phrasal v. 돌아서다, 몸을 돌리다; 회전하다
When you turn around, you move your head and shoulders or your whole body so that you face in the opposite direction.

cannot help

idiom ~하지 않을 수 없다
If you cannot help doing something, it is impossible to prevent or avoid.

figure*
[fígjər]

v. 생각하다, 판단하다, 계산하다; n. 형태, 형상; 수치, 숫자
If you figure that something is the case, you think or guess that it is the case.

trot*
[trat]

v. 빠른 걸음으로 가다, 총총걸음 치다; n. 빠른 걸음
When an animal such as a horse trots, it moves fairly fast, taking quick small steps.

sit up

phrasal v. 일어나 앉다
If you sit up, you move yourself into a sitting position, for example, from lying down.

hard stare

idiom 냉랭한 눈길, 노려봄
If someone gives you a hard stare, he or she gazes you face with anger.

make fun of

phrasal v. 놀리다, 비웃다
If you make fun of someone, you make unkind remarks or jokes about somebody.

honest*
[ánist]

a. 정직한, 솔직한
If you describe someone as honest, you mean that they always tell the truth, and do not try to deceive people or break the law.

cereal*
[síəriəl]

n. 시리얼; 곡물
Cereal or breakfast cereal is a food made from grain. It is mixed with milk and eaten for breakfast.

aisle*
[ail]

n. 통로, 측면의 복도
An aisle is a long narrow gap that people can walk along between rows of seats in a public building.

cashier*
[kæʃíər]

n. 출납원, 회계원
A cashier is a person who customers pay money to or get money from in places such as shops or banks.

skinny
[skíni]

a. 말라빠진, 비쩍 마른
A skinny person is extremely thin, often in a way that you find unattractive.

rib[*]
[rib]

n. 갈비(뼈), 늑골
Your ribs are the 12 pairs of curved bones that surround your chest.

bald[*]
[bɔːld]

a. (머리 등이) 벗어진, 대머리의; vi. 머리가 벗어지다
Someone who is bald has little or no hair on the top of their head.

patch[*]
[pætʃ]

n. (주변과는 다른 조그만) 부분; 조각; 안대; 자그만 땅
A patch on a surface is a part of it which is different in appearance from the area around it.

fur[*]
[fəːr]

n. 부드러운 털; 모피
Fur is the thick and usually soft hair that grows on the bodies of many mammals.

mess[*]
[mes]

n. 엉망진창, 난잡함; v. 망쳐놓다, 방해하다
If you say that something is a mess or in a mess, you think that it is in an untidy state.

bet[*]
[bet]

v. ~임이 틀림없다; 걸다, 내기를 하다; n. 내기, 건 돈
You use expressions such as 'I bet', 'I'll bet', and 'you can bet' to indicate that you are sure something is true.

belong^{***}
[bilɔ́ːŋ]

v. (~에) 속하다; 제자리[알맞은 위치]에 있다
If something belongs to you, you own it.

sneeze[*]
[sniːz]

vi. 재채기하다; n. 재채기
When you sneeze, you suddenly take in your breath and then blow it down your nose noisily without being able to stop yourself, for example because you have a cold.

immediately^{**}
[imíːdiətli]

a. 곧 바로, 즉시
If something happens immediately, it happens without any delay.

humor^{**}
[hjúːmər]

n. 유머, 익살, 해학
You can refer to the amusing things that people say as their humor.

Check Your Reading Speed

1분에 몇 단어를 읽는지 리딩 속도를 측정해보세요.

$$\frac{833 \text{ words}}{\text{reading time ( ) sec}} \times 60 = (\quad) \text{ WPM}$$

Build Your Vocabulary

preacher^{복습}
[príːtʃər]

n. 목사, 설교자, 전도자
A preacher is a person, usually a member of the clergy, who preaches sermons as part of a church service.

preach*
[príːtʃ]

v. 설교하다, 전도하다
When a member of the clergy preaches a sermon, he or she gives a talk on a religious or moral subject during a religious service.

missionary*
[míʃənèri]

n. 선교사
A missionary is a Christian who has been sent to a foreign country to teach people about Christianity.

distract*
[distrǽkt]

v. (마음 · 주의를) 흐트러뜨리다, 딴 데로 돌리다 (distracted a. 정신이 산만한)
If something distracts you or your attention from something, it takes your attention away from it.

sermon*
[sə́ːrmən]

n. 설교; 잔소리
A sermon is a talk on a religious or moral subject that is given by a member of the clergy as part of a church service.

prayer*
[prέər]

n. 기도(문), 빌기; (pl.) 예배
A prayer is the words a person says when they speak to God.

suffer***
[sʌ́fər]

vi. 시달리다, 고통 받다; 겪다, 당하다
If you suffer pain, you feel it in your body or in your mind.

grocery
[gróusəri]

n. (pl.) 식료 잡화류; 식료 잡화점
Groceries are foods you buy at a grocer's or at a supermarket such as flour, sugar, and tinned foods.

wag^{복습}
[wǽg]

v. (꼬리 등을) 흔들다, 흔들리다; n. 흔들기
When a dog wags its tail, it repeatedly waves its tail from side to side.

tail^{복습}
[teil]

n. (동물의) 꼬리
The tail of an animal, bird, or fish is the part extending beyond the end of its body.

limp
[limp]

v. 다리를 절다, 절뚝거리다; a. 기운 없는, 축 늘어진
If a person or animal limps, they walk with difficulty or in an uneven way because one of their legs or feet is hurt.

admit***
[ədmít]

v. 인정하다
If you admit that something bad, unpleasant, or embarrassing is true, you agree, often unwillingly, that it is true.

18

stink
[stiŋk]

v. (stunk/stank—stunk) 냄새가 나다, 구린내가 나다; 수상쩍다
To stink means to smell extremely unpleasant.

trailer*
[tréilər]

n. 트레일러하우스, (자동차가 끌고 다니는) 이동식 주택
A trailer is a container on wheels which is pulled by a car or other vehicle and which is used for transporting large or heavy items.

behave**
[bihéiv]

v. 행동하다, 처신하다; 예의바르게 굴다
If you behave or behave yourself, you act in the way that people think is correct and proper.

exception**
[iksépʃən]

n. 예외, 이례, 특례; 제외
An exception is a particular thing, person, or situation that is not included in a general statement, judgment, or rule.

specific*
[spisífik]

a. 명확한, 구체적인, 특정의 (specifically ad. 명확하게, 특히)
You use specific to refer to a particular fixed area, problem, or subject.

pick a fight

phrasal v. 싸움을 걸다, 시비를 걸다
If you pick a fight, you deliberately start a fight or an argument with someone.

yappy
[jǽpi]

a. (개가) 사납게 짖어대는; 잡담하는
If a dog is yappy, it makes short loud sounds in an excited way.

swear**
[swɛər]

v. 단언하다, 맹세하다; n. 맹세, 선서
If you swear that something is true or you can swear to it, you are saying very firmly that it is true.

manner***
[mǽnər]

n. (pl.) 예의(범절); 방식, 풍습; 태도
If someone has good manners, they are polite and observe social customs.

foldout
[fóuldàut]

a. 접는 방식의
If something is foldout, it has extra sections that can be folded out to make it larger, supported on legs that swing out from the center.

spread***
[spred]

v. 펼치다, 퍼지다, 뻗다; 뿌리다; n. 퍼짐, 폭, 넓이
If something spreads or is spread by people, it gradually reaches or affects a larger and larger area or more and more people.

rub**
[rʌb]

v. 비비다, 문지르다; 스치다; n. 문지르기
If you rub a part of your body, you move your hand or fingers backward and forward over it while pressing firmly.

fortunate**
[fɔ́ːrtʃənət]

a. 운이 좋은, 행운의, 복 받은
If you say that someone is fortunate, you mean that they are lucky.

grocery store 복습
[gróusəri stɔːr]

n. 식품점, 슈퍼마켓
A grocery store is a store that retails food.

stare*
[stɛər]

v. 응시하다, 똘어지게 보다
If you stare at someone or something, you look at them for a long time.

remind[**]
[rimáind]

vt. 생각나게 하다, 상기시키다, 일깨우다
If someone reminds you of a fact or event that you already know about, they say something which makes you think about it.

turtle[*]
[tɔ́:rtl]

n. [동물] 거북, 바다거북
A turtle is a large reptile which has a thick shell covering its body and which lives in the sea most of the time.

shell[**]
[ʃel]

n. 껍데기; 조가비; v. 껍데기를 벗기다
The shell of an animal such as a tortoise, snail, or crab is the hard protective covering that it has around its body or on its back.

stick[**]
[stik]

① v. 내밀다; 찔러 넣다, 찌르다; 붙이다, 달라붙다; 고수하다 ② n. 막대기, 지팡이
If something is sticking out from a surface or object, it extends up or away from it.

wonder[***]
[wʌ́ndə:r]

v. 호기심을 가지다, 이상하게 여기다; n. 경탄할 만한 것, 경이
If you wonder about something, you think about it because it interests you and you want to know more about it.

holler[복습]
[hálər]

v. 고함지르다; 큰 소리로 부르다; n. 외침, 큰 소리
If you holler, you shout loudly.

shoot up

phrasal v. 갑자기 올라가다, 급등하다
If something shoots up, it rises or increases very quickly.

grin[**]
[grin]

v. (이를 드러내고) 싱긋 웃다, 활짝 웃다; n. 싱긋 웃음
When you grin, you smile broadly.

sneeze[복습]
[sni:z]

vi. 재채기하다; n. 재채기
When you sneeze, you suddenly take in your breath and then blow it down your nose noisily without being able to stop yourself, for example because you have a cold.

lap[*]
[læp]

① n. 무릎; (트랙의) 한 바퀴 ② v. (파도가) 찰싹거리다; (할짝할짝) 핥다
If you have something on your lap, it is on top of your legs and near to your body.

pile[**]
[pail]

n. 쌓아 올린 더미; 다수; v. 쌓아 올리다; 쌓이다
A pile of things is a mass of them that is high in the middle and has sloping sides.

rib[복습]
[rib]

n. 갈비(뼈), 늑골
Your ribs are the 12 pairs of curved bones that surround your chest.

matted
[mǽtid]

a. (특히 물에 젖었거나 더러워서) 엉겨 붙은
If you describe someone's hair as matted, you mean that it has become a thick untidy mass, often because it is wet or dirty.

fur[복습]
[fə:r]

n. 부드러운 털; 모피
Fur is the thick and usually soft hair that grows on the bodies of many mammals.

bald[복습]
[bɔ:ld]

a. (머리 등이) 벗어진, 대머리의; vi. 머리가 벗어지다
Someone who is bald has little or no hair on the top of their head.

wrinkle*
[ríŋkl]

v. 주름이 지다, 구겨지다; n. 주름, 잔주름
When someone's skin wrinkles or when something wrinkles it, lines start to form in it because the skin is getting old or damaged.

pretty*
[príti]

a. 꽤, 상당히; a. 귀여운, 예쁜
You can use pretty before an adjective or adverb to mean 'quite' or 'rather'.

pull back복습
phrasal v. 뒤로 끌어당기다; 후퇴하다
If you pull back something, you move it back from a place.

crooked
[krúkid]

a. 구부러진, 비뚤어진; 마음이 비뚤어진, 부정직한
If you describe something as crooked, especially something that is usually straight, you mean that it is bent or twisted.

knock off복습
phrasal v. 넘어뜨리다, 바닥에 떨어뜨리다; 때려눕히다
If you knock something off, you remove it and usually make it fall to the ground, by hitting it.

flutter*
[flʌ́tə:r]

v. 펄럭이다, 흔들다; (새 등이) 파닥이다, 날갯짓하다; n. 펄럭임
If something thin or light flutters, or if you flutter it, it moves up and down or from side to side with a lot of quick, light movements.

whisper*
[hwíspə:r]

v. 속삭이다
When you whisper, you say something very quietly.

effect*
[ifékt]

n. 영향, 효과, 결과; vt. 초래하다, 달성하다, 이루다
If you say that someone is doing something for effect, you mean that they are doing it in order to impress people and to draw attention to themselves.

poke*
[pouk]

v. 쑥 내밀다; 찌르다, 쑤시다; 들이대다; n. 찌름, 쑤심
If you poke your head through an opening or if it pokes through an opening, you push it through, often so that you can see something more easily.

stray**
[strei]

n. 길을 잃은[주인이 없는] 동물; a. (애완동물이) 길을 잃은, 주인이 없는;
v. 제 위치를 벗어나다, 옆길로 새다
A stray dog or cat has wandered away from its owner's home.

Chapters Three & Four

1. Opal's mother left when she was _____ years old.
   A. one
   B. two
   C. three
   D. four

2. Why did NOT Opal have any friends?
   A. Opal wasn't a nice girl.
   B. Her friends were in Watley, the town where she used to live.
   C. She didn't want any friends.
   D. Her father wouldn't let her play with other children.

3. Why did NOT Opal ask about her mother?
   A. She didn't want to be sad.
   B. Her father didn't remember her mother.
   C. Opal didn't know she had a mother.
   D. She didn't want her father to get angry.

4. How old is Opal?
   A. 8
   B. 9
   C. 10
   D. 11

5. What color is Opal's hair?
   A. Red
   B. Brown
   C. Blond
   D. Black

6. What was NOT true about Opal's mother?
   A. She could run fast.
   B. She could make people laugh.
   C. She could cook well.
   D. She drank alcohol.

7. Why did Opal memorize ten things about her mother?
   A. So she could recognize her mother if she came back.
   B. She wanted to make her father happy.
   C. So she could write a letter to her mother.
   D. She wanted to write a book about her mother.

Check Your Reading Speed

1분에 몇 단어를 읽는지 리딩 속도를 측정해보세요.

$$\frac{775 \text{ words}}{\text{reading time ( ) sec}} \times 60 = (\quad) \text{ WPM}$$

Build Your Vocabulary

start in

phrasal v. 시작하다. 착수하다
If you start in something, you begin to do it.

give a bath

phrasal v. 남을 목욕시키다
If you give someone a bath, you wash them to make them clean.

hose*
[houz]

n. 호스; v. 호스로 물을 뿌리다
A hose is a long, flexible pipe made of rubber or plastic. Water is directed through a hose in order to do things such as put out fires, clean cars, or water gardens.

insult*
[insʌlt]

vt. 모욕하다. ~에게 무례한 짓을 하다; n. 모욕
If someone insults you, they say or do something that is rude or offensive.

brush**
[brʌʃ]

v. 솔질하다. 솔질로 털다; n. 붓, 솔
If you brush something or brush something such as dirt off it, you clean it or tidy it using a brush.

hairbrush
[héərbrʌʃ]

n. 머리빗
A hairbrush is a brush that you use to brush your hair.

knot**
[nat]

n. 매듭; 나무 마디; v. 얽히게 하다. 매다
If you tie a knot in a piece of string, rope, cloth, or other material, you pass one end or part of it through a loop and pull it tight.

patch*
[pætʃ]

n. (주변과는 다른 조그만) 부분; 조각; 안대; 자그만 땅
A patch on a surface is a part of it which is different in appearance from the area around it.

stick*
[stik]

① v. (stuck-stuck) 달라붙다. 붙이다; 내밀다; 찔러 넣다. 찌르다; 고수하다
② n. 막대기, 지팡이
If one thing sticks to another, it becomes attached to it and is difficult to remove.

mind***
[maind]

v. 언짢아하다. 상관하다; 주의하다; n. 마음, 정신
If you do not mind something, you are not annoyed or bothered by it.

wiggle
[wigl]

v. (몸을) 뒤흔들다. (좌우로) 움직이다; n. 뒤흔듦
If you wiggle something or if it wiggles, it moves up and down or from side to side in small quick movements.

pretty*
[príti]

a. 꽤, 상당히; a. 귀여운. 예쁜
You can use pretty before an adjective or adverb to mean 'quite' or 'rather'.

24

neither ***
[níːðər]

conj. (부정문을 만들며) ~도 마찬가지이다; pron. (둘 중) 어느 것도 ~이 아니다
If you say that one person or thing does not do something and neither does another, what you say is true of all the people or things that you are mentioning.

hardly ***
[háːrdli]

a. 거의 ~할 수 없다; 거의 ~이 아니다
When you say you can hardly do something, you are emphasizing that it is very difficult for you to do it.

bet 복습
[bet]

v. ~임이 틀림없다; 걸다, 내기를 하다; n. 내기, 건 돈
You use expressions such as 'I bet', 'I'll bet', and 'you can bet' to indicate that you are sure something is true.

orphan *
[ɔ́ːrfən]

n. 고아
An orphan is a child whose parents are dead.

relieve *
[rilíːv]

vt. (걱정 · 고통 등을) 덜다, 안도하게 하다, 완화하다
(relieved a. 안도하는, 다행으로 여기는)
If something relieves an unpleasant feeling or situation, it makes the feeling or situation less unpleasant or disappear completely.

situation **
[sitʃuéiʃən]

n. 상태, 정세; 위치, 환경
You use situation to refer generally to what is happening in a particular place at a particular time, or to refer to what is happening to you.

nod **
[nɔd]

v. 끄덕이다, 끄덕여 표시하다; n. (동의 · 인사 · 신호 · 명령의) 끄덕임
If you nod, you move your head downward and upward to show agreement, understanding, or approval.

go on

phrasal v. 계속하다; 앞으로 가다, 나아가다; 자자, 어서
When you go on what you are doing, you continue or proceed it.

extra **
[ékstrə]

ad. 특별히, 각별히; a. 추가의, 여분의
You can use extra in front of adjectives and adverbs to emphasize the quality that they are describing.

twitch
[twitʃ]

vi. (손가락 · 근육 따위가) 씰룩거리다; 홱 잡아당기다, 잡아채다; n. 씰룩거림, 경련
If something, especially a part of your body, twitches or if you twitch it, it makes a little jumping movement.

eyebrow *
[áibràu]

n. 눈썹
Your eyebrows are the lines of hair which grow above your eyes.

stare 복습
[stɛər]

v. 응시하다, 뚫어지게 보다
If you stare at someone or something, you look at them for a long time.

spot **
[spɑt]

n. 반점, 얼룩; 장소, 지점; vt. 발견하다, 분별하다
Spots are small, round, colored areas on a surface.

shiny *
[ʃáini]

a. 빛나는; 해가 비치는; 광택이 있는
Shiny things are bright and reflect light.

rib 복습
[rib]

n. 늑골, 갈빗대; [요리] 갈비
Your ribs are the 12 pairs of curved bones that surround your chest.

intend*** [inténd]
v. ~할 작정이다, ~하려고 생각하다; 의도하다
If you intend to do something, you have decided or planned to do it.

crooked [krúkid]
a. 구부러진, 비뚤어진; 마음이 비뚤어진, 부정직한
If you describe something as crooked, especially something that is usually straight, you mean that it is bent or twisted.

fit* [fit]
① n. 발작, 경련 ② v. 끼우다, 맞게 하다, 적합하다; a. 적합한
If someone has a fit, they suddenly lose consciousness and their body makes uncontrollable movements.

toothbrush* [tú:θbrʌʃ]
n. 칫솔
A toothbrush is a small brush that you use for cleaning your teeth.

give up
phrasal v. 포기하다, 단념하다
If you give up, you decide that you cannot do something and stop trying to do it.

trailer [tréilər]
n. 트레일러하우스, (자동차가 끌고 다니는) 이동식 주택
A trailer is a container on wheels which is pulled by a car or other vehicle and which is used for transporting large or heavy items.

sermon [sə́:rmən]
n. 설교; 잔소리
A sermon is a talk on a religious or moral subject that is given by a member of the clergy as part of a church service.

mutter* [mʌtər]
v. 중얼거리다, 불평하다; n. 중얼거림, 불평
If you mutter, you speak very quietly so that you cannot easily be heard, often because you are complaining about something.

rub [rʌb]
v. 비비다, 문지르다; 스치다; n. 문지르기
If you rub a part of your body, you move your hand or fingers backward and forward over it while pressing firmly.

lap [læp]
① n. 무릎; (트랙의) 한 바퀴 ② v. (파도가) 찰싹거리다; (할짝할짝) 핥다
If you have something on your lap, it is on top of your legs and near to your body.

lose one's nerve
idiom 주눅 들다, 겁내다
If you lost your nerve, you are feeling timid and lacked of courage.

still*** [stil]
a. 움직이지 않는; 조용한, 고요한; ad. 조용히; 여전히, 아직도
If you stay still, you stay in the same position and do not move.

shell [ʃel]
n. 껍데기; 조가비; v. 껍데기를 벗기다
The shell of an animal such as a tortoise, snail, or crab is the hard protective covering that it has around its body or on its back.

nudge [nʌdʒ]
n. (팔꿈치로) 살짝 밀기, 가볍게 찌르기; vt. (주의를 끌기 위해 팔꿈치로) 찌르다
If you nudge someone, you push them gently, usually with your elbow, in order to draw their attention to something.

sigh* [sai]
v. 한숨 쉬다; n. 한숨, 탄식
When you sigh, you let out a deep breath, as a way of expressing feelings such as disappointment, tiredness, or pleasure.

1분에 몇 단어를 읽는지 리딩 속도를 측정해보세요.

$$\frac{629 \text{ words}}{\text{reading time ( ) sec}} \times 60 = (\quad) \text{ WPM}$$

Build Your Vocabulary

preacher^{복습}
[priːtʃər]

n. 목사, 설교자, 전도자
A preacher is a person, usually a member of the clergy, who preaches sermons as part of a church service.

couch*
[kautʃ]

n. 소파, 긴 의자
A couch is a long, comfortable seat for two or three people.

freckle
[frekl]

n. 주근깨, 반점
Freckles are small light brown spots on someone's skin, especially on their face.

nod^{복습}
[nɔd]

v. 끄덕이다, 끄덕여 표시하다; n. (동의 · 인사 · 신호 · 명령의) 끄덕임
If you nod, you move your head downward and upward to show agreement, understanding, or approval.

talent*
[tǽlənt]

n. 재능, 재주
Talent is a natural ability to do something well.

chew*
[tʃuː]

v. 물다, 씹다, 물어뜯다
If you chew on something, you bite something continuously, especially because you are nervous or to test your teeth.

paw*
[pɔː]

n. (갈고리 발톱이 있는 동물의) 발; v. 앞발로 차다
The paws of an animal such as a cat, dog, or bear are its feet, which have claws for gripping things and soft pads for walking on.

tap*
[tæp]

① v. 가볍게 두드리다; n. 가볍게 두드리기 ② n. 주둥이, (수도 등의) 꼭지
If you tap something, you hit it with a quick light blow or a series of quick light blows.

get a head start

idiom 남보다 유리한 출발을 하다
If you have a head start on other people, you have an advantage over them in something such as a competition or race.

beat**
[biːt]

v. 이기다, 패배시키다; 치다, 두드리다; n. [음악] 박자, 고동
If you beat someone in a competition or election, you defeat them.

sore loser

idiom 패배를 인정하지 않는 사람
A sore loser refers to one who doesn't take failure well, especially one who complains or contests it.

can't make head nor tail of

idiom 도무지 종잡을 수 없다
If you can't make head nor tail, you are not able to understand something at all.

ceiling[**] [síːliŋ]
n. 천장
A ceiling is the horizontal surface that forms the top part or roof inside a room.

especially[**] [ispéʃəli]
a. 특히, 각별히
You use especially to emphasize that what you are saying applies more to one person, thing, or area than to any others.

constellation [kὰnstəléiʃən]
n. [천문] 별자리, 성좌
A constellation is a group of stars which form a pattern and have a name.

planet[**] [plǽnit]
n. 행성
A planet is a large, round object in space that moves around a star.

name[***] [neim]
v. (정확히) 말하다, 지정하다; 이름을 지어주다; n. 이름; 평판
If you name someone, you identify them by stating their name.

point out
phrasal v. ~을 지적하다
If you point out a fact or mistake, you tell someone about it or draw their attention to it.

get tired of
idiom 싫증내다, 권태를 느끼다; 피곤하다
If you get tired of something, you get bored or annoyed with it.

stand[***] [stænd]
vi. 참다, 견디다; 서다, 일어서다; n. 가판대, 좌판; 관람석
If you cannot stand something, you cannot bear it or tolerate it.

judge[***] [dʒʌdʒ]
v. 평가하다, 심사하다; 재판하다; n. 심판, 심사원; 재판관
If you judge something or someone, you form an opinion about them after you have examined the evidence or thought carefully about them.

microscope[*] [máikrəskòup]
n. 현미경
A microscope is a scientific instrument which makes very small objects look bigger so that more detail can be seen.

lie[복습] [lai]
vi. (lay-lain) 눕다, 누워 있다; 놓여 있다, 위치하다; 거짓말하다; n. 거짓말
If you are lying somewhere, you are in a horizontal position and are not standing or sitting.

sigh[복습] [sai]
n. 한숨, 탄식; v. 한숨 쉬다
When you sigh, you let out a deep breath, as a way of expressing feelings such as disappointment, tiredness, or pleasure.

turtle[복습] [təːrtl]
n. [동물] 거북, 바다거북
A turtle is a large reptile which has a thick shell covering its body and which lives in the sea most of the time.

hop[*] [hap]
v. 깡충 뛰다, 뛰어오르다; n. 깡충깡충 뜀
If you hop, you move along by jumping.

memorize[*] [méməràiz]
vt. 기억하다, 암기하다
If you memorize something, you learn it so that you can remember it exactly.

inside and out
idiom 완전히, 모두 다
If you know something inside and out, you know it very thoroughly.

recognize[**] [rékəgnaiz]

vt. 인지하다, 알아보다
If you recognize someone or something, you know who that person is or what that thing is.

grab[복습] [græb]

v. 부여잡다, 움켜쥐다; n. 부여잡기
If you grab something, you take it or pick it up suddenly and roughly.

hold on to

phrasal v. 지키다, 고수하다; 보유하다
If you hold on to something or someone, you keep them not to lose.

tight[**] [tait]

ad. 단단히, 꽉; a. 단단한, 팽팽한, 빈틈없는
If you hold someone or something tight, you hold them firmly and securely.

get away

phrasal v. 떠나다, 탈출하다
If you get away from something, you escape from it.

Chapters Five & Six

1. What did Opal and her father find out about Winn-Dixie?
   A. They found that Winn-Dixie didn't want to be left alone.
   B. They found that Winn-Dixie liked the preacher.
   C. They found that Winn-Dixie didn't like other people.
   D. They found that Winn-Dixie wanted to go to the church.

2. Why did Opal call the church "Pick-It-Quick"?
   A. Pick-It-Quick was Opal's favorite store.
   B. There was a Pick-It-Quick sign on the church's door.
   C. The church used to be a Pick-It-Quick store.
   D. The preacher wrote Pick-It-Quick on the floor.

3. Why did the preacher bring Winn-Dixie into the church?
   A. The preacher didn't want Winn-Dixie to be lonely outside.
   B. Winn-Dixie howled outside.
   C. Opal wouldn't tie Winn-Dixie to a tree.
   D. It started to rain.

4. When Winn-Dixie caught the mouse, what did he do?
   A. He held it carefully in his mouth.
   B. He killed it and put it outside.
   C. He gave it to Opal.
   D. He ate it.

5. Which of the following is NOT true?
   A. Opal prayed for her mother.
   B. Opal prayed for the mouse.
   C. Opal talked to God about being lonely.
   D. Opal asked God for new friends.

6. When Opal went into the library, _____.
   A. Winn-Dixie howled outside
   B. she left Winn-Dixie at home
   C. she secretly took Winn-Dixie inside
   D. Winn-Dixie looked in the window

7. What did Miss Franny do after she saw Winn-Dixie?
   A. She thought Winn-Dixie was a bear.
   B. She told Opal that she hated dogs.
   C. She didn't let Winn-Dixie into the library.
   D. She said that she didn't know any stories and ran away.

1분에 몇 단어를 읽는지 리딩 속도를 측정해보세요.

$$\frac{1{,}138 \text{ words}}{\text{reading time (} \quad \text{) sec}} \times 60 = (\quad) \text{ WPM}$$

Build Your Vocabulary

stand^{복습}
[stænd]

vi. 참다, 견디다; 서다, 일어서다; n. 가판대, 좌판; 관람석
If you cannot stand something, you cannot bear it or tolerate it.

go off

phrasal v. 떠나다; (알람 · 경보기) 울리다; 발생하다
If you go off, you leave a place, especially in order to do something.

by oneself

idiom 혼자, 다른 사람 없이
If you are by yourself, you are alone.

pull off

phrasal v. 뜯어내다, 벗다; ~을 달성하다, 성공하다
If you pull off something, you remove it forcefully.

couch^{복습}
[kautʃ]

n. 소파, 긴 의자
A couch is a long, comfortable seat for two or three people.

tie up

phrasal v. (동물을 도망가지 못하게) 묶어 놓다; 꽁꽁 묶다
If you tie something up, you make it secure by putting string or rope around it, or attaching it to something else.

howl[*]
[haul]

v. 짖다, 울부짖다; n. 울부짖는 소리
If an animal such as a wolf or a dog howls, it makes a long, loud, crying sound.

empty^{복습}
[émpti]

a. 빈, 공허한; vt. 비우다
If you feel empty, you feel unhappy and have no energy, usually because you are very tired or have just experienced something upsetting.

give in

phrasal v. 굴복하다, 따르다, 항복하다
If you give in, you admit that you are defeated or that you cannot do something.

used to

phrasal v. ~ 하곤 했다; 과거 한때는 ~이었다
If someone used to do something, it suggests habitual or accustomed actions or states, taking place in the past but not continuing into the present.

motto[*]
[mátou]

n. 좌우명, 표어, 모토
A motto is a short sentence or phrase that expresses a rule for sensible behavior, especially a way of behaving in a particular situation.

tiny^{**}
[táini]

a. 몹시 작은
Something or someone that is tiny is extremely small.

cover up	phrasal v. 덮다, 가리다; (나쁜 짓 등을) 은폐하다 If you cover up something, you put something over it in order to hide or protect it.
give up^{복습}	phrasal v. 포기하다, 단념하다 If you give up, you decide that you cannot do something and stop trying to do it.
pew [pju:]	n. (교회의, 길게 나무로 된) 좌석, 신도석 A pew is a long wooden seat with a back, which people sit on in church.
foldup [fóuldʌp]	a. 접을 수 있는 A foldup piece of furniture or equipment is one that is specially designed so that it can be folded into a smaller shape in order to be stored.
lawn[*] [lɔ:n]	n. 잔디(밭) A lawn is an area of grass that is kept cut short and is usually part of someone's garden or backyard, or part of a park.
congregation[*] [kàŋgrigéiʃən]	n. (종교적인) 집회, 모임, 화합 The people who are attending a church service or who regularly attend a church service are referred to as the congregation.
fit in	phrasal v. (~와) 자연스럽게 어울리다, 맞다 If someone fits in, they are accepted by the other people in a group.
all the way	idiom 내내, 시종 If you have been doing something all the way, you are emphasizing the period of time during the whole journey.
belong^{복습} [bilɔ́:ŋ]	v. (~에) 속하다; 제자리[알맞은 위치]에 있다 If something belongs to you, you own it.
shade^{**} [ʃeid]	n. 그늘, 음영; 색조; vt. 그늘지게 하다 Shade is an area of darkness under or next to an object such as a tree, where sunlight does not reach.
service^{***} [sə́:rvis]	n. (종교적인) 의식, 예배; (상업적인) 서비스 A service is a religious ceremony that takes place in a church.
pray^{**} [prei]	v. 기도하다, 기원하다, 빌다 When people pray, they speak to God in order to give thanks or to ask for his help.
preach^{복습} [pri:tʃ]	v. 설교하다, 전도하다 When a member of the clergy preaches a sermon, he or she gives a talk on a religious or moral subject during a religious service.
sermon^{복습} [sə́:rmən]	n. 설교; 잔소리 A sermon is a talk on a religious or moral subject that is given by a member of the clergy as part of a church service.
terrible[*] [térəbl]	a. 극심한, 지독한; 무서운, 끔찍한 If something is terrible, it is very bad or of very poor quality.

ignore[**] [ignɔ́ːr]
vt. 무시하다, 모르는 체하다
If you ignore someone or something, you pay no attention to them.

wail [weil]
v. 울부짖다, 통곡하다; n. 울부짖음, 통곡
If someone wails, they make long, loud, high-pitched cries which express sorrow or pain.

one another
pron. 서로(서로)
One another refers to each other.

yell[*] [jel]
v. 소리치다, 고함치다; n. 고함소리, 부르짖음
If you yell, you shout loudly, usually because you are excited, angry, or in pain.

untie [ʌntái]
vt. 풀다; 자유롭게 하다
If you untie something such as string or rope, you undo it so that there is no knot or so that it is no longer tying something.

cannot help[복습]
idiom ~하지 않을 수 없다
If you cannot help doing something, it is impossible to prevent or avoid.

effect[복습] [ifékt]
n. 영향, 효과, 결과; vt. 초래하다, 달성하다, 이루다
If you say that someone is doing something for effect, you mean that they are doing it in order to impress people and to draw attention to themselves.

start in[복습]
phrasal v. 시작하다, 착수하다
If you start in something, you begin to do it.

wiggle[복습] [wigl]
v. (몸을) 뒤흔들다, (좌우로) 움직이다; n. 뒤흔듦
If you wiggle something or if it wiggles, it moves up and down or from side to side in small quick movements.

except[***] [iksépt]
prep. ~을 제외하고, ~외에는; vt. ~을 빼다, 제외하다
You use except for to introduce the only thing or person that prevents a statement from being completely true.

leftover [léftòuvər]
a. 나머지의, 남은; n. (pl.) 나머지, 찌꺼기
You use leftover to describe an amount of something that remains after the rest of it has been used or eaten.

crumb [krʌm]
n. 빵 부스러기, 빵가루
Crumbs are tiny pieces that fall from bread, biscuits, or cake when you cut it or eat it.

supper[***] [sʌ́pər]
n. 저녁 식사, (가벼운) 만찬
Supper is a simple meal eaten just before you go to bed at night.

keep on[복습]
phrasal v. 계속하다
When you keep on doing something, you continue or persist doing it.

up[***] [ʌp]
a. 명랑한, 기분 좋은, 신이 난; 위쪽의
If you are up, you are cheerful, happy or excited.

on and on
idiom 쉬지 않고, 계속해서
If you do something on and on, you do it without stopping.

34

furry
[fə́:ri]

a. 털로 덮인, 부드러운 털의
If you describe something as furry, you mean that it has a soft rough texture like fur.

bullet**
[búlit]

n. (소총 · 권총의) 총탄, 탄환
A bullet is a small piece of metal with a pointed or rounded end, which is fired out of a gun.

chase**
[tʃeis]

v. 뒤쫓다, 추적하다
If you chase someone, or chase after them, you run after them or follow them quickly in order to catch or reach them.

bark*
[ba:rk]

v. (개가) 짖다; n. (개 등이) 짖는[우는] 소리; 나무껍질
When a dog barks, it makes a short, loud noise, once or several times.

skid복습
[skid]

v. 미끄러지다; n. 미끄럼, 옆으로 미끄러짐
If a vehicle skids, it slides sideways or forward while moving, for example when you are trying to stop it suddenly on a wet road.

polish*
[páliʃ]

v. 닦다, 윤내다; n. 광택 (polished a. 광이 나는)
If you polish something, you rub it with a cloth to make it shine.

clap*
[klæp]

v. 박수를 치다
When you clap, you hit your hands together to show appreciation or attract attention.

holler복습
[hálər]

v. 고함지르다; 큰 소리로 부르다; n. 외침, 큰 소리
If you holler, you shout loudly.

go wild

idiom 열광하다, 들뜨다; ~에 미친 듯 열중하다
If someone go wild, they behave in an uncontrolled or excited manner.

imagine***
[imǽdʒin]

v. 생각하다, 여기다; 상상하다
If you imagine that something is the case, you think that it is the case.

wag복습
[wæg]

v. (꼬리 등을) 흔들다, 흔들리다; n. 흔들기
When a dog wags its tail, it repeatedly waves its tail from side to side.

tail복습
[teil]

n. (동물의) 꼬리
The tail of an animal, bird, or fish is the part extending beyond the end of its body.

hold on to복습

phrasal v. 지키다, 고수하다; 보유하다
If you hold on to something or someone, you keep them not to lose.

tight복습
[tait]

ad. 단단히, 꽉; a. 단단한, 팽팽한, 빈틈없는
If you hold someone or something tight, you hold them firmly and securely.

squish
[skwiʃ]

v. 찌부러뜨리다, 으깨다
If something soft squishes or is squished, it is crushed out of shape when it is pressed.

retriever
[ritríːvər]

n. 사냥감을 찾아 가져오는 사냥개; 되찾는 사람[것]
A retriever is a kind of dog. Retrievers are traditionally used to bring back birds and animals which their owners have shot.

get away^{복습}

phrasal v. 떠나다, 탈출하다
If you get away from something, you escape from it.

paw^{복습}
[pɔː]

n. (갈고리 발톱이 있는 동물의) 발; v. 앞발로 차다
The paws of an animal such as a cat, dog, or bear are its feet, which have claws for gripping things and soft pads for walking on.

rub^{복습}
[rʌb]

v. 비비다, 문지르다; 스치다; n. 문지르기
If you rub a part of your body, you move your hand or fingers backward and forward over it while pressing firmly.

pick up

phrasal v. 줍다, 들다; 되찾다, 회복하다; 알아채다
When you pick up something, you take hold of and lift it.

applaud*
[əplɔ́ːd]

v. 박수를 보내다, 성원하다
When a group of people applaud, they clap their hands in order to show approval, for example when they have enjoyed a play or concert.

pinch*
[pintʃ]

v. 여위게 하다, 초췌하게 하다; 꼬집다; n. 꼬집기
(pinched a. (가난 등으로) 수척해진)
If someone's face is pinched, it looks thin and pale, usually because they are ill or old.

tell on

phrasal v. ~를 고자질하다
If you tell on someone, you tell a teacher or someone else in authority that they have done something wrong.

land*
[lænd]

v. 내려앉다, 상륙하다, 착륙하다; n. 육지, 국토, 나라
When someone or something lands, they come down to the ground after moving through the air or falling.

patch^{복습}
[pætʃ]

n. 자그만 땅; (주변과는 다른 조그만) 부분; 조각; 안대
A patch of land is a small area of land where a particular plant or crop grows.

Check Your Reading Speed

1분에 몇 단어를 읽는지 리딩 속도를 측정해보세요.

$$\frac{598 \text{ words}}{\text{reading time (\quad) sec}} \times 60 = (\qquad) \text{ WPM}$$

Build Your Vocabulary

memorial
[məmɔ́:riəl]

a. (죽은 사람을) 기념하기 위한, 추도[추모]의; n. 기념비(적인 것)
A memorial event, object, or prize is in honor of someone who has died, so that they will be remembered.

fancy^{**}
[fǽnsi]

a. 화려한, 고급스러운; v. 공상[상상]하다; 좋아하다; n. 공상; 기호, 선호
If you describe something as fancy, you mean that it is very expensive or of very high quality.

in charge of

idiom ~을 맡고 있는, 담당의
If you have charge of or are in charge of something or someone, you have responsibility for them.

hind^{복습}
[haind]

a. 뒤쪽의, 후방의
An animal's hind legs are at the back of its body.

select^{**}
[silékt]

v. 선택하다, 골라내다; 선출하다; a. 엄선된
If you select something, you choose it from a number of things of the same kind.

pick out^{복습}

phrasal v. (여럿 가운데에서 신중하게) ~을 고르다, 선발하다
If you pick out something, you choose it from a number of people or things.

hum[*]
[hʌm]

v. 콧노래를 부르다; (벌 · 기계 등이) 윙윙거리다; n. 윙윙(소리)
When you hum a tune, you sing it with your lips closed.

scary
[skéəri]

a. 무서운, 두려운
Something that is scary is rather frightening.

positive^{**}
[pázətiv]

a. 확신하고 있는; 명백한; 긍정적인
If you are positive about something, you are completely sure about it.

tremble[*]
[trembl]

v. 떨다; 떨리다
If something trembles, it shakes slightly.

stick^{복습}
[stik]

① v. (stuck-stuck) 내밀다; 찔러 넣다, 찌르다; 붙이다, 달라붙다; 고수하다
② n. 막대기, 지팡이
If something is sticking out from a surface or object, it extends up or away from it.

pull up

phrasal v. 잡아당기다; 차를 세우다, (말 · 차 등이) 서다
If you pull someone up, you move them from a lower to a higher position.

weigh[**]
[wei]

v. 무게가 ~이다, 무게를 달다; 신중히 고려하다
If someone or something weighs a particular amount, this amount is how heavy they are.

hardly[복습]
[háːrdli]

a. 거의 ~이 아니다; 거의 ~할 수 없다
You use hardly in expressions such as hardly ever, hardly any, and hardly anyone to mean almost never, almost none, or almost no-one.

embarrass[**]
[imbǽrəs]

v. 부끄럽게[무안하게] 하다; 어리둥절하게 하다; 당황하다
(embarrassed a. 당혹한, 창피한)
If something or someone embarrasses you, they make you feel shy or ashamed.

silly[**]
[síli]

a. 어리석은, 바보 같은; 익살맞은; n. 바보, 멍청이
If you say that someone or something is silly, you mean that they are foolish, childish, or ridiculous.

get over

phrasal v. ~을 극복하다, 회복하다
If you get over something, you return to your usual state of health or happiness.

allow[***]
[əláu]

v. 허락하다, ~하게 두다; 인정하다
If someone is allowed to do something, it is all right for them to do it and they will not get into trouble.

bend[**]
[bend]

v. (bent—bent) 구부리다, 돌리다; 구부러지다, 휘다; n. 커브, 굽음
When you bend a part of your body such as your arm or leg, or when it bends, you change its position so that it is no longer straight.

pat[*]
[pæt]

n. 쓰다듬기; v. 톡톡 가볍게 치다, (애정을 담아) 쓰다듬다
Pat refers to a gentle friendly touch with your open hand or with a flat object.

back and forth

a. 앞뒤(좌우)로의; 여기저기의
If something moves back and forth, it moves in one direction and then in the opposite one, repeatedly.

snuffle
[snʌfl]

v. 코를 킁킁거리다, 훌쩍이다; n. 코를 킁킁거리는 소리; 콧소리
If a person or an animal snuffles, they breathe in noisily through their nose, for example because they have a cold.

38

1. What did Miss Franny want for her birthday?
   A. A pet dog
   B. A library
   C. A new bookshelf
   D. Hundreds of books that only she could read

2. What did the bear do?
   A. He tried to eat Miss Franny.
   B. He took Miss Franny's book.
   C. He sniffed Miss Franny's books.
   D. He jumped onto a desk.

3. The men in town used to _____.
   A. tease Miss Franny
   B. buy Miss Franny new books
   C. call Miss Franny a liar
   D. help Miss Franny at the library

4. What did Amanda Wilkinson want?
   A. To pet Winn-Dixie
   B. An easier book
   C. To talk to Opal
   D. A more difficult book

5. What did Opal want from the pet store?
   A. A food bowl
   B. Treats for Winn-Dixie
   C. A nametag for Winn-Dixie
   D. A collar and leash

6. How will Opal pay for the item at the pet store?
   A. She will sweep the pet store's floors.
   B. She will save her allowance for one month.
   C. She will give her allowance to the pet store every week.
   D. She will ask the preacher for money.

7. What did Sweetie Pie do when she bumped into Opal and Winn-Dixie?
   A. She said she wanted a pet goldfish.
   B. She asked to buy Winn-Dixie.
   C. She invited Opal to her party.
   D. She stopped sucking her knuckle.

1분에 몇 단어를 읽는지 리딩 속도를 측정해보세요.

$$\frac{973 \ words}{reading \ time \ (\quad) \ sec} \times 60 = (\qquad) \ WPM$$

Build Your Vocabulary

consist**
[kənsíst]

vi. 이루어지다, 구성되다
If something consists of other things, it is formed from the things or people mentioned.

mosquito*
[məskí:tou]

n. 모기
Mosquitoes are small flying insects which bite people and animals in order to suck their blood.

start in^{복습}

phrasal v. 시작하다, 착수하다
If you start in something, you begin to do it.

lean^{복습}
[li:n]

① v. 몸을 구부리다, 기울다; 기대다, 의지하다 ② a. 야윈, 마른
When you lean in a particular direction, you bend your body in that direction.

pride**
[praid]

vt. 자랑하다; n. 자존심, 긍지; 만족감 (prideful a. 거만한, 자랑스러운)
If you pride yourself on a quality or skill that you have, you are very proud of it.

nod^{복습}
[nɔd]

v. 끄덕이다, 끄덕여 표시하다; n. (동의 · 인사 · 신호 · 명령의) 끄덕임
If you nod, you move your head downward and upward to show agreement, understanding, or approval.

share**
[ʃɛər]

vt. 공유하다, 분배하다; n. 몫, 분담
If you share something with another person, you both have it, use it, or occupy it.

librarian*
[laibréəriən]

n. (도서관의) 사서
A librarian is a person who is in charge of a library or who has been specially trained to work in a library.

mention***
[ménʃən]

vt. 말하다, 언급하다; n. 언급, 진술
If you mention something, you say something about it, usually briefly.

shadow**
[ʃǽdou]

n. 그림자; 어둠, 그늘
A shadow is a dark shape on a surface that is made when something stands between a light and the surface.

aware**
[əwɛ́ər]

a. 알아차린; 알고 있는, 의식하고 있는
If you are aware of something, you realize that it is present or is happening because you hear it, see it, smell it, or feel it.

peculiar*
[pikjú:ljər]

a. 이상한, 특이한; 특유한, 고유의
If you describe someone or something as peculiar, you think that they are strange or unusual, sometimes in an unpleasant way.

sniff* [snif]

v. 코를 킁킁거리다, 냄새를 맡다; 콧방귀를 뀌다; n. 냄새 맡음; 콧방귀
If you sniff something or sniff at it, you smell it by sniffing.

in the mood

idiom ~할 기분이 나는
If you are in the mood to do something, you have a strong desire to do something or feel like doing something.

intend^{복습} [inténd]

v. ~할 작정이다, ~하려고 생각하다; 의도하다
If you intend to do something, you have decided or planned to do it.

aim* [eim]

v. 겨냥을 하다, 목표삼다; n. 겨냥, 조준; 목적, 뜻
If you aim a weapon or object at something or someone, you point it toward them before firing or throwing it.

snatch* [snætʃ]

v. 잡아채다, 와락 붙잡다; n. 잡아챔, 강탈
If you snatch something or snatch at something, you take it or pull it away quickly.

tease* [ti:z]

v. 놀리다, 괴롭히다; 졸라대다; n. 골리기
To tease someone means to laugh at them or make jokes about them in order to embarrass, annoy, or upset them.

used to^{복습}

phrasal v. ~하곤 했다; 과거 한때는 ~이었다
If someone used to do something, it suggests habitual or accustomed actions or states, taking place in the past but not continuing into the present.

sigh^{복습} [sai]

v. 한숨 쉬다; n. 한숨, 탄식
When you sigh, you let out a deep breath, as a way of expressing feelings such as disappointment, tiredness, or pleasure.

imagine^{복습} [imædʒin]

v. 생각하다, 여기다; 상상하다
If you imagine that something is the case, you think that it is the case.

recall* [rikɔ́:l]

vt. 생각해내다, 상기하다; n. 회상, 상기
When you recall something, you remember it and tell others about it.

wrinkle^{복습} [riŋkl]

v. 주름이 지다, 구겨지다; n. 주름, 잔주름 (wrinkled a. 주름진, 구김살이 있는)
When someone's skin wrinkles or when something wrinkles it, lines start to form in it because the skin is getting old or damaged.

friendless [fréndlis]

a. 친구가 없는
Someone who is friendless has no friends.

comfort** [kʌ́mfərt]

vt. 위로[위안]하다; n. 마음이 편안함, 안락; 위로, 위안
If you comfort someone, you make them feel less worried, unhappy, or upset, for example by saying kind things to them.

paw^{복습} [pɔ:]

n. (갈고리 발톱이 있는 동물의) 발; v. 앞발로 차다
The paws of an animal such as a cat, dog, or bear are its feet, which have claws for gripping things and soft pads for walking on.

back and forth^{복습}

a. 앞뒤(좌우)로의; 여기저기의
If something moves back and forth, it moves in one direction and then in the opposite one, repeatedly.

sit up ^{복습}

phrasal v. 일어나 앉다
If you sit up, you move yourself into a sitting position, for example, from lying down.

talent ^{복습}
[tǽlənt]

n. 재능, 재주
Talent is a natural ability to do something well.

grand**
[grænd]

a. 아주 즐거운; 웅장한, 장려한
If you describe an activity or experience as grand, you mean that it is very pleasant and enjoyable.

march***
[mɑːrtʃ]

① v. 당당하게 걷다, 행진하다; n. 행진, 행군 ② n. 3월
If you say that someone marches somewhere, you mean that they walk there quickly and in a determined way, for example because they are angry.

memorial ^{복습}
[məmɔ́ːriəl]

a. (죽은 사람을) 기념하기 위한, 추도[추모]의; n. 기념비(적인 것)
A memorial event, object, or prize is in honor of someone who has died, so that they will be remembered.

pinch
[pintʃ]

v. 여위게 하다, 초췌하게 하다; 꼬집다; n. 꼬집기 (pinch-faced a. 파리한 얼굴의)
If someone's face is pinched, it looks thin and pale, usually because they are ill or old.

advance**
[ædvǽns]

v. 진보하다; 전진하다, 나아가다 (advanced a. 고급의, 상급의)
An advanced student has already learned the basic facts of a subject and is doing more difficult work.

pretend***
[priténd]

v. ~인 체하다, 가장하다; a. 가짜의
If you pretend that something is the case, you act in a way that is intended to make people believe that it is the case, although in fact it is not.

stare ^{복습}
[stɛər]

v. 응시하다, 뚫어지게 보다
If you stare at someone or something, you look at them for a long time.

allow ^{복습}
[əláu]

v. 허락하다, ~하게 두다; 인정하다
If someone is allowed to do something, it is all right for them to do it and they will not get into trouble.

select ^{복습}
[silékt]

a. 엄선된; v. 선택하다, 골라내다; 선출하다
A select group is a small group of some of the best people or things of their kind.

turn around ^{복습}

phrasal v. 돌아서다, 몸을 돌리다; 회전하다
When you turn around, you move your head and shoulders or your whole body so that you face in the opposite direction.

mess up

phrasal v. 망쳐놓다, 어질러놓다
If you mess something up or if you mess up, you cause something to fail or be spoiled.

1분에 몇 단어를 읽는지 리딩 속도를 측정해보세요.

$$\frac{1{,}073 \text{ words}}{\text{reading time } (\quad) \text{ sec}} \times 60 = (\qquad) \text{ WPM}$$

Build Your Vocabulary

bald^{복습}
[bɔːld]

a. (머리 등이) 벗어진, 대머리의; vi. 머리가 벗어지다
Someone who is bald has little or no hair on the top of their head.

spot^{복습}
[spɑt]

n. 반점, 얼룩; 장소, 지점; vt. 발견하다, 분별하다
Spots are small, round, coloured areas on a surface.

fur^{복습}
[fəːr]

n. 부드러운 털; 모피
Fur is the thick and usually soft hair that grows on the bodies of many mammals.

shiny^{복습}
[ʃáini]

a. 빛나는; 해가 비치는; 광택이 있는
Shiny things are bright and reflect light.

limp^{복습}
[limp]

v. 다리를 절다, 절뚝거리다; a. 기운 없는, 축 늘어진
If a person or animal limps, they walk with difficulty or in an uneven way because one of their legs or feet is hurt.

stray^{복습}
[strei]

n. 길을 잃은[주인이 없는] 동물; a. (애완동물이) 길을 잃은, 주인이 없는; v. 제 위치를 벗어나다, 옆길로 새다
A stray dog or cat has wandered away from its owner's home.

collar**
[kálər]

n. (개 등의 목에 거는) 목걸이; 칼라, 깃
A collar is a band of leather or plastic which is put round the neck of a dog or cat.

leash
[liːʃ]

n. 가죽 끈, 사슬; 속박, 통제
A dog's leash is a long thin piece of leather or a chain, which you attach to the dog's collar so that you can keep the dog under control.

lizard
[lízərd]

n. [동물] 도마뱀
A lizard is a reptile with short legs and a long tail.

supply**
[səplái]

n. (pl.) 필수품; 공급(량), 보급(량); vt. 공급하다, 지급하다
You can use supplies to refer to food, equipment, and other essential things that people need, especially when these are provided in large quantities.

leather**
[léðər]

n. 가죽
Leather is treated animal skin which is used for making shoes, clothes, bags, and furniture.

allow^{복습}
[əláu]

v. 허락하다, ~하게 두다; 인정하다
If someone is allowed to do something, it is all right for them to do it and they will not get into trouble.

pull up 복습

phrasal v. 잡아당기다; 차를 세우다. (말 · 차 등이) 서다
If you pull up something, you move it from a lower to a higher position.

sneeze 복습
[sni:z]

vi. 재채기하다; n. 재채기
When you sneeze, you suddenly take in your breath and then blow it down your nose noisily without being able to stop yourself, for example because you have a cold.

wag 복습
[wæg]

v. (꼬리 등을) 흔들다, 흔들리다; n. 흔들기
When a dog wags its tail, it repeatedly waves its tail from side to side.

tail 복습
[teil]

n. (동물의) 꼬리
The tail of an animal, bird, or fish is the part extending beyond the end of its body.

furious*
[fjúəriəs]

a. 맹렬한; 격노한, 몹시 화가 난
Furious is used to describe something that is done with great energy, effort, speed, or violence.

absolute*
[æbsəlu:t]

a. 절대적인; 완전한; 무조건의 (absolutely ad. 절대적으로, 무조건)
Absolute means total and complete.

combination**
[kàmbənéiʃən]

n. 조합, 결합, 화합
A combination of things is a mixture of them.

expensive***
[ikspénsiv]

a. 비싼, 비용이 많이 드는
If something is expensive, it costs a lot of money.

explain***
[ikspléin]

v. 설명하다, 분명하게 하다
If you explain something, you give details about it or describe it so that it can be understood.

situation 복습
[sitʃuéiʃən]

n. 상태, 정세; 위치, 환경
You use situation to refer generally to what is happening in a particular place at a particular time, or to refer to what is happening to you.

allowance*
[əláuəns]

n. 용돈; 수당, 급여; 허락, 허가
A child's allowance is money that is given to him or her every week or every month by his or her parents.

afford**
[əfɔ́:rd]

vt. ~할 여유가 있다; 주다, 공급하다
If you cannot afford something, you do not have enough money to pay for it.

fancy 복습
[fǽnsi]

a. 화려한, 고급스러운; v. 공상[상상]하다; 좋아하다; n. 공상; 기호, 선호
If you describe something as fancy, you mean that it is very expensive or of very high quality.

set (someone) up

idiom (필요한 자금을) ~에게 제공하다; 함정에 빠뜨리다
If you set someone up, you provide them with the money they need, for example to start a business, or buy a home.

installment
[instɔ́:lmənt]

a. 할부지급 방식의; n. 할부. 납입금. 분할 불입
If you pay for something in instalments, you pay small sums of money at regular intervals over a period of time, rather than paying the whole amount at once.

**irritate*
[írətèit]

vt. 짜증나게 하다. 화나게 하다 (irritating a. 짜증나게 하는)
If something irritates you, it keeps annoying you.

**parrot*
[pǽrət]

n. [동물] 앵무새
A parrot is a tropical bird with a curved beak and brightly-colored or grey feathers.

fish tank
[fiʃ tæŋk]

n. (물고기 · 수생 동물의) 수조
A fish tank is a container housing fish.

ignore복습
[ignɔ́:r]

vt. 무시하다. 모르는 체하다
If you ignore someone or something, you pay no attention to them.

promise*
[prámis]

vt. 약속하다; n. 약속. 계약
If you promise that you will do something, you say to someone that you will definitely do it.

owner**
[óunər]

n. 주인. 소유주
The owner of something is the person to whom it belongs.

slick back

phrasal v. (머리카락을) 뒤로 빗어 넘기다
If you slick your hair back or down, you make it lie flat by putting oil or water on it.

sweep**
[swi:p]

v. (swept–swept) 청소하다. 쓸어내리다; 휙 지나가다; n. 청소; 한 번 휘두름
If you sweep an area of floor or ground, you push dirt or rubbish off it using a brush with a long handle.

**dust*
[dʌst]

v. 먼지를 털다; n. 먼지. 가루. 티끌
When you dust something such as furniture, you remove dust from it, usually using a cloth.

shelf**
[ʃelf]

n. (pl. shelves) 선반
A shelf is a flat piece which is attached to a wall or to the sides of a cupboard for keeping things on.

take out

phrasal v. 제거하다. 버리다; 꺼내다
If you take out something, you remove it from its place.

shell복습
[ʃel]

n. 껍데기; 조가비; v. 껍데기를 벗기다
The shell of a nut or egg is the hard covering which surrounds it.

**trustworthy*
[trʌ́stwə̀:rði]

a. 신뢰할 수 있는
A trustworthy person is reliable, responsible, and can be trusted completely.

preacher복습
[prí:tʃər]

n. 목사. 설교자. 전도자
A preacher is a person, usually a member of the clergy, who preaches sermons as part of a church service.

honest복습
[ánist]

a. 정직한. 솔직한
If you describe someone as honest, you mean that they always tell the truth, and do not try to deceive people or break the law.

separate[**] [sépəreit]

v. 가르다, 떼어놓다, 분리하다 (separated a. 따로 떨어져)
If you separate people or things that are together, or if they separate, they move apart.

howl[복습] [haul]

v. 짖다, 울부짖다; n. 울부짖는 소리
A howl is a long, loud, crying sound.

terrible[복습] [térəbl]

a. 극심한, 지독한; 무서운, 끔찍한
If something is terrible, it is very bad or of very poor quality.

name[복습] [neim]

v. 이름을 지어주다; (정확히) 말하다, 지정하다; n. 이름; 평판
If you name someone, you identify them by stating their name.

get along

idiom 사이좋게 지내다, 의기투합하다; 지내다, 살아가다
When you get along with someone, you're friendly or compatible with them.

mumble [mʌmbl]

v. 중얼거리다, 웅얼거리다; n. 중얼거림
If you mumble, you speak very quietly and not at all clearly with the result that the words are difficult to understand.

trot[복습] [trat]

v. 빠른 걸음으로 가다, 총총걸음 치다; n. 빠른 걸음
When an animal such as a horse trots, it moves fairly fast, taking quick small steps.

cock[*] [kɔk]

v. 위로 치올리다, (귀·꽁지를) 쫑긋 세우다; n. 수탉; 마개
If you cock a part of your body in a particular direction, you lift it or point it in that direction.

spread[복습] [spred]

v. (spread–spread) 펼치다, 뻗다, 퍼지다; 뿌리다; n. 퍼짐, 폭, 넓이
If you spread your arms, hands, fingers, or legs, you stretch them out until they are far apart.

land[복습] [lænd]

v. 내려앉다, 상륙하다, 착륙하다; n. 육지, 국토, 나라
When someone or something lands, they come down to the ground after moving through the air or falling.

croak [krouk]

v. (까마귀가) 깍깍 울다; 쉰 목소리를 내다
When a frog or bird croaks, it makes a harsh, low sound.

tiny[복습] [táini]

a. 몹시 작은
Something or someone that is tiny is extremely small.

neither[복습] [ní:ðər]

pron. (둘 중) 어느 것도 ~ 아니다; conj. (부정문을 만들며) ~도 마찬가지이다
You use neither to refer to each of two things or people, when you are making a negative statement that includes both of them.

bump into[복습]

phrasal v. 부닥치다; 우연히 만나다
If you bump into something or someone, you accidentally hit them while you are moving.

suck[**] [sʌk]

v. 빨다, 흡수하다; 삼키다; n. 빨아들임
If you suck on something, you hold it in your mouth and pull at it with the muscles in your cheeks and tongue, for example in order to get liquid out of it.

48

knuckle
[nʌkl]

n. 손가락 관절[마디]; v. 손가락 마디로 치다
Your knuckles are the rounded pieces of bone that form lumps on your hands where your fingers join your hands, and where your fingers bend.

ponytail
[póunitèil]

n. 포니테일(뒤에서 묶어 아래로 드리운 머리)
A ponytail is a hair style in which someone's hair is tied up at the back of the head and hangs down like a tail.

strand*
[strænd]

n. (실 · 전선 · 머리카락 등의) 가닥, 끈 줄
A strand of something such as hair, wire, or thread is a single thin piece of it.

goldfish
[góuldfiʃ]

n. 금붕어
A goldfish is a small orange or red fish. Goldfish are kept as pets in bowls or ponds.

pet**
[pet]

v. (사람 · 동물을) 어루만지다; (동물을) 귀여워하다; n. 애완동물
If you pet a person or animal, you touch them in an affectionate way.

stroke*
[strouk]

① vt. 쓰다듬다, 어루만지다; n. 쓰다듬기, 달램 ② n. 타격, 일격, 치기
If you stroke someone or something, you move your hand slowly and gently over them.

droop*
[dru:p]

v. (특히 지치거나 약해져서) 아래로 처지다; 풀이 죽다
If something droops, it hangs or leans downward with no strength or firmness.

drool
[dru:l]

n. 군침; v. 군침을 흘리다, 침이 나오다
Drool is saliva spilling from the mouth.

theme**
[θi:m]

n. 주제, 테마; a. 특정 분위기를 살린
A theme in a piece of writing, a talk, or a discussion is an important idea or subject that runs through it.

bet복습
[bet]

v. ~임이 틀림없다; 걸다, 내기를 하다; n. 내기, 건 돈
You use expressions such as 'I bet', 'I'll bet', and 'you can bet' to indicate that you are sure something is true.

invitation**
[invitéiʃən]

n. 초대
An invitation is a written or spoken request to come to an event such as a party, a meal, or a meeting.

Chapters Nine & Ten

1. Why did the Dewberry brothers have shaved heads?
   A. They were too hot in the summertime.
   B. Dunlap got fleas in his hair once.
   C. They wanted to look the same.
   D. They always got their hair dirty.

2. What did the brothers say to Opal?
   A. Winn-Dixie would be eaten by the witch.
   B. The witch would eat Opal.
   C. Opal would get lost in the yard.
   D. They won't tell the preacher what happened to Opal.

3. Winn-Dixie liked to eat _____ at Gloria's house.
   A. vegetables
   B. bread
   C. flowers
   D. peanut butter

4. Gloria couldn't _____ well.
   A. see
   B. hear
   C. cook
   D. chew

5. What did Opal and Gloria do together?

   A. They made sandwiches.

   B. They planted a tree.

   C. They washed Winn-Dixie.

   D. They fixed Gloria's garden.

6. Which of the following is NOT true?

   A. Opal was invited to Sweetie Pie's party.

   B. Opal made friends that day.

   C. Opal was teased by Gloria Dump.

   D. Opal got a job at the pet store.

7. At bedtime, Winn-Dixie _____.

   A. looked like he was laughing

   B. sneezed all over the bed

   C. licked the preacher's face

   D. took a long time to fall asleep

Check Your Reading Speed

1분에 몇 단어를 읽는지 리딩 속도를 측정해보세요.

$$\frac{827 \text{ words}}{\text{reading time (\quad) sec}} \times 60 = (\qquad) \text{ WPM}$$

Build Your Vocabulary

for instance

idiom 예를 들어, 예컨대
You use for instance to introduce a particular event, situation, or person that is an example of what you are talking about.

whisper^{복습}
[hwíspər]

v. 속삭이다
When you whisper, you say something very quietly.

neither^{복습}
[níːðər]

pron. (둘 중) 어느 것도 ~ 아니다; conj. (부정문을 만들며) ~도 마찬가지이다
You use neither to refer to each of two things or people, when you are making a negative statement that includes both of them.

shave^{**}
[ʃeiv]

v. (머리카락을) 깎다; 면도하다
If someone shaves a part of their body, they remove the hair from it so that it is smooth.

flea[*]
[fiː]

n. [곤충] 벼룩
A flea is a very small jumping insect that has no wings and feeds on the blood of humans or animals.

identical^{**}
[aidéntikəl]

a. 동일한, 꼭 같은
Things that are identical are exactly the same.

holler^{복습}
[hálər]

v. 고함지르다; 큰 소리로 부르다; n. 외침, 큰 소리
If you holler, you shout loudly.

watch out

idiom 조심해라
You say 'watch out', when you warn someone about something dangerous.

head^{***}
[hed]

v. 특정 방향으로 가다; 앞서다; n. 한발 앞선 출발, 우위
If you are headed for a particular place, you are going toward that place.

witch^{**}
[witʃ]

n. 마녀
In fairy stories, a witch is a woman, usually an old woman, who has evil magic powers.

keep on^{복습}

phrasal v. 계속하다
When you keep on doing something, you continue or persist doing it.

hop^{복습}
[hap]

v. 깡충 뛰다, 뛰어오르다; n. 깡충깡충 뜀
If you hop, you move along by jumping.

52

overgrown
[òuvərgróun]

a. (풀 · 잡초 등이) 마구[제멋대로] 자란
If a garden or other place is overgrown, it is covered with a lot of untidy plants because it has not been looked after.

get off

phrasal v. (탈것에서) 내리다, 하차하다
If you get off you vehicle, you descend from it.

back off

phrasal v. 뒤로 물러나다[뒷걸음질 치다]
When you back off, you move away from someone or something frightening or unpleasant.

deal**
[di:l]

v. (~를) 상대하다; 처리하다; 거래하다; n. 대우; 거래
When you deal with someone, you take appropriate action in a particular situation or according to who you are talking to.

dessert**
[dizə́:rt]

n. 디저트, 후식
Dessert is something sweet, such as fruit or a pudding, that you eat at the end of a meal.

vegetable복습
[védʒətəbl]

n. 야채
Vegetables are plants such as cabbages, potatoes, and onions which you can cook and eat.

vine**
[vain]

n. 덩굴식물, 포도나무
A vine is a plant that grows up or over things, especially one which produces grapes.

moss**
[mɔːs]

n. 이끼
Moss is a very small soft green plant which grows on damp soil, or on wood or stone.

crinkly
[kríŋkli]

a. 잔주름이 많은, 쪼글쪼글한
A crinkly object has many small creases or folds in it or in its surface.

floppy
[flápi]

a. 퍼덕퍼덕 펄럭이는; 늘어진, 느슨한
Something that is floppy is loose rather than stiff, and tends to hang downward.

company***
[kámpəni]

n. 함께 있음; 동료, 일행; 회사; v. 따르다, 동행하다
Company is having another person or other people with you, usually when this is pleasant or stops you feeling lonely.

terrible복습
[térəbl]

a. 극심한, 지독한; 무서운, 끔찍한
If something is terrible, it is very bad or of very poor quality.

thump
[θʌmp]

v. 탁 치다, 부딪치다; n. 탁[쿵] 하는 소리; 때림, 세게 쥐어박음
If you thump something, you hit it hard, usually with your fist.

grocery store복습
[gróusəri stɔːr]

n. 식품점, 슈퍼마켓
A grocery store is a store that retails food.

prize***
[praiz]

n. 상; 상품; vt. 높이 평가하다, 소중히 여기다
A prize is money or something valuable that is given to someone who has the best results in a competition or game, or as a reward for doing good work.

fix[***]
[fiks]

vt. (식사 등을) 준비하다; 고치다; 고정시키다
If you fix some food or a drink for someone, you make it or prepare it for them.

go on[복습]

phrasal v. 자자, 어서; 계속하다; 앞으로 가다, 나아가다
People use 'go on' to encourage or dare someone to do something.

lawn[복습]
[lɔːn]

n. 잔디(밭)
A lawn is an area of grass that is kept cut short and is usually part of someone's garden or backyard, or part of a park.

bust[*]
[bʌst]

v. 부수다; 고장 내다; 불시 단속을 벌이다, 급습하다
If you bust something, you break it or damage it so badly that it cannot be used.

general[***]
[dʒénərəl]

a. 대강의, 대체적인; 일반적인, 보편적인
If you talk about the general situation somewhere or talk about something in general terms, you are describing the situation as a whole rather than considering its details or exceptions.

shape[***]
[ʃeip]

n. 형태, 모양
The shape of an object, a person, or an area is the appearance of their outside edges or surfaces, for example whether they are round, square, curved, or fat.

rely on

phrasal v. ~에 의지[의존]하다, ~을 필요로 하다
If you rely on someone or something, you need them and depend on them in order to live or work properly.

54

1분에 몇 단어를 읽는지 리딩 속도를 측정해보세요.

$$\frac{635 \text{ words}}{\text{reading time ( ) sec}} \times 60 = (\quad) \text{ WPM}$$

Build Your Vocabulary

preacher^{복습}
[príːtʃər]

n. 목사, 설교자, 전도자
A preacher is a person, usually a member of the clergy, who preaches sermons as part of a church service.

explain^{복습}
[ikspléin]

v. 설명하다, 분명하게 하다
If you explain something, you give details about it or describe it so that it can be understood.

turtle^{복습}
[təːrtl]

n. [동물] 거북, 바다거북
A turtle is a large reptile which has a thick shell covering its body and which lives in the sea most of the time.

shell^{복습}
[ʃel]

n. 껍데기; 조가비; v. 껍데기를 벗기다
The shell of an animal such as a tortoise, snail, or crab is the hard protective covering that it has around its body or on its back.

produce^{복습}
[prədjúːs]

n. 농작물, 농산물, 생산품; v. 생산하다
Produce is food or other things that are grown in large quantities to be sold.

name^{복습}
[neim]

v. 이름을 지어주다; (정확히) 말하다, 지정하다; n. 이름; 평판
If you name someone, you identify them by stating their name.

invite***
[inváit]

vt. 초청하다, 초대하다
If you invite someone to something such as a party or a meal, you ask them to come to it.

witch^{복습}
[witʃ]

n. 마녀
In fairy stories, a witch is a woman, usually an old woman, who has evil magic powers.

mean***
[miːn]

① a. 비열한; 성질이 나쁜, 심술궂은 ② vt. 의미하다, 뜻하다 ③ a. 평균의, 중간의
If you describe a behavior as mean, you are saying that it is very bad and evil.

anyhow**
[énihàu]

a. 어쨌든, 아무튼
You use anyhow to correct or modify a statement, for example to limit it to what you definitely know to be true.

nod^{복습}
[nɔd]

v. 끄덕이다, 끄덕여 표시하다; n. (동의 · 인사 · 신호 · 명령의) 끄덕임
If you nod, you move your head downward and upward to show agreement, understanding, or approval.

frown[**]
[fraun]

vi. 얼굴을 찡그리다, 눈살을 찌푸리다; n. 찌푸린 얼굴
When someone frowns, their eyebrows become drawn together, because they are annoyed or puzzled.

freckle[복습]
[frekl]

n. 주근깨, 반점
Freckles are small light brown spots on someone's skin, especially on their face.

thumb[**]
[θʌm]

n. 엄지손가락
Your thumb is the short thick part on the side of your hand next to your four fingers.

dig[***]
[dig]

v. 파다, 파헤치다; 찌르다; (구어) 마음에 들다, 좋아하다; n. 파기
If people or animals dig, they make a hole in the ground or in a pile of earth, stones, or rubbish.

pat[복습]
[pæt]

v. 톡톡 가볍게 치다, (애정을 담아) 쓰다듬다; n. 쓰다듬기
If you pat something or someone, you tap them lightly, usually with your hand held flat.

dirt[**]
[dəːrt]

n. 흙, 진흙, 먼지; 쓰레기
You can refer to the earth on the ground as dirt, especially when it is dusty.

tight[복습]
[tait]

ad. 단단히, 꽉; a. 단단한, 팽팽한, 빈틈없는
If you hold someone or something tight, you hold them firmly and securely.

tuck[*]
[tʌk]

v. 밀어 넣다, 쑤셔 넣다; n. 접어 넣은 단
If you tuck something somewhere, you put it there so that it is safe, comfortable, or neat.

whisker[*]
[hwískər]

n. (고양이 · 쥐 등의) 수염; 구레나룻
The whiskers of an animal such as a cat or a mouse are the long stiff hairs that grow near its mouth.

yawn[*]
[jɔːn]

vi. 하품하다; n. 하품
If you yawn, you open your mouth very wide and breathe in more air than usual, often when you are tired or when you are not interested in something.

stretch[**]
[stretʃ]

v. 쭉 펴다, 뻗다, 늘이다; n. 뻗침
When you stretch, you put your arms or legs out straight and tighten your muscles.

lick[복습]
[lik]

vt. 핥다; (불길이 혀처럼) 날름거리다, 넘실거리다; n. 핥기
When people or animals lick something, they move their tongue across its surface.

lie[복습]
[lai]

vi. (lay-lain) 눕다, 누워 있다, 놓여 있다, 위치하다; 거짓말하다; n. 거짓말
If you are lying somewhere, you are in a horizontal position and are not standing or sitting.

hop[복습]
[hap]

v. 깡충 뛰다, 뛰어오르다; n. 깡충깡충 뜀
If you hop, you move along by jumping.

lean^{복습}
[li:n]

① v. 몸을 구부리다, 가울다; 기대다, 의지하다 ② a. 야윈, 마른
When you lean in a particular direction, you bend your body in that direction.

amaze[*]
[əméiz]

vt. 깜짝 놀라게 하다
If something amazes you, it surprises you very much.

turn out

phrasal v. (전기 · 난방기를) 끄다
When you turn out something, you switch it off such as a light or a source of heat.

notice^{***}
[nóutis]

vt. 알아차리다, 주의하다; n. 주의, 주목
If you notice something or someone, you become aware of them.

asleep^{***}
[əslí:p]

a. 잠이 든, 자고 있는
Someone who is asleep is sleeping.

snore[*]
[snɔ:r]

v. 코를 골다
When someone who is asleep snores, they make a loud noise each time they breathe.

Chapters Eleven & Twelve

1. Why did Opal wake up?

   A. Winn-Dixie was howling and clawing at the door.

   B. The thunderstorm was very loud.

   C. Winn-Dixie was running around in the trailer.

   D. Winn-Dixie was hitting his head against the door.

2. What did Winn-Dixie do when there was thunder?

   A. He howled and barked.

   B. He ran through the trailer.

   C. He climbed onto the bed.

   D. He jumped on the preacher.

3. Why was Winn-Dixie acting strangely?

   A. He didn't like rain.

   B. He was scared of thunderstorms.

   C. He wanted to go outside.

   D. He was scared that Opal and the preacher would leave him.

4. What was NOT true when Opal entered the pet store?

   A. The animals were out of their cages.

   B. Gertrude said, "Dog."

   C. Winn-Dixie barked at Otis.

   D. Otis was playing the guitar.

5. What was true about Otis?

  A. He made animals nervous.

  B. He wore sandals.

  C. He had been to jail.

  D. He could speak with animals.

6. What did Opal do after leaving the pet store?

  A. She wanted to go home with Sweetie Pie.

  B. She waved back at Sweetie Pie's mother.

  C. She put a leash on Winn-Dixie.

  D. She played the guitar with Otis.

7. Opal thought her mother would like _____.

  A. to see Opal with her new friend

  B. to see Opal work at the pet store

  C. to pet Winn-Dixie

  D. to hear Opal's stories

Check Your Reading Speed

1분에 몇 단어를 읽는지 리딩 속도를 측정해보세요.

$$\frac{975 \text{ words}}{\text{reading time ( ) sec}} \times 60 = (\quad) \text{ WPM}$$

Build Your Vocabulary

thunderstorm
[θʌ́ndərstɔ̀:rm]

n. 폭풍우
A thunderstorm is a storm in which there is thunder and lightning and a lot of heavy rain.

thunder**
[θʌ́ndə:r]

n. 천둥; v. 천둥이 치다; 우르릉거리다
Thunder is the loud noise that you hear from the sky after a flash of lightning, especially during a storm.

lightning**
[làitniŋ]

n. 번개, 번갯불; a. 번개의, 번개 같은; 매우 빠른
Lightning is the very bright flashes of light in the sky that happen during thunderstorms.

whine*
[hwain]

v. 낑낑거리다, 우는 소리를 하다, 푸념하다; 윙 소리를 내다
If something or someone whines, they make a long, high-pitched noise, especially one which sounds sad or unpleasant.

butt*
[bʌt]

v. (머리로) 들이받다, 부딪히다; n. (구어) 엉덩이; 뭉툭한 끝 부분
If a person or animal butts you, they hit you with the top of their head.

pay attention

phrasal v. 주의를 기울이다, 유의하다
When you pay attention to something, you are attentive and focusing on it.

beat***
[bi:t]

v. 치다, 두드리다; 이기다, 패배시키다; n. [음악] 박자, 고동
If you beat someone or something, you hit them very hard.

whimper*
[hwímpər]

v. 낑낑거리다; 훌쩍이다, 울먹이다
If someone whimpers, they make quiet unhappy or frightened sounds, as if they are about to start crying.

tremble***
[trembl]

v. 떨다; 떨리다
If something trembles, it shakes slightly.

kneel*
[ni:l]

v. (knelt/kneeled–knelt/kneeled) 무릎을 꿇다
When you kneel, you bend your legs so that your knees are touching the ground.

wrap**
[ræp]

v. 감싸다; 포장하다; n. 싸개, 덮개
If someone wraps their arms, fingers, or legs around something, they put them firmly around it.

sneeze^{복습}
[sni:z]

vi. 재채기하다; n. 재채기
When you sneeze, you suddenly take in your breath and then blow it down your nose noisily without being able to stop yourself, for example because you have a cold.

wag^{복습}
[wæg]

v. (꼬리 등을) 흔들다, 흔들리다; n. 흔들기
When a dog wags its tail, it repeatedly waves its tail from side to side.

tail^{복습}
[teil]

n. (동물의) 꼬리
The tail of an animal, bird, or fish is the part extending beyond the end of its body.

normal**
[nɔ́:rməl]

a. 보통의, 평범한, 정상적인
Something that is normal is usual and ordinary, and is what people expect.

mean^{복습}
[mi:n]

① a. 비열한; 성질이 나쁜, 심술궂은 ② vt. 의미하다, 뜻하다 ③ a. 평균의, 중간의
If you describe a behavior as mean, you are saying that it is very bad and evil.

chase^{복습}
[tʃeis]

v. 뒤쫓다, 추적하다
If you chase someone, or chase after them, you run after them or follow them quickly in order to catch or reach them.

hiss*
[his]

v. 쉿 하는 소리를 내다; n. 쉿(제지·힐책의 소리)
To hiss means to make a sound like a long 's'.

trailer^{복습}
[tréilər]

n. 트레일러하우스, (자동차가 끌고 다니는) 이동식 주택
A trailer is a container on wheels which is pulled by a car or other vehicle and which is used for transporting large or heavy items.

last**
[læst]

vi. 계속하다, 오래가다; a. 최후의, 마지막의
If an event, situation, or problem lasts for a particular length of time, it continues to exist or happen for that length of time.

tear**
[tɛər]

① v. 부리나케 가다; 찢다, 찢어지다; n. 찢음 ② n. 눈물
If you tear somewhere, you move there very quickly, often in an uncontrolled or dangerous way.

pant**
[pænt]

vi. 헐떡거리다, 숨차다; n. 헐떡거림, 숨 가쁨
If you pant, you breathe quickly and loudly with your mouth open, because you have been doing something energetic.

grab^{복습}
[græb]

v. 부여잡다, 움켜쥐다; n. 부여잡기
If you grab something, you take it or pick it up suddenly and roughly.

crack**
[kræk]

n. 갑작스런 날카로운 소리; 갈라진 금; v. 날카로운 소리가 나다; 금이 가다, 깨다
A crack is a sharp sound, like the sound of a piece of wood breaking.

watch out^{복습}

idiom 조심해라
You say 'watch out', when you warn someone about something dangerous.

confuse**
[kənfjú:z]

v. 어리둥절하게 하다, 혼동하다 (confused a. 당황한, 어리둥절한)
To confuse someone means to make it difficult for them to know exactly what is happening or what to do.

barrel**
[bǽrəl]

v. 쏜살같이 달리다[질주하다]; n. 통; 배럴
If a vehicle or person is barreling in a particular direction, they are moving very quickly in that direction.

stomach**
[stʌ́mək]

n. 복부, 배; 위
You can refer to the front part of your body below your waist as your stomach.

pathological
[pæθəlάdʒikəl]

a. 병적인, 걷잡을 수 없는
You describe a person or their behavior as pathological when they behave in an extreme and unacceptable way, and have very powerful feelings which they cannot control.

rub^수능
[rʌb]

v. 비비다, 문지르다; 스치다; n. 문지르기
If you rub a part of your body, you move your hand or fingers backward and forward over it while pressing firmly.

reason out

phrasal v. (논리적으로) ~을 추론[도출]해 내다
If you reason something out, you think carefully about it in a logical way in order to understand it.

poke^수능
[pouk]

v. 찌르다, 쑤시다; 들이대다; 쑥 내밀다; n. 찌름, 쑤심
If you poke someone or something, you quickly push them with your finger or with a sharp object.

sit up^수능

phrasal v. 일어나 앉다
If you sit up, you move yourself into a sitting position, for example, from lying down.

sentence***
[séntəns]

n. 문장, 글; 판결, 판정; vt. 판결을 내리다, 선고하다
A sentence is a group of words which, when they are written down, begin with a capital letter and end with a full stop, question mark, or exclamation mark. Most sentences contain a subject and a verb.

in time

idiom 때맞추어, 제시간에; 늦지 않고
When you do something in time, you are not late and early enough to make it.

back and forth^수능

a. 앞뒤(좌우)로의; 여기저기의
If something moves back and forth, it moves in one direction and then in the opposite one, repeatedly.

terrorize
[térəràiz]

vt. 위협하다, 공포의 도가니로 몰아넣다
If someone terrorizes you, they keep you in a state of fear by making it seem likely that they will attack you.

storm***
[stɔːrm]

n. 폭풍우; vi. 돌진하다; 격노하다
A storm is very bad weather, with heavy rain, strong winds, and often thunder and lightning.

rumble*
[rʌ́mbl]

n. 우르르 하는 소리; 소음; v. 우르르 울리(게 하)다; (차 등이) 덜거덕거리며 가다
A rumble is a low continuous noise.

go away

phrasal v. 없어지다; 떠나다
If something goes away, it disappear gradually.

quit**
[kwit]

v. (quit-quit) 그만두다; (술 · 담배 등을) 끊다
If you quit an activity or quit doing something, you stop doing it.

62

cock^{복습}
[kɔk]

v. 위로 치올리다, (귀 · 꽁지를) 쫑긋 세우다; n. 수탉; 마개
If you cock a part of your body in a particular direction, you lift it or point it in that direction.

creep**
[kri:p]

vi. (crept-crept) 살금살금 걷다, 기다; n. 포복
If something creeps somewhere, it moves very slowly.

couch^{복습}
[kautʃ]

n. 소파, 긴 의자
A couch is a long, comfortable seat for two or three people.

slide**
[slaid]

v. 미끄러지다, 미끄러지듯 움직이다
If you slide somewhere, you move there smoothly and quietly.

by accident

idiom 우연히
If you say that something happens by accident, you mean that it has not been planned.

intend^{복습}
[inténd]

v. ~할 작정이다, ~하려고 생각하다; 의도하다
If you intend to do something, you have decided or planned to do it.

awful***
[ɔ́:fəl]

a. 지독한, 대단한; 무서운
If you say that something is awful, you mean that it is extremely unpleasant, shocking, or bad.

keep an eye on

idiom ~을 주목하다, 감시하다
If you keep an eye on someone or something, you watch them or it carefully.

run away

phrasal v. 도망치다, 탈주하다; 떠나다, 가출하다
When you run away, you escape from someone or a place.

forgive**
[fərgív]

v. (사람 · 죄 등을) 용서하다, 관대히 봐주다; (빚 등을) 면제하다, 탕감하다
If you forgive someone who has done something bad or wrong, you stop being angry with them and no longer want to punish them.

Check Your Reading Speed

1분에 몇 단어를 읽는지 리딩 속도를 측정해보세요.

$$\frac{1{,}014 \text{ words}}{\text{reading time ( ) sec}} \times 60 = (\quad) \text{ WPM}$$

Build Your Vocabulary

swing*** [swiŋ]	**v.** (swung–swung) 휙 움직이다, (한 점을 축으로 하여) 빙 돌다, 휘두르다 If something swings in a particular direction or if you swing it in that direction, it moves in that direction with a smooth, curving movement.
go on^{복습}	**phrasal v.** 앞으로 가다, 나아가다; 계속하다; 자자, 어서 If you go on to somewhere, you move forward it.
notice^{복습} [nóutis]	**vt.** 알아차리다, 주의하다; **n.** 주의, 주목 If you notice something or someone, you become aware of them.
cage** [keidʒ]	**n.** 우리, 새장; **vt.** 새장에 넣다 A cage is a structure of wire or metal bars in which birds or animals are kept.
lizard^{복습} [lízərd]	**n.** [동물] 도마뱀 A lizard is a reptile with short legs and a long tail.
skinny^{복습} [skíni]	**a.** 말라빠진, 비쩍 마른 A skinny person is extremely thin, often in a way that you find unattractive.
pointy-toed [pɔ́inti-tóud]	**a.** 발가락 부분이 뾰족한 모양의 Pointy-toed shoes refer to shoes with long and sharp front part.
tap^{복습} [tæp]	① **v.** 가볍게 두드리다; **n.** 가볍게 두드리기 ② **n.** 주둥이, (수도 등의) 꼭지 If you tap something, you hit it with a quick light blow or a series of quick light blows.
dreamy* [drí:mi]	**a.** 꿈꾸는 듯한, 꿈 많은 If you say that someone has a dreamy expression, you mean that they look as if they are thinking about something pleasant.
whisker^{복습} [hwískər]	**n.** (고양이 · 쥐 등의) 수염; 구레나룻 The whiskers of an animal such as a cat or a mouse are the long stiff hairs that grow near its mouth.
fuzzy [fʌzi]	**a.** 흐트러진; (머리가) 곱슬곱슬한; 흐릿한, 불분명한 Fuzzy hair sticks up in a soft, curly mass.
sigh^{복습} [sai]	**v.** 한숨 쉬다; **n.** 한숨, 탄식 When you sigh, you let out a deep breath, as a way of expressing feelings such as disappointment, tiredness, or pleasure.
catch sight of	**idiom** (~을) 발견하다, 눈에 띄다 If you catch sight of something, you see it for a brief time.

64

croak^{복습}
[krouk]

v. (까마귀가) 깍깍 울다; 쉰 목소리를 내다
When a frog or bird croaks, it makes a harsh, low sound.

land^{복습}
[lænd]

v. 내려앉다, 상륙하다, 착륙하다; n. 육지, 국토, 나라
When someone or something lands, they come down to the ground after moving through the air or falling.

spell**
[spel]

n. 주문(呪文), 주술; 마력, 마법; v. (낱말을) 맞춤법에 따라 쓰다
A spell is a situation in which events are controlled by a magical power.

hop^{복습}
[hap]

v. 깡충 뛰다, 뛰어오르다; n. 깡충깡충 뜀
If you hop, you move along by jumping.

leap***
[liːp]

v. 껑충 뛰다; 뛰어넘다; n. 뜀, 도약
If you leap, you jump high in the air or jump a long distance.

slither
[slíðər]

v. 미끄러지듯 나아가다, 미끄러지게 하다
If an animal such as a snake slithers, it moves along in a curving way.

bark^{복습}
[baːrk]

v. (개가) 짖다; n. 나무껍질; (개 등이) 짖는[우는] 소리
When a dog barks, it makes a short, loud noise, once or several times.

chase^{복습}
[tʃeis]

v. 뒤쫓다, 추적하다
If you chase someone, or chase after them, you run after them or follow them quickly in order to catch or reach them.

keep on^{복습}

phrasal v. 계속하다
When you keep on doing something, you continue or persist doing it.

bump into^{복습}

phrasal v. 부닥치다; 우연히 만나다
If you bump into something or someone, you accidentally hit them while you are moving.

trip***
[trip]

v. 걸려 넘어지다; 경쾌한 걸음걸이로 걷다; n. 여행
If you trip when you are walking, you knock your foot against something and fall or nearly fall.

slam^{복습}
[slæm]

v. (문 따위를) 탕 닫다; 털썩 내려놓다; 세게 치다; n. 쾅 (하는 소리)
If you slam a door or window or if it slams, it shuts noisily and with great force.

silly^{복습}
[síli]

a. 어리석은, 바보 같은; 익살맞은; n. 바보, 멍청이
If you say that someone or something is silly, you mean that they are foolish, childish, or ridiculous.

yell^{복습}
[jel]

v. 소리치다, 고함치다; n. 고함소리, 부르짖음
If you yell, you shout loudly, usually because you are excited, angry, or in pain.

blink*
[bliŋk]

v. 눈을 깜박거리다; (등불·별 등이) 깜박이다; n. 깜박거림
When you blink or when you blink your eyes, you shut your eyes and very quickly open them again.

still^{복습}
[stil]

a. 움직이지 않는; 조용한, 고요한; ad. 조용히; 여전히, 아직도
If you stay still, you stay in the same position and do not move.

pick up^{복습}

phrasal v. 줍다, 들다; 되찾다, 회복하다; 알아채다
When you pick up something, you take hold of and lift it.

escape***
[iskéip]

v. 달아나다; 벗어나다; n. 탈출, 도망
If you escape from a place, you succeed in getting away from it.

take out^{복습}

phrasal v. 꺼내다; 제거하다, 버리다
If you take out something, you remove it from its place.

lock up

phrasal v. 철창 안에 가두다; 안전한 곳에 넣어 두다
If something is being locked up, it is locked or secured by the doors or windows.

jail**
[dʒeil]

n. 교도소, 감옥, 구치소
A jail is a place where criminals are kept in order to punish them, or where people waiting to be tried are kept.

never mind

idiom 신경 쓰지 마라, 걱정하지 마라
Never mind is used to tell someone not to worry or be upset.

sweep^{복습}
[swi:p]

v. 청소하다; 쓸어내리다; 휙 지나가다; n. 청소; 한 번 휘두름
If you sweep an area of floor or ground, you push dirt or rubbish off it using a brush with a long handle.

dig^{복습}
[dig]

v. 파헤치다, 파다; 찌르다; (구어) 마음에 들다, 좋아하다; n. 파기
If you dig into something such as a deep container, you put your hand in it to search for something.

pile^{복습}
[pail]

n. 쌓아 올린 더미; 다수; v. 쌓아 올리다; 쌓이다
A pile of things is a mass of them that is high in the middle and has sloping sides.

broom*
[bru:m]

n. 빗자루
A broom is a kind of brush with a long handle. You use a broom for sweeping the floor.

confuse^{복습}
[kənfjú:z]

v. 어리둥절하게 하다, 혼동하다 (confused a. 당황한, 어리둥절한)
To confuse someone means to make it difficult for them to know exactly what is happening or what to do.

blush**
[blʌʃ]

v. 얼굴을 붉히다; (얼굴이) 빨개지다; n. 얼굴을 붉힘, 홍조
When you blush, your face becomes redder than usual because you are ashamed or embarrassed.

hand***
[hænd]

v. 건네주다, 넘겨주다; n. 손; 도움의 손길
If you hand something to someone, you pass it to them.

sweeper*
[swi:pər]

n. 청소부; 청소기
A sweeper refers to an employee who sweeps floors or street.

dust^{복습}
[dʌst]

v. 먼지를 털다; n. 먼지, 가루, 티끌
When you dust something such as furniture, you remove dust from it, usually using a cloth.

66

shelf ^{복습}
[ʃelf]

n. (pl. shelves) 선반
A shelf is a flat piece which is attached to a wall or to the sides of a cupboard for keeping things on.

preacher ^{복습}
[príːtʃər]

n. 목사, 설교자, 전도자
A preacher is a person, usually a member of the clergy, who preaches sermons as part of a church service.

criminal**
[krímənl]

n. 범죄자, 범인
A criminal is a person who regularly commits crimes.

suck ^{복습}
[sʌk]

v. 빨다, 흡수하다; 삼키다; n. 빨아들임
If you suck on something, you hold it in your mouth and pull at it with the muscles in your cheeks and tongue, for example in order to get liquid out of it.

knuckle ^{복습}
[nʌkl]

n. 손가락 관절[마디]; v. 손가락 마디로 치다
Your knuckles are the rounded pieces of bone that form lumps on your hands where your fingers join your hands, and where your fingers bend.

stare ^{복습}
[steər]

v. 응시하다, 뚫어지게 보다
If you stare at someone or something, you look at them for a long time.

grocery store ^{복습}
[gróusəri stɔːr]

n. 식품점, 슈퍼마켓
A grocery store is a store that retails food.

theme ^{복습}
[θiːm]

n. 주제, 테마; a. 특정 분위기를 살린
A theme in a piece of writing, a talk, or a discussion is an important idea or subject that runs through it.

porch***
[pɔːrtʃ]

n. (본 건물 입구에 달린 지붕이 있는) 현관, 포치
A porch is a sheltered area at the entrance to a building, which has a roof and sometimes has walls.

wave ^{복습}
[weiv]

v. 흔들다, 신호하다; 파도치다; n. 파도, 물결
If you wave or wave your hand, you move your hand from side to side in the air, usually in order to say hello or goodbye to someone.

run off

phrasal v. 서둘러 떠나다; 달아나다, 꽁무니를 빼다
When you run off, you depart in haste.

charm***
[tʃaːrm]

v. 마법으로 ~을 사로잡다; 주문[마법]을 걸다; n. 매력; 작은 장식물; 마법
If you charm someone, you please them, especially by using your charm.

Chapters Thirteen & Fourteen

1. What was Opal's favorite place?
   A. The pet store
   B. The Herman W. Block memorial Library
   C. Church
   D. Gloria Dump's yard

2. Opal said the preacher knew that _____, but he didn't.
   A. Winn-Dixie liked peanut butter
   B. Gloria wasn't a witch
   C. she went to the library to see Miss Franny
   D. Otis had been in jail

3. Why didn't Opal play with the Dewberry boys?
   A. She thought they were ignorant.
   B. The boys didn't like Winn-Dixie.
   C. Gloria thought that the boys didn't want to be friends with Opal.
   D. They boys lived too far away.

4. What was special about the big tree?
   A. It was the biggest tree Opal had ever seen.
   B. The tree had big leaves.
   C. There were bottles hanging from the tree.
   D. There were ghosts floating around the tree.

5. Which of the following is true about Gloria?
   A. She was the nicest person Opal knew.
   B. She drank whisky in her coffee.
   C. She told Opal to stop speaking to the Dewberry boys.
   D. She said that Otis was a bad person.

6. What did Gloria used to do?
   A. She taught at a school.
   B. She drank a lot of alcohol.
   C. She owned a restaurant.
   D. She drove a school bus.

7. Gloria told Opal to _____.
   A. judge people by what they're doing now
   B. tell the preacher about Otis's past
   C. always think about what people have done in the past
   D. make friends with the Dewberry boys

Check Your Reading Speed

1분에 몇 단어를 읽는지 리딩 속도를 측정해보세요.

$$\frac{698 \text{ words}}{\text{reading time ( ) sec}} \times 60 = (\quad) \text{ WPM}$$

Build Your Vocabulary

daily[**]
[déili]

a. 매일의, 일상적인
If something happens daily, it happens every day.

routine[*]
[ruːtíːn]

n. 일과, 일상적인 일
A routine is the usual series of things that you do at a particular time.

trailer[복습]
[tréilər]

n. 트레일러하우스, (자동차가 끌고 다니는) 이동식 주택
A trailer is a container on wheels which is pulled by a car or other vehicle and which is used for transporting large or heavy items.

in time[복습]

idiom 제시간에, 늦지 않고, 때맞추어
When you do something in time, you are not late and early enough to make it.

sneak[*]
[sniːk]

v. (snuck/sneaked–snuck/sneaked) 살금살금 가다; 몰래 하다[가져가다]
If you sneak somewhere, you go there very quietly on foot, trying to avoid being seen or heard.

wrap[복습]
[ræp]

v. 감싸다; 포장하다; n. 싸개, 덮개
If someone wraps their arms, fingers, or legs around something, they put them firmly around it.

rock[**]
[rɑk]

① v. 흔들다, 진동하다 ② n. 바위, 암석
When something rocks or when you rock it, it shakes violently.

pick out[복습]

phrasal v. (여럿 가운데에서 신중하게) ~을 고르다, 선발하다
If you pick out something, you choose it from a number of people or things.

give up[복습]

phrasal v. 포기하다, 단념하다
If you give up, you decide that you cannot do something and stop trying to do it.

arrange[***]
[əréindʒ]

v. 가지런히 하다, 배열하다; 준비하다
If you arrange things somewhere, you place them in a particular position, usually in order to make them look attractive or tidy.

shelf[복습]
[ʃelf]

n. (pl. shelves) 선반
A shelf is a flat piece which is attached to a wall or to the sides of a cupboard for keeping things on.

mark***
[ma:rk]

v. 표를 하다; 채점하다; n. 표적, 과녁; 표, 흔적
If you mark something with a particular word or symbol, you write that word or symbol on it.

leather^{복습}
[léðər]

n. 가죽
Leather is treated animal skin which is used for making shoes, clothes, bags, and furniture.

collar^{복습}
[kálər]

n. (개 등의 목에 거는) 목걸이; 칼라, 깃
A collar is a band of leather or plastic which is put round the neck of a dog or cat.

leash^{복습}
[li:ʃ]

n. 가죽 끈, 사슬; 속박, 통제
A dog's leash is a long thin piece of leather or a chain, which you attach to the dog's collar so that you can keep the dog under control.

criminal^{복습}
[krímənl]

n. 범죄자, 범인
A criminal is a person who regularly commits crimes.

memorial^{복습}
[məmɔ́:riəl]

a. (죽은 사람을) 기념하기 위한, 추도[추모]의; n. 기념비(적인 것)
A memorial event, object, or prize is in honor of someone who has died, so that they will be remembered.

figure^{복습}
[fígjər]

v. 생각하다, 판단하다, 계산하다; n. 형태, 형상; 수치, 숫자
If you figure that something is the case, you think or guess that it is the case.

break away

idiom (~에서) 달아나다; 독립하다
If an object breaks away from something that is holding it in place, it becomes separated from it.

for all one is worth

idiom 전력을 기울여
If you do something for all you are worth, you do it with as much energy and effort as possible.

head^{복습}
[hed]

v. 특정 방향으로 가다; 앞서다; n. 한발 앞선 출발, 우위
If you are headed for a particular place, you are going toward that place.

spoonful
[spú:nfʊl]

n. 한 스푼 가득한 양
You can refer to an amount of food resting on a spoon as a spoonful of food.

holler^{복습}
[hálər]

v. 고함지르다; 큰 소리로 부르다; n. 외침, 큰 소리
If you holler, you shout loudly.

witch^{복습}
[witʃ]

n. 마녀
In fairy stories, a witch is a woman, usually an old woman, who has evil magic powers.

coop
[ku:p]

v. 가두다, 감금하다; n. 닭장, 우리
If a person or an animal is cooped up, they are kept in a small place or inside a building.

lay off

idiom 내버려둬, 그만둬
If you say 'lay off' to someone, you tell them to stop doing something that irritates or annoys you.

shame**
[ʃeim]

vt. 부끄러워하게 하다, 망신시키다; n. 부끄럼, 수치, 치욕
If something shames you, it causes you to feel ashamed.

retarded
[ritá:rdid]

a. 지능 발달이 늦은, 정신 지체의
Someone who is retarded is much less advanced mentally than most people of their age.

jail 복습
[dʒeil]

n. 교도소, 감옥, 구치소
A jail is a place where criminals are kept in order to punish them, or where people waiting to be tried are kept.

wonder 복습
[wʌ́ndər]

v. 호기심을 가지다, 이상하게 여기다; n. 경탄할 만한 것, 경이
If you wonder about something, you think about it because it interests you and you want to know more about it.

lie 복습
[lai]

n. 거짓말; vi. 거짓말하다; 눕다, 누워 있다; 놓여 있다, 위치하다
A lie is something that someone says or writes which they know is untrue.

tell on 복습
phrasal v. ~를 고자질하다
If you tell on someone, you tell a teacher or someone else in authority that they have done something wrong.

bald 복습
[bɔ:ld]

a. (머리 등이) 벗어진, 대머리의; vi. 머리가 벗어지다
Someone who is bald has little or no hair on the top of their head.

swear 복습
[swɛər]

v. 단언하다, 맹세하다; n. 맹세, 선서
If you swear that something is true or you can swear to it, you are saying very firmly that it is true.

wear (someone) out
phrasal v. 지치게 하다; 해지다, 낡아서 떨어지다
If you wear someone out, they become really tired.

yell 복습
[jel]

v. 소리치다, 고함치다; n. 고함소리, 부르짖음
If you yell, you shout loudly, usually because you are excited, angry, or in pain.

soldier 복습
[sóuldʒər]

n. 군인, 병사
A soldier is a person who works in an army, especially a person who is not an officer.

battle**
[bætl]

n. 전투, 싸움; 싸우다
A battle is a violent fight between groups of people, especially one between military forces during a war.

straight off
idiom 즉시; 서슴없이
When you do something straight off, you do it without deliberation or hesitation.

pour**
[pɔ:r]

v. 따르다, 붓다, 쏟아지다; 흐르듯이 이동하다, 쇄도하다
If you pour a liquid or other substance, you make it flow steadily out of a container by holding the container at an angle.

refresh*
[rifréʃ]

v. 상쾌하게 하다, 기운이 나게 하다
If something refreshes you when you have become hot, tired, or thirsty, it makes you feel cooler or more energetic.

72

ignorant[**]
[ígnərənt]

a. 무지한, 예의를 모르는; (어떤 일을) 모르는

If you describe someone as ignorant, you mean that they do not know things they should know.

roundabout[*]
[ráundəbàut]

a. 간접의, 우회적인; 빙 도는; n. 완곡한[간접적인] 말씨

If you do or say something in a roundabout way, you do not do or say it in a simple, clear, and direct way.

1분에 몇 단어를 읽는지 리딩 속도를 측정해보세요.

$$\frac{745 \text{ words}}{\text{reading time (} \quad \text{) sec}} \times 60 = (\quad) \text{ WPM}$$

Build Your Vocabulary

imitate**
[ímitèit]

vt. 모방하다, 흉내 내다; 따르다, 본받다
If you imitate someone, you copy what they do or produce.

tap^{복습}
[tæp]

① v. 가볍게 두드리다; n. 가볍게 두드리기 ② n. 주둥이, (수도 등의) 꼭지
If you tap something, you hit it with a quick light blow or a series of quick light blows.

pointy-toed^{복습}
[pɔ́inti-tóud]

a. 발가락 부분이 뾰족한 모양의
Pointy-toed shoes refer to shoes with long and sharp front part.

all the way^{복습}

idiom 내내, 시종
If you have been doing something all the way, you are emphasizing the period of time during the whole journey.

used to^{복습}

phrasal v. ~하곤 했다; 과거 한때는 ~이었다
If someone used to do something, it suggests habitual or accustomed actions or states, taking place in the past but not continuing into the present.

storytelling
[stɔ́:ritèliŋ]

n. 이야기하기
Storytelling is the activity of telling or writing stories.

criminal^{복습}
[krímənl]

n. 범죄자, 범인
A criminal is a person who regularly commits crimes.

jail^{복습}
[dʒeil]

n. 교도소, 감옥, 구치소
A jail is a place where criminals are kept in order to punish them, or where people waiting to be tried are kept.

hang***
[hæŋ]

v. 매달리다; 걸다, 달아매다; 교수형에 처하다
If something hangs in a high place or position, or if you hang it there, it is attached there so it does not touch the ground.

branch***
[bræntʃ]

n. 가지; 지점; 분파; v. 가지를 내다
The branches of a tree are the parts that grow out from its trunk and have leaves, flowers, or fruit growing on them.

string***
[striŋ]

n. 끈, 실; (악기의) 현[줄]; v. 묶다, 매달다
String is thin rope made of twisted threads, used for tying things together or tying up parcels.

clank
[klæŋk]

v. 철커덕 하는 소리가 나다
When large metal objects clank, they make a noise because they are hitting together or hitting against something hard.

spooky
[spúːki]

a. 유령(이 나올 것) 같은, 으스스한, 무시무시한
A place that is spooky has a frightening atmosphere, and makes you feel that there are ghosts around.

growl^{**}
[graul]

v. 으르렁거리다; n. 으르렁거리는 소리
When a dog or other animal growls, it makes a low noise in its throat, usually because it is angry.

throat^{***}
[θrout]

n. 목(구멍)
Your throat is the back of your mouth and the top part of the tubes that go down into your stomach and your lungs.

cane^{**}
[kein]

n. 지팡이
A cane is a long thin stick with a curved or round top which you can use to support yourself when you are walking.

keep away

phrasal v. 떨어지게 하다, 멀리 하다
When you keep something away from you, you prevent it from coming near you.

whisper^{복습}
[hwíspəːr]

v. 속삭이다
When you whisper, you say something very quietly.

preacher^{복습}
[príːtʃər]

n. 목사, 설교자, 전도자
A preacher is a person, usually a member of the clergy, who preaches sermons as part of a church service.

folk^{***}
[fouk]

n. (pl.) (특정 국가 · 지역 출신 또는 특정한 생활방식을 가진) 사람들
You can refer to people as folk or folks.

alcohol^{**}
[ǽlkəhɔ́ːl]

n. 술, 알코올
Drinks that can make people drunk, such as beer, wine, and whisky, can be referred to as alcohol.

in the meantime

idiom (두 가지 시점 · 사건들) 그 동안[사이]에
In the meantime or meantime means in the period of time between two events.

judge^{복습}
[dʒʌdʒ]

v. 평가하다, 심사하다; 재판하다; n. 심판, 심사원; 재판관
If you judge something or someone, you form an opinion about them after you have examined the evidence or thought carefully about them.

harsh^{**}
[haːrʃ]

a. 냉혹한, 가혹한; 거친, (소리 따위가) 귀에 거슬리는
Harsh actions or speech are unkind and show no understanding or sympathy.

nudge^{복습}
[nʌdʒ]

vt. (주의를 끌기 위해 팔꿈치로) 찌르다; n. (팔꿈치로) 살짝 밀기, 가볍게 찌르기
If you nudge someone, you push them gently, usually with your elbow, in order to draw their attention to something.

wet^{***}
[wet]

a. 젖은, 축축한
If something is wet, it is covered in water, rain, sweat, tears, or another liquid.

wag^{복습}
[wæg]

v. (꼬리 등을) 흔들다, 흔들리다; n. 흔들기
When a dog wags its tail, it repeatedly waves its tail from side to side.

tail ^{복습}
[teil]

n. (동물의) 꼬리
The tail of an animal, bird, or fish is the part extending beyond the end of its body.

trot ^{복습}
[trat]

v. 빠른 걸음으로 가다, 총총걸음 치다; n. 빠른 걸음
When an animal such as a horse trots, it moves fairly fast, taking quick small steps.

76

Chapters Fifteen & Sixteen

1. What would sometimes happen to Miss Franny?
   A. She would fall over.
   B. She would forget her story and stop talking until the next day.
   C. She would have trouble breathing.
   D. She would have a shaking fit.

2. How did Opal want to comfort Gloria Dump?
   A. She wanted to read Gloria a book.
   B. She wanted to cut the bottles from the tree.
   C. She wanted to tell Gloria about her mother.
   D. She wanted to visit Gloria during thunderstorms.

3. The civil war was NOT about _____.
   A. slavery
   B. an evil leader
   C. states' rights
   D. money

4. Why did Littmus lie about his age?
   A. He wanted to fight in the war.
   B. He didn't like his family and he wanted to leave home.
   C. He wanted to buy a gun.
   D. He wanted to build a new home.

5. During the war, Littmus was NOT _____.
   A. hungry all the time
   B. shot at
   C. very cold in the winter
   D. killed

6. What happened to Littmus's home?
   A. It was burned down.
   B. It was flooded.
   C. It belonged to someone else.
   D. It was robbed.

7. What happened to Littmus's sisters?
   A. They moved to Virginia.
   B. They died on the battlefield.
   C. They died of typhoid fever.
   D. They were killed in a fire.

1분에 몇 단어를 읽는지 리딩 속도를 측정해보세요.

$$\frac{772 \text{ words}}{\text{reading time ( ) sec}} \times 60 = (\quad) \text{ WPM}$$

Build Your Vocabulary

air-conditioning
[éər-kəndíʃəniŋ]

n. 공기 조절, 냉난방
Air-conditioning is a method of providing buildings and vehicles with cool dry air.

unit**
[júːnit]

n. 장치, 설비, 기구
A unit is a small machine which has a particular function, often part of a larger machine.

fan*
[fæn]

n. 선풍기, 부채; vt. 부채꼴로 펴다; 부채질하다
A fan is a piece of electrical or mechanical equipment with blades that go round and round. It keeps a room or machine cool or gets rid of unpleasant smells.

hog*
[hɔːg]

v. 독차지하다; 탐욕부리다; n. 돼지
If you hog something, you take all of it in a greedy or impolite way.

fur***
[fəːr]

n. 부드러운 털; 모피
Fur is the thick and usually soft hair that grows on the bodies of many mammals.

pretty***
[príti]

a. 꽤, 상당히; a. 귀여운, 예쁜
You can use pretty before an adjective or adverb to mean 'quite' or 'rather'.

puff*
[pʌf]

n. 훅 날아오는 작은 양의 공기; (담배 · 파이프 등을) 피우기;
v. (담배 · 파이프 등을) 피우다; (연기 · 김을) 내뿜다
A puff of something such as air or smoke is a small amount of it that is blown out from somewhere.

fit***
[fit]

① n. 발작, 경련 ② v. 끼우다, 맞게 하다, 적합하다; a. 적합한
If someone has a fit they suddenly lose consciousness and their body makes uncontrollable movements.

last***
[læst]

vi. 계속하다, 오래가다; a. 최후의, 마지막의
If an event, situation, or problem lasts for a particular length of time, it continues to exist or happen for that length of time.

leaf**
[liːf]

n. 잎, 한 장
The leaves of a tree or plant are the parts that are flat, thin, and usually green.

sit up***

phrasal v. 일어나 앉다
If you sit up, you move yourself into a sitting position, for example, from lying down.

80

protect[**]
[prətékt]

v. 보호하다, 막다, 지키다
To protect someone or something means to prevent them from being harmed or damaged.

soldier[급]
[sóuldʒər]

n. 군인, 병사
A soldier is a person who works in an army, especially a person who is not an officer.

lick[복습]
[lik]

vt. 핥다; (불길이 허처럼) 날름거리다, 넘실거리다; n. 핥기
When people or animals lick something, they move their tongue across its surface.

remind[복습]
[rimáind]

vt. 생각나게 하다, 상기시키다, 일깨우다
If someone reminds you of a fact or event that you already know about, they say something which makes you think about it.

thunderstorm[복습]
[θʌndərstɔ́:rm]

n. 폭풍우
A thunderstorm is a storm in which there is thunder and lightning and a lot of heavy rain.

hold on to[복습]

phrasal v. 지키다, 고수하다; 보유하다
If you hold on to something or someone, you keep them not to lose.

comfort[복습]
[kʌmfərt]

vt. 위로[위안]하다; n. 마음이 편안함, 안락; 위로, 위안
If you comfort someone, you make them feel less worried, unhappy, or upset, for example by saying kind things to them.

rock[복습]
[rak]

① v. 흔들다, 진동하다 ② n. 바위, 암석
When something rocks or when you rock it, it shakes violently.

tight[복습]
[tait]

ad. 단단히, 꽉; a. 단단한, 팽팽한, 빈틈없는
If you hold someone or something tight, you hold them firmly and securely.

run away[복습]

phrasal v. 도망치다, 탈주하다; 떠나다, 가출하다
When you run away, you escape from someone or a place.

knock[**]
[nak]

v. 부딪치다, 충돌시키다; (문을) 두드리다, 노크하다
If you knock something, you touch or hit it roughly, especially so that it falls or moves.

chatter[*]
[tʃǽtər]

v. 수다를 떨다, 재잘거리다; 지저귀다; n. 재잘거림, 수다
If you chatter, you talk quickly and continuously, usually about things which are not important.

grown-up[*]
[gróun-ʌp]

a. 어른이 된, 성숙한; n. (pl.) (구어) 어른, 성인
Someone who is grown-up is physically and mentally mature and no longer depends on their parents or another adult.

suggestion[**]
[səgdʒéstʃən]

n. 제안, 암시, 시사
If you make a suggestion, you put forward an idea or plan for someone to think about.

faint[*]
[feint]

vi. 기절하다; n. 기절, 졸도; a. 희미한, 어렴풋한
If you faint, you lose consciousness for a short time, especially because you are hungry, or because of pain, heat, or shock.

wave^{복습}
[weiv]

v. 흔들다, 신호하다; 파도치다; n. 파도, 물결
If you wave or wave your hand, you move your hand from side to side in the air, usually in order to say hello or goodbye to someone.

slavery*
[sléivəri]

n. 노예 제도, 노예(상태); 굴종, 예속
Slavery is the system by which people are owned by other people as slaves.

right***
[rait]

n. 권리, 정의; a. 옳은, 올바른, 오른쪽
Your rights are what you are morally or legally entitled to do or to have.

terrible^{복습}
[térəbl]

a. 극심한, 지독한; 무서운, 끔찍한
If something is terrible, it is very bad or of very poor quality.

yawn^{복습}
[jɔːn]

vi. 하품하다; n. 하품
If you yawn, you open your mouth very wide and breathe in more air than usual, often when you are tired or when you are not interested in something.

thump^{복습}
[θʌmp]

n. 탁[쿵] 하는 소리; 때림, 세게 쥐어박음; v. 탁 치다, 부딪치다
A thump is a loud, dull sound by hitting something.

sigh^{복습}
[sai]

n. 한숨, 탄식; v. 한숨 쉬다
When you sigh, you let out a deep breath, as a way of expressing feelings such as disappointment, tiredness, or pleasure.

swear^{복습}
[swɛər]

v. 단언하다, 맹세하다; n. 맹세, 선서
If you swear that something is true or you can swear to it, you are saying very firmly that it is true.

phrase**
[freiz]

n. 구절, 관용구
A phrase is a short group of words that people often use as a way of saying something.

cross-legged
[krɔːs-légd]

ad. 책상다리를 하고
If someone is sitting cross-legged, they are sitting on the floor with their legs bent so that their knees point outward.

share^{복습}
[ʃɛər]

vt. 공유하다, 분배하다; n. 몫, 분담
If you share something with another person, you both have it, use it, or occupy it.

pretend^{복습}
[priténd]

v. ~인 체하다, 가장하다; a. 가짜의
If you pretend that something is the case, you act in a way that is intended to make people believe that it is the case, although in fact it is not.

asleep^{복습}
[əslíːp]

a. 잠이 든, 자고 있는
Someone who is asleep is sleeping.

settle***
[setl]

v. (편하게) 앉다, 자리를 잡다; (논쟁 등을) 해결하다, 끝내다; 안정되다, 진정되다
If you settle yourself somewhere or settle somewhere, you sit down or make yourself comfortable.

bang*
[bæŋ]

v. 쾅 닫(히)다, 탕 치다, 부딪치다; n. 쾅 하는 소리
If you bang a door or if it bangs, it closes suddenly with a loud noise.

82

pinch^{복습}
[pintʃ]

v. 여위게 하다, 초췌하게 하다; 꼬집다; n. 꼬집기 (pinch-faced a. 파리한 얼굴의)
If someone's face is pinched, it looks thin and pale, usually because they are ill or old.

stare^{복습}
[stɛər]

v. 응시하다, 뚫어지게 보다
If you stare at someone or something, you look at them for a long time.

slam^{복습}
[slæm]

v. 털썩 내려놓다; (문 따위를) 탕 닫다; 세게 치다; n. 쾅 (하는 소리)
If you slam something down, you put it there quickly and with great force.

mind^{복습}
[maind]

v. 언짢아하다, 상관하다; 주의하다; n. 마음, 정신
If you do not mind something, you are not annoyed or bothered by it.

dramatic**
[drəmǽtik]

a. 과장된, 호들갑스러운; 극적인, 감격스러운
Dramatic action, event, or situation is exciting and impressive.

suit yourself

idiom 마음대로 해라, 네 멋대로 해라
If you say 'suit yourself', you tell someone to do what they want, even though it annoys you.

shrug*
[ʃrʌg]

v. (어깨를) 으쓱하다; n. (양 손바닥을 내보이면서 어깨를) 으쓱하기
If you shrug, you raise your shoulders to show that you are not interested in something or that you do not know or care about something.

Check Your Reading Speed

1분에 몇 단어를 읽는지 리딩 속도를 측정해보세요.

$$\frac{708\ words}{reading\ time\ (\quad)\ sec} \times 60 = (\quad)\ WPM$$

Build Your Vocabulary

fire***
[faiər]

v. 발사하다; 불을 지르다; 해고하다; n. 불, 화재 (firing n. 발사, 발포)
If someone fires a gun or a bullet, or if they fire, a bullet is sent from a gun that they are using.

occur**
[əkə́:r]

vi. 일어나다, 생기다; 생각이 떠오르다
When something occurs, it happens.

start in복습
phrasal v. 시작하다, 착수하다
If you start in something, you begin to do it.

shrug복습
[ʃrʌg]

v. (어깨를) 으쓱하다; n. (양 손바닥을 내보이면서 어깨를) 으쓱하기
If you shrug, you raise your shoulders to show that you are not interested in something or that you do not know or care about something.

enlist
[inlíst]

v. 입대하다. (징병에) 응하다; 적극적으로 협력하다; 도움을 얻다
If someone enlists or is enlisted, they join the army, navy, marines, or air force.

stand by
phrasal v. (방관하며) 가만히[그냥] 있다
When you are just standing by, you are present when something bad or unpleasant is happening, but not become involved.

beat복습
[bi:t]

v. (beat–beat/beaten) 패배시키다, 이기다; 치다, 두드리다; n. [음악] 박자, 고동
If you beat someone in a competition or election, you defeat them.

abide**
[əbáid]

v. 지속하다; 머무르다; 참다, 감수하다 (abiding a. 지속적인, 변치 않는)
An abiding feeling, memory, or interest is one that you have for a very long time.

notion*
[nóuʃən]

n. 생각, 개념, 관념
A notion is an idea or belief about something.

convince*
[kənvíns]

vt. 설득하다; 확신시키다, 납득시키다
If someone or something convinces you to do something, they persuade you to do it.

lie복습
[lai]

vi. 거짓말하다; 눕다, 누워 있다; 놓여 있다, 위치하다; n. 거짓말
If someone is lying, they are saying something which they know is not true.

army복습
[á:rmi]

n. 군대; 특정 목적을 위한 사람들, 집단
An army is a large organized group of people who are armed and trained to fight on land in a war.

84

go off^{복습}

phrasal v. 떠나다; (알람 · 경보가) 울리다; 발생하다
If you go off, you leave a place, especially in order to do something.

hell[*]
[hel]

n. 지옥
If you say that a particular situation or place is hell, you are emphasizing that it is extremely unpleasant.

pure^{***}
[pjuər]

a. 순전한, 완전한; 순수한, 맑은
Pure means complete and total.

steal a look

idiom (~을) 몰래 훔쳐보다
When you steal a look at someone's face, you look quickly at it so that nobody notices you looking.

neither^{복습}
[níːðər]

pron. (둘 중) 어느 것도 ~ 아니다; conj. (부정문을 만들며) ~도 마찬가지이다
You use neither to refer to each of two things or people, when you are making a negative statement that includes both of them.

imagine^{복습}
[imǽdʒin]

v. 상상하다; 생각하다, 여기다
If you imagine something, you think about it and your mind forms a picture or idea of it.

all manner of

idiom 온갖 종류의
If you say all manner of something, you mean many different types of them.

flea^{복습}
[fliː]

n. [곤충] 벼룩
A flea is a very small jumping insect that has no wings and feeds on the blood of humans or animals.

freeze^{**}
[friːz]

v. 얼다, 얼어붙다; 얼게 하다; n. 결빙
If you freeze, you feel extremely cold.

stink^{복습}
[stiŋk]

v. 냄새가 나다, 구린내가 나다; 수상쩍다
To stink means to smell extremely unpleasant.

itchy
[íʧi]

a. 가려운; 가렵게 하는
If a part of your body or something you are wearing is itchy, you have an unpleasant feeling on your skin that makes you want to scratch.

grief[*]
[griːf]

n. 슬픔, 비탄
Grief is a feeling of extreme sadness.

exist^{***}
[igzíst]

v. 존재하다, 실재하다, 현존하다
If something exists, it is present in the world as a real thing.

except^{복습}
[iksépt]

prep. ~를 제외하고, ~외에는; vt. ~을 빼다, 제외하다
You use except for to introduce the only thing or person that prevents a statement from being completely true.

fever^{**}
[fíːvər]

n. 열, 발열; 열중, 열광
If you have a fever when you are ill, your body temperature is higher than usual.

battlefield
[bǽtlfiːld]

n. 싸움터, 전장
A battlefield is a place where a battle is fought.

orphan ^{복습}
[ɔ́ːrfən]

n. 고아
An orphan is a child whose parents are dead.

amaze ^{복습}
[əméiz]

vt. 깜짝 놀라게 하다 (amazed a. 깜짝 놀란)
If something amazes you, it surprises you very much.

snore ^{복습}
[snɔːr]

v. 코를 골다
When someone who is asleep snores, they make a loud noise each time they breathe.

nudge ^{복습}
[nʌdʒ]

vt. (주의를 끌기 위해 팔꿈치로) 찌르다; n. (팔꿈치로) 살짝 밀기, 가볍게 찌르기
If you nudge someone, you push them gently, usually with your elbow, in order to draw their attention to something.

quit ^{복습}
[kwit]

v. 그만두다; (술 · 담배 등을) 끊다
If you quit an activity or quit doing something, you stop doing it.

rest ***
[rest]

① n. 나머지, 잔여 ② v. 쉬다, 쉬게 하다, 멈추게 하다; n. 휴식, 휴양
The rest is used to refer to all the parts of something or all the things in a group that remain or that you have not already mentioned.

survive **
[sərváiv]

v. 살아남다, 생존하다
If a person or living thing survives in a dangerous situation such as an accident or an illness, they do not die.

Chapters Seventeen & Eighteen

1. When Littmus stopped crying, he wanted to _____.
   A. go for a walk
   B. eat something sweet
   C. fight in another war
   D. build a new home

2. What did Littmus build in Florida?
   A. A medicine factory
   B. The Herman W. Block memorial Library
   C. A candy factory
   D. A hospital

3. According to Miss Franny, what was the secret ingredient in Littmus Lozenges?
   A. Strawberry
   B. Happiness
   C. Sorrow
   D. Loneliness

4. Which of the following is true about Amanda?
   A. She borrowed another book.
   B. She took Littmus Lozenges home for her family.
   C. She didn't like Miss Franny.
   D. She missed Carson.

5. What did the Preacher think of when he ate the candy?
   A. Opal
   B. Opal's mother
   C. Winn-Dixie
   D. His mother

6. The preacher thought that Opal should _____.
   A. get more candy from Miss Franny
   B. apologize to Stevie
   C. give Mrs. Dewberry a Littmus Lozenge
   D. find out more about Amanda

7. What happened to Amanda's brother?
   A. He drowned.
   B. He died from disease.
   C. He hurt his legs in an accident.
   D. He was hurt in a fire.

1분에 몇 단어를 읽는지 리딩 속도를 측정해보세요.

$$\frac{1{,}003 \text{ words}}{\text{reading time (} \quad \text{) sec}} \times 60 = (\quad) \text{ WPM}$$

Build Your Vocabulary

go on^{복습}

phrasal v. 계속하다; 앞으로 가다, 나아가다; 자자, 어서
When you go on what you are doing, you continue or proceed it.

used to^{복습}

phrasal v. ~ 하곤 했다; 과거 한때는 ~이었다
If someone used to do something, it suggests habitual or accustomed actions or states, taking place in the past but not continuing into the present.

sensation*
[senséiʃən]

n. 감각, 느낌, 기분
You can use sensation to refer to the general feeling or impression caused by a particular experience.

decision**
[disíʒən]

n. 결정, 결심
When you make a decision, you choose what should be done or which is the best of various possible actions.

figure^{복습}
[fígjər]

v. 생각하다, 판단하다, 계산하다; n. 형태, 형상; 수치, 숫자
If you figure that something is the case, you think or guess that it is the case.

concentrate**
[kánsəntrèit]

v. 집중하다, 전념하다
If you concentrate on something, you give all your attention to it.

all the way^{복습}

idiom 내내, 시종
If you have been doing something all the way, you are emphasizing the period of time during the whole journey.

factory**
[fǽktəri]

n. 공장
A factory is a large building where machines are used to make large quantities of goods.

stand out

phrasal v. 두드러지다, 눈에 띄다
If something stands out, it is much better or more important than other things.

spooky^{복습}
[spúːki]

a. 으스스한, 무시무시한, 유령(이 나올 것) 같은
A place that is spooky has a frightening atmosphere, and makes you feel that there are ghosts around.

birthplace*
[bɔ́ːrθplèis]

n. 발생지; 생가, 출생지
The birthplace of something is the place where it began.

90

fortune**
[fɔ́:rtʃən]

n. 부, 재산; 운, 행운
If you talk about someone's fortunes or the fortunes of something, you are talking about the extent to which they are doing well or being successful.

manufacture**
[mænjufǽktʃər]

vt. 제조하다; n. 제조, (pl.) 제품
To manufacture something means to make it in a factory, usually in large quantities.

appetite*
[ǽpitait]

n. 욕구, 식욕
Someone's appetite for something is their strong desire for it.

happen to

phrasal v. 우연히 ~하다
If you happen to do something, you do it by chance not by your intention.

drawer**
[drɔ:r]

n. 서랍
A drawer is part of a desk, chest, or other piece of furniture that is shaped like a box and is designed for putting things in.

would you care for

idiom ~하시겠어요?; ~을 좋아하다
People use 'would you care for' to ask someone if they would like something to eat or drink.

unwrap
[ʌnrǽp]

v. (포장 등을) 풀다
When you unwrap something, you take off the paper, plastic, or other covering that is around it.

hold out

phrasal v. (손 혹은 손에 든 것을) 내밀다, 내뻗다
If you hold out your hand, you move your hand away from your body, for example to shake hands.

sniff복습
[snif]

v. 코를 킁킁거리다, 냄새를 맡다; 콧방귀를 뀌다; n. 냄새 맡음; 콧방귀
If you sniff something or sniff at it, you smell it by sniffing.

wag복습
[wæg]

v. (꼬리 등을) 흔들다, 흔들리다; n. 흔들기
When a dog wags its tail, it repeatedly waves its tail from side to side.

chew복습
[tʃu:]

v. 물다, 씹다, 물어뜯다
If you chew on something, you bite something continuously, especially because you are nervous or to test your teeth.

swallow**
[swálou]

v. 삼키다, 목구멍으로 넘기다; (초조해서) 마른침을 삼키다
If you swallow something, you cause it to go from your mouth down into your stomach.

gulp*
[gʌlp]

n. 한입; 꿀꺽꿀꺽 마심; v. 꿀꺽 삼키다[마시다]; 꾹 참다
A gulp of air, food, or drink, is a large amount of it that you swallow at once.

suck복습
[sʌk]

v. 빨다, 흡수하다; 삼키다; n. 빨아들임
If you suck on something, you hold it in your mouth and pull at it with the muscles in your cheeks and tongue, for example in order to get liquid out of it.

wonder ^{복습}
[wʌ́ndər]

v. 호기심을 가지다, 이상하게 여기다; n. 경탄할 만한 것, 경이
If you wonder about something, you think about it because it interests you and you want to know more about it.

ingredient [*]
[ingrí:diənt]

n. 재료, 성분, 원료
Ingredients are the things that are used to make something, especially all the different foods you use when you are cooking a particular dish.

sorrow [*]
[sárou]

n. 슬픔, 비통; 후회
Sorrow is a feeling of deep sadness or regret.

especially ^{복습}
[ispéʃəli]

a. 특히, 각별히
You use especially to emphasize that what you are saying applies more to one person, thing, or area than to any others.

share ^{복습}
[ʃɛər]

n. 몫, 분담; vt. 분배하다, 공유하다
If you have or do your share of something, you have or do an amount that seems reasonable to you, or to other people.

sadness [*]
[sǽdnis]

n. 슬픔, 비애
Sadness refers to the feeling of being sad, or something which makes you sad.

pick on

phrasal v. (구어) 괴롭히다, 못살게 굴다; ~을 선택하다, 고르다
If you pick on someone, you treat them badly or unfairly, especially repeatedly.

hardly ^{복습}
[háːrdli]

a. 거의 ~ 할 수 없다; 거의 ~ 아니다
When you say you can hardly do something, you are emphasizing that it is very difficult for you to do it.

memorial ^{복습}
[məmɔ́:riəl]

a. (죽은 사람을) 기념하기 위한, 추도[추모]의; n. 기념비(적인 것)
A memorial event, object, or prize is in honor of someone who has died, so that they will be remembered.

preacher ^{복습}
[prí:tʃər]

n. 목사, 설교자, 전도자
A preacher is a person, usually a member of the clergy, who preaches sermons as part of a church service.

stuff [*]
[stʌf]

vt. 채워 넣다, 속을 채우다; n. 일[것](일반적으로 말하거나 생각하는 것); 물건, 물질
If you stuff a container or space with something, you fill it with something or with a quantity of things until it is full.

check out

phrasal v. (도서관 등에서) 대출받다; 확인하다, 조사하다
If you check something out, you borrow it such as a book or a video from a library.

stick ^{복습}
[stik]

① v. 내밀다; 찔러 넣다, 찌르다; 붙이다, 달라붙다; 고수하다 ② n. 막대기, 지팡이
If something is sticking out from a surface or object, it extends up or away from it.

tongue ^{복습}
[tʌŋ]

n. 혀; 말, 말씨
Your tongue is the soft movable part inside your mouth which you use for tasting, eating, and speaking.

hell [복습]
[hel]

n. 지옥

If you say that a particular situation or place is hell, you are emphasizing that it is extremely unpleasant.

judge [복습]
[dʒʌdʒ]

v. 평가하다, 심사하다; 재판하다; n. 심판, 심사원; 재판관

If you judge something or someone, you form an opinion about them after you have examined the evidence or thought carefully about them.

wave [복습]
[weiv]

v. 흔들다, 신호하다; 파도치다; n. 파도, 물결

If you wave or wave your hand, you move your hand from side to side in the air, usually in order to say hello or goodbye to someone.

stare [복습]
[stɛər]

v. 응시하다, 뚫어지게 보다

If you stare at someone or something, you look at them for a long time.

holler [복습]
[hálər]

v. 고함지르다; 큰 소리로 부르다; n. 외침, 큰 소리

If you holler, you shout loudly.

neat **
[ni:t]

a. 굉장한, 훌륭한; 산뜻한, 깔끔한

If you say that something is neat, you mean that it is very good.

Check Your Reading Speed

1분에 몇 단어를 읽는지 리딩 속도를 측정해보세요.

$$\frac{1{,}122 \text{ words}}{\text{reading time (} \quad \text{) sec}} \times 60 = (\qquad) \text{ WPM}$$

Build Your Vocabulary

hand^{복습}
[hænd]

v. 건네주다, 넘겨주다; n. 손; 도움의 손길
If you hand something to someone, you pass it to them.

used to^{복습}

phrasal v. ~ 하곤 했다; 과거 한때는 ~이었다
If someone used to do something, it suggests habitual or accustomed actions or states, taking place in the past but not continuing into the present.

unwrap^{복습}
[ʌnrǽp]

v. (포장 등을) 풀다
When you unwrap something, you take off the paper, plastic, or other covering that is around it.

nod^{복습}
[nɔd]

v. 끄덕이다, 끄덕여 표시하다; n. (동의 · 인사 · 신호 · 명령의) 끄덕임
If you nod, you move your head downward and upward to show agreement, understanding, or approval.

sorrow^{복습}
[sɑ́rou]

n. 슬픔, 비통; 후회
Sorrow is a feeling of deep sadness or regret.

sorrowful**
[sɑ́rəfəl]

a. 슬퍼하는, 비탄에 잠긴
Sorrowful means very sad.

mention^{복습}
[ménʃən]

vt. 말하다, 언급하다; n. 언급, 진술
If you mention something, you say something about it, usually briefly.

suck^{복습}
[sʌk]

v. 빨다, 흡수하다; 삼키다; n. 빨아들임
If you suck on something, you hold it in your mouth and pull at it with the muscles in your cheeks and tongue, for example in order to get liquid out of it.

lean^{복습}
[liːn]

① v. 기대다, 의지하다; 몸을 구부리다, 기울다 ② a. 야윈, 마른
If you lean on or against someone or something, you rest against them so that they partly support your weight.

stomach^{복습}
[stʌ́mək]

n. 복부, 배; 위
You can refer to the front part of your body below your waist as your stomach.

invent***
[invént]

vt. 발명하다, 고안하다; (상상력으로) 만들다
If you invent something such as a machine or process, you are the first person to think of it or make it.

rub^{복습}
[rʌb]

v. 비비다, 문지르다; 스치다; n. 문지르기
If you rub a part of your body, you move your hand or fingers backward and forward over it while pressing firmly.

94

peculiar^{복습}
[pikjúːljər]

a. 기묘한, 특이한; 특유한, 고유의
If you describe someone or something as peculiar, you think that they are strange or unusual, sometimes in an unpleasant way.

flavor[*]
[fléivər]

n. 맛, 풍미, 향
The flavor of a food or drink is its taste.

odd^{**}
[ɑd]

a. 이상한, 기묘한
If you describe someone or something as odd, you think that they are strange or unusual.

get away^{복습}

phrasal v. 떠나다, 탈출하다
If you get away from something, you escape from it.

further^{**}
[fɔ́ːrðər]

a. (far–further–furthest) 더욱 더, 더 멀리
Further means to a greater extent or degree.

hunch
[hʌntʃ]

v. 둥글게 구부리다; n. 예감, 직감
If you hunch forward, you raise your shoulders, put your head down, and lean forward, often because you are cold, ill, or unhappy.

lower^{**}
[louər]

v. 낮추다, 내리다
If you lower something, you move it slowly downward.

chin^{**}
[tʃin]

n. 아래턱, 턱 끝
Your chin is the part of your face that is below your mouth and above your neck.

shell^{복습}
[ʃel]

n. 껍데기; 조가비; v. 껍데기를 벗기다
The shell of an animal such as a tortoise, snail, or crab is the hard protective covering that it has around its body or on its back.

melancholy[*]
[mélənkɑli]

a. 우울한, 슬픈, 구슬픈; n. 우울(증), 침울
You describe something that you see or hear as melancholy when it gives you an intense feeling of sadness.

sniff^{복습}
[snif]

v. 코를 킁킁거리다, 냄새를 맡다; 콧방귀를 뀌다; n. 냄새 맡음; 콧방귀
If you sniff something or sniff at it, you smell it by sniffing.

wrapper
[rǽpər]

n. 포장지, 보자기
A wrapper is a piece of paper, plastic, or thin metal which covers and protects something that you buy, especially food.

sigh^{복습}
[sai]

v. 한숨 쉬다; n. 한숨, 탄식
When you sigh, you let out a deep breath, as a way of expressing feelings such as disappointment, tiredness, or pleasure.

batch
[bætʃ]

n. 한 묶음, 한 회분, 집단
A batch of things is a group of things of the same kind, dealt with at the same time.

sit up^{복습}

phrasal v. 일어나 앉다
If you sit up, you move yourself into a sitting position, for example, from lying down.

disease^{**}
[dizíːz]

n. 병, 질환
A disease is an illness which affects people, animals, or plants, for example one which is caused by bacteria or infection.

factory [복습]
[fǽktəri]

n. 공장
A factory is a large building where machines are used to make large quantities of goods.

snuffle [복습]
[snʌfl]

v. 코를 킁킁거리다, 훌쩍이다; n. 코를 킁킁거리는 소리; 콧소리
If a person or an animal snuffles, they breathe in noisily through their nose, for example because they have a cold.

chew [복습]
[ʧuː]

v. 물다, 씹다, 물어뜯다
If you chew on something, you bite something continuously, especially because you are nervous or to test your teeth.

give up [복습]

phrasal v. 포기하다, 단념하다
If you give up, you decide that you cannot do something and stop trying to do it.

reach ***
[riːʧ]

v. (손·팔을 ~쪽으로) 뻗다, 내밀다; 도착하다, 도달하다; n. 뻗침, 범위
If you reach somewhere, you move your arm and hand to take or touch something.

throat [복습]
[θrout]

n. 목(구멍) (clear one's throat idiom 목을 가다듬다)
Your throat is the back of your mouth and the top part of the tubes that go down into your stomach and your lungs.

bald [복습]
[bɔːld]

a. (머리 등이) 벗어진, 대머리의; vi. 머리가 벗어지다
Someone who is bald has little or no hair on the top of their head.

witch [복습]
[wiʧ]

n. 마녀
In fairy stories, a witch is a woman, usually an old woman, who has evil magic powers.

retarded [복습]
[ritάːrdid]

a. 지능 발달이 늦은, 정신 지체의
Someone who is retarded is much less advanced mentally than most people of their age.

apologize **
[əpάlədʒàiz]

v. 사과하다, 사죄하다
When you apologize to someone, you say that you are sorry that you have hurt them or caused trouble for them.

name [복습]
[neim]

v. 이름을 지어주다; (정확히) 말하다, 지정하다; n. 이름; 평판
If you name someone, you identify them by stating their name.

drown **
[draun]

v. 익사하다, 물에 빠지다
When someone drowns or is drowned, they die because they have gone or been pushed under water and cannot breathe.

suffer [복습]
[sʌ́fər]

vi. 시달리다, 고통 받다; 겪다, 당하다
If you suffer pain, you feel it in your body or in your mind.

great deal

idiom 상당량, 다량
A great deal of something means that there's a lot of them.

tragedy *
[trǽdʒidi]

n. 비극, 비극적인 이야기
A tragedy is an extremely sad event or situation.

subject **
[sʌ́bdʒikt]

n. 주제; 백성, 국민; 과목; vt. 복종시키다
The subject of something such as a conversation, letter, or book is the thing that is being discussed or written about.

96

idle***
[áidl]

a. 무의미한; 한가한, 게으른
Idle is used to describe something that you do for no particular reason, often because you have nothing better to do.

conversation**
[kὰnvərséiʃən]

n. 대화, 회화
If you have a conversation with someone, you talk with them, usually in an informal situation.

explain^{복습}
[ikspléin]

v. 설명하다, 분명하게 하다
If you explain something, you give details about it or describe it so that it can be understood.

wonder^{복습}
[wΛ́ndə:r]

n. 경이, 경탄할 만한 것; v. 호기심을 가지다, 이상하게 여기다
If you say that it is a wonder that something happened, you mean that it is very surprising and unexpected.

pinch^{복습}
[pintʃ]

v. 여위게 하다, 초췌하게 하다; 꼬집다; n. 꼬집기 (pinch-faced a. 파리한 얼굴의)
If someone's face is pinched, it looks thin and pale, usually because they are ill or old.

sadness^{복습}
[sǽdnis]

n. 슬픔, 비애
Sadness refers to the feeling of being sad, or something which makes you sad.

breath**
[breθ]

n. 숨, 호흡
Your breath is the air that you let out through your mouth when you breathe.

pat^{복습}
[pæt]

v. 톡톡 가볍게 치다, (애정을 담아) 쓰다듬다; n. 쓰다듬기
If you pat something or someone, you tap them lightly, usually with your hand held flat.

lie^{복습}
[lai]

vi. (lay-lain) 눕다, 누워 있다; 놓여 있다, 위치하다; 거짓말하다; n. 거짓말
If you are lying somewhere, you are in a horizontal position and are not standing or sitting.

separate^{복습}
[sépəreit]

v. 가르다, 떼어놓다, 분리하다
If you separate people or things that are together, or if they separate, they move apart.

confuse^{복습}
[kənfjú:z]

v. 어리둥절하게 하다, 혼동하다 (confusing a. 혼란스러운)
To confuse someone means to make it difficult for them to know exactly what is happening or what to do.

eyebrow^{복습}
[áibràu]

n. 눈썹
Your eyebrows are the lines of hair which grow above your eyes.

repeat**
[ripí:t]

vt. 되풀이하다, 반복하다
To say or write something again or more than once.

hidden*
[hidn]

a. 숨겨진, 숨은, 비밀의; 신비한
Hidden facts, feelings, activities, or problems are not easy to notice or discover.

Chapters Nineteen & Twenty

1. The Littmus Lozenge reminded Otis of _____.
   A. his family
   B. his mistakes
   C. jail
   D. Gertrude

2. Otis went to jail because he _____
   and _____.
   A. killed a policeman; then he played guitar in jail
   B. robbed a music store; played guitar on the street
   C. begged for money on the street; stole a guitar
   D. played guitar on the street; hit a police man

3. What did Opal think as she swept the floor?
   A. It seemed like everyone in the world was lonely.
   B. Gertrude was wrong for giving Otis a job.
   C. Otis shouldn't have told her why he went to jail.
   D. She didn't want to clean the pet store anymore.

4. Sweet Pie said the Littmus Lozenge tasted like _____.
   A. lemon
   B. sadness
   C. Rootbeer
   D. not having a dog

5. Opal couldn't stand to think about _____.
   A. her mother anymore
   B. things that couldn't be helped anymore
   C. her old friends anymore
   D. Gloria's ghosts anymore

6. What did Opal promise Gloria?
   A. She would invite Otis.
   B. She would make egg-salad sandwiches.
   C. She would clean Gloria's yard for the party.
   D. She would invite the Dewberry boys.

7. Which of the following is NOT true?
   A. Amanda wanted to come to the party.
   B. Opal invited the Dewberry boys to the party.
   C. Otis liked parties.
   D. Sweetie Pie thought the party should have a theme.

1분에 몇 단어를 읽는지 리딩 속도를 측정해보세요.

$$\frac{656 \text{ words}}{\text{reading time (} \quad \text{) sec}} \times 60 = (\qquad) \text{ WPM}$$

Build Your Vocabulary

sweep^{복습}
[swi:p]

v. 청소하다; 쓸어내리다; 휙 지나가다; n. 청소; 한 번 휘두름
If you sweep an area of floor or ground, you push dirt or rubbish off it using a brush with a long handle.

unwrap^{복습}
[ʌnrǽp]

v. (포장 등을) 풀다
When you unwrap something, you take off the paper, plastic, or other covering that is around it.

jail^{복습}
[dʒeil]

n. 교도소, 감옥, 구치소
A jail is a place where criminals are kept in order to punish them, or where people waiting to be tried are kept.

squawk
[skwɔ:k]

v. (오리 등이) 꽥꽥 울다; 불평하다; n. 꽥꽥거리는 소리
When a bird squawks, it makes a loud harsh noise.

pick up^{복습}

phrasal v. 줍다, 들다; 되찾다, 회복하다; 알아채다
When you pick up something, you take hold of and lift it.

wrapper^{복습}
[rǽpər]

n. 포장지, 보자기
A wrapper is a piece of paper, plastic, or thin metal which covers and protects something that you buy, especially food.

beak**
[bi:k]

n. 새의 부리
A bird's beak is the hard curved or pointed part of its mouth.

lose one's nerve^{복습}

idiom 주눅 들다, 겁내다
If you lost your nerve, you are feeling timid and lacked of courage.

murder***
[mə́:rdə:r]

v. 죽이다, 살해하다; n. 살인 (murderer n. 살인자)
To murder someone means to commit the crime of killing them deliberately.

burglar**
[bə́:rglər]

n. 강도, 밤도둑
A burglar is a thief who enters a house or other building by force.

suck^{복습}
[sʌk]

v. 빨다, 흡수하다; 삼키다; n. 빨아들임
If you suck on something, you hold it in your mouth and pull at it with the muscles in your cheeks and tongue, for example in order to get liquid out of it.

stare^{복습}
[steər]

v. 응시하다, 뚫어지게 보다
If you stare at someone or something, you look at them for a long time.

pointy-toed ^{복습}
[pɔ́inti-tóud]

a. 발가락 부분이 뾰족한 모양의
Pointy-toed shoes refer to shoes with long and sharp front part.

wonder ^{복습}
[wʌ́ndə:r]

v. 호기심을 가지다, 이상하게 여기다; n. 경탄할 만한 것, 경이
If you wonder about something, you think about it because it interests you and you want to know more about it.

broom ^{복습}
[bru:m]

n. 빗자루
A broom is a kind of brush with a long handle. You use a broom for sweeping the floor.

on account of

idiom ~때문에
If something is on account of another thing, the latter is the cause of the former.

used to ^{복습}

phrasal v. ~하곤 했다; 과거 한때는 ~이었다
If someone used to do something, it suggests habitual or accustomed actions or states, taking place in the past but not continuing into the present.

break a law

idiom 범법 행위를 저지르다, 법률을 위반하다
If you break a law, you do something that you should not do according to the system of rules that a society or government develops.

handcuff
[hǽndkʌ̀f]

n. 수갑, 쇠고랑; vt. ~에게 수갑을 채우다
Handcuffs are two metal rings which are joined together and can be locked round someone's wrists, usually by the police during an arrest.

whisper ^{복습}
[hwíspə:r]

v. 속삭이다
When you whisper, you say something very quietly.

knock out

phrasal v. 때려눕히다, 나가떨어지게 하다; 녹초가 되게 하다
To knock someone out means to cause them to become unconscious.

lock up ^{복습}

phrasal v. 철창 안에 가두다, 안전한 곳에 넣어 두다
If something is being locked up, it is locked or secured by the doors or windows.

promise ^{복습}
[prάmis]

vt. 약속하다; n. 약속, 계약
If you promise that you will do something, you say to someone that you will definitely do it.

mind ^{복습}
[maind]

v. 상관하다, 언짢아하다; 주의하다; n. 마음, 정신
If you do not mind something, you are not annoyed or bothered by it.

spit *
[spit]

v. (spit/spat–spit/spat) 뱉다, 내뿜다
If you spit liquid or food somewhere, you force a small amount of it out of your mouth.

keep someone company

idiom ~의 곁에 있어 주다, 친구가 되어 주다
When you keep someone company, you spend time with them so that they are not alone.

keep on^{복습}

phrasal v. 계속하다
When you keep on doing something, you continue or persist doing it.

tongue^{복습}
[tʌŋ]

n. 혀; 말, 말씨
Your tongue is the soft movable part inside your mouth which you use for tasting, eating, and speaking.

tooth**
[tuːθ]

n. 이, 치아, 이빨
Your teeth are the hard white objects in your mouth, which you use for biting and chewing.

empty^{복습}
[émpti]

a. 빈, 공허한; vt. 비우다
An empty place, vehicle, or container is one that has no people or things in it.

spot^{복습}
[spɑt]

n. 장소, 지점; 반점, 얼룩; vt. 발견하다, 분별하다
You can refer to a particular place as a spot.

1분에 몇 단어를 읽는지 리딩 속도를 측정해보세요.

$$\frac{1,193 \ words}{reading \ time \ (\quad) \ sec} \times 60 = (\qquad) \ WPM$$

Build Your Vocabulary

arrest[**]
[ərést]

vt. 체포하다; 저지하다; (주의 · 이목 · 흥미 등을) 끌다; n. 체포, 검거, 구속
If the police arrest you, they take charge of you and take you to a police station, because they believe you may have committed a crime.

grab[*]
[græb]

v. 부여잡다, 움켜쥐다; n. 부여잡기
If you grab something, you take it or pick it up suddenly and roughly.

criminal[복습]
[krímənl]

n. 범죄자, 범인
A criminal is a person who regularly commits crimes.

wipe[*]
[waip]

vt. 닦다, 닦아 내다; n. 닦기
If you wipe something, you rub its surface to remove dirt or liquid from it.

hem
[hem]

n. (천 · 옷의) 옷단, 가장자리; vt. 옷단을 대다; 둘러싸다
A hem on something such as a piece of clothing is an edge that is folded over and stitched down to prevent threads coming loose.

pinch[복습]
[pintʃ]

v. 여위게 하다, 초췌하게 하다; 꼬집다; n. 꼬집기 (pinch-faced a. 파리한 얼굴의)
If someone's face is pinched, it looks thin and pale, usually because they are ill or old.

drown[복습]
[draun]

v. 익사하다, 물에 빠지다
When someone drowns or is drowned, they die because they have gone or been pushed under water and cannot breathe.

ache[*]
[eik]

vi. 쑤시다, 아프다; n. 아픔, 쑤심 (aching a. 아픈, 쑤시는; 마음 아픈)
If you ache or a part of your body aches, you feel a steady, fairly strong pain.

indeed[***]
[indíd]

a. 실로, 참으로, 정말; 과연
You use indeed to confirm or agree with something that has just been said.

look forward to

idiom ~을 고대하다, 기대하다, 즐거이 기다리다
If you are looking forward to do something, you are excited about it because you expect to enjoy it.

allow[복습]
[əláu]

v. 허락하다, ~하게 두다; 인정하다
If someone is allowed to do something, it is all right for them to do it and they will not get into trouble.

slam ^{복습}
[slæm]

v. (문 따위를) 탕 닫다; 털썩 내려놓다; 세게 치다; n. 쾅 (하는 소리)
If you slam a door or window or if it slams, it shuts noisily and with great force.

shoot up ^{복습}

phrasal v. 갑자기 올라가다, 급등하다
If something shoots up, it rises or increases very quickly.

underneath **
[ʌndərníːθ]

prep. ~의 아래에; ~의 지배하에; ~에 숨어서
If one thing is underneath another, it is directly under it, and may be covered or hidden by it.

nervous **
[nɔ́ːrvəs]

a. 불안해하는, 걱정하는; 신경이 과민한
If someone is nervous, they are frightened or worried about something that is happening or might happen, and show this in their behavior.

invite ^{복습}
[inváit]

vt. 초청하다, 초대하다
If you invite someone to something such as a party or a meal, you ask them to come to it.

preacher ^{복습}
[príːtʃər]

n. 목사, 설교자, 전도자
A preacher is a person, usually a member of the clergy, who preaches sermons as part of a church service.

triangle *
[tráiæŋgl]

n. 삼각형; [음악] 트라이앵글(악기)
A triangle is an object, arrangement, or flat shape with three straight sides and three angles.

fancy ^{복습}
[fǽnsi]

a. 고급스러운, 화려한; v. 공상[상상]하다; 좋아하다; n. 공상; 기호, 선호
If you describe something as fancy, you mean that it is very expensive or of very high quality.

bet ^{복습}
[bet]

v. ~임이 틀림없다; 걸다, 내기를 하다; n. 내기, 건 돈
You use expressions such as 'I bet', 'I'll bet', and 'you can bet' to indicate that you are sure something is true.

squeeze **
[skwiːz]

vt. 꽉 쥐다[죄다]; 비집고 들어가다; n. 압착, 짜냄; 꽉 끌어안음
If you squeeze something, you press it firmly, usually with your hands.

wag ^{복습}
[wæg]

v. (꼬리 등을) 흔들다, 흔들리다; n. 흔들기
When a dog wags its tail, it repeatedly waves its tail from side to side.

tail ^{복습}
[teil]

n. (동물의) 꼬리
The tail of an animal, bird, or fish is the part extending beyond the end of its body.

stand ^{복습}
[stænd]

vi. 참다, 견디다; 서다, 일어서다; n. 가판대, 좌판; 관람석
If you cannot stand something, you cannot bear it or tolerate it.

rub ^{복습}
[rʌb]

v. 비비다, 문지르다; 스치다; n. 문지르기
If you rub a part of your body, you move your hand or fingers backward and forward over it while pressing firmly.

sigh ^{복습}
[sai]

v. 한숨 쉬다; n. 한숨, 탄식
When you sigh, you let out a deep breath, as a way of expressing feelings such as disappointment, tiredness, or pleasure.

clap^{복습}
[klæp]

v. 박수를 치다
When you clap, you hit your hands together to show appreciation or attract attention.

stuff^{복습}
[stʌf]

n. 일[것](일반적으로 말하거나 생각하는 것); 물건, 물질; vt. 채워 넣다, 속을 채우다
You can use stuff to refer to things such as a substance, a collection of things, events, or ideas, or the contents of something in a general way without mentioning the thing itself by name.

knock^{복습}
[nak]

v. 부딪치다, 충돌시키다; (문을) 두드리다, 노크하다
To knock someone into a particular position or condition means to hit them very hard so that they fall over or become unconscious.

elbow^{**}
[élbou]

n. 팔꿈치; vt. 팔꿈치로 쿡 찌르다
Your elbow is the part of your arm where the upper and lower halves of the arm are joined.

pot^{**}
[pɑt]

n. 항아리, 단지; v. 화분에 심다; 병에 넣다
A pot is a deep round container used for cooking stews, soups, and other food.

theme^{복습}
[θi:m]

n. 주제, 테마; a. 특정 분위기를 살린
A theme in a piece of writing, a talk, or a discussion is an important idea or subject that runs through it.

stick^{복습}
[stik]

① v. (stuck-stuck) 찔러 넣다, 찌르다; 내밀다; 붙이다, 달라붙다; 고수하다
② n. 막대기, 지팡이
If you stick something somewhere, you put it there in a rather casual way.

knuckle^{복습}
[nʌkl]

n. 손가락 관절[마디]; v. 손가락 마디로 치다
Your knuckles are the rounded pieces of bone that form lumps on your hands where your fingers join your hands, and where your fingers bend.

wrap^{복습}
[ræp]

v. 감싸다; 포장하다; n. 싸개, 덮개
If someone wraps their arms, fingers, or legs around something, they put them firmly around it.

pop[*]
[pap]

v. 튀어나오다; 불쑥 움직이다; 뻥 하고 터뜨리다; n. 뻥[탁] 하는 소리; 발포
If your eyes pop, you look very surprised or excited when you see something.

beg[*]
[beg]

vt. 부탁[간청]하다; 구걸하다, 빌다
If you beg someone to do something, you ask them very anxiously or eagerly to do it

unless^{**}
[ənlés]

conj. ~하지 않는 한, ~이 아닌 한
You use unless to introduce the only circumstances in which an event you are mentioning will not take place or in which a statement you are making is not true.

sweep^{복습}
[swi:p]

v. 청소하다; 쓸어내리다; 휙 지나가다; n. 청소; 한 번 휘두름
If you sweep an area of floor or ground, you push dirt or rubbish off it using a brush with a long handle.

arrange ^{복습}
[əréindʒ]

v. 가지런히 하다, 배열하다; 준비하다
If you arrange things somewhere, you place them in a particular position, usually in order to make them look attractive or tidy.

dust ^{복습}
[dʌst]

v. 먼지를 털다; n. 먼지, 가루, 티끌
When you dust something such as furniture, you remove dust from it, usually using a cloth.

Chapters Twenty-One & Twenty-Two

1. What did NOT Opal and Gloria do for preparing the party?
   A. They put crepe paper in the trees.
   B. They put candles in bags of sand.
   C. They made sandwiches together.
   D. They put flowers on the table.

2. Who wore a green dress to the party?
   A. Gloria
   B. Opal
   C. Miss Franny
   D. Amanda

3. What did Sweetie Pie bring to the party?
   A. Candy
   B. Pictures of dogs
   C. A cake
   D. Sandwiches

4. What did NOT Otis bring to the party?
   A. Treats for Winn-Dixie
   B. His guitar
   C. Pickles
   D. Gertrude

5. What did the preacher do at the party?
   A. He blessed the party.
   B. He gave Winn-Dixie a sandwich.
   C. He helped Sweetie Pie hang pictures.
   D. He put Otis's guitar on the ground.

6. Opal thought the Dewberry boys weren't coming because the boys _____.
   A. didn't like egg-salad sandwiches
   B. thought Gloria was a witch
   C. didn't like Opal
   D. weren't allowed to come

7. What happened at the party?
   A. Winn-Dixie knocked over the sandwiches.
   B. Otis played his guitar.
   C. Opal wasn't nice to Amanda.
   D. It started to rain.

Check Your Reading Speed

1분에 몇 단어를 읽는지 리딩 속도를 측정해보세요.

$$\frac{967 \text{ words}}{\text{reading time (\quad) sec}} \times 60 = (\qquad) \text{ WPM}$$

Build Your Vocabulary

convince ^{복습}
[kənvíns]

vt. 설득하다; 확신시키다, 납득시키다
If someone or something convinces you to do something, they persuade you to do it.

rest ^{복습}
[rest]

① n. 나머지, 잔여 ② v. 쉬다, 쉬게 하다, 멈추게 하다; n. 휴식, 휴양
The rest is used to refer to all the parts of something or all the things in a group that remain or that you have not already mentioned.

triangle ^{복습}
[tráiæŋgl]

n. 삼각형; [음악] 트라이앵글(악기)
A triangle is an object, arrangement, or flat shape with three straight sides and three angles.

crust *
[krʌst]

n. 빵 껍질; 딱딱한 표면, 겉껍질
The crust on a loaf of bread is the outside part.

toothpick
[túːθpik]

n. 이쑤시개
A toothpick is a small stick which you use to remove food from between your teeth.

frill
[fril]

n. 주름 장식 (frilly a. 주름 장식이 달린)
A frill is a long narrow strip of cloth or paper with many folds in it, which is attached to something as a decoration.

keep on ^{복습}

phrasal v. 계속하다
When you keep on doing something, you continue or persist doing it.

wag ^{복습}
[wæg]

v. (꼬리 등을) 흔들다, 흔들리다; n. 흔들기
When a dog wags its tail, it repeatedly waves its tail from side to side.

tail ^{복습}
[teil]

n. (동물의) 꼬리
The tail of an animal, bird, or fish is the part extending beyond the end of its body.

soda *
[sóudə]

n. 탄산음료, 소다수
Soda is a sweet fizzy drink.

bowl **
[boul]

n. 사발, 그릇, 공기
A bowl is a round container with a wide uncovered top.

decorate **
[dekəréit]

vt. 장식하다, 꾸미다
If you decorate something, you make it more attractive by adding things to it.

110

string ^{복습}
[striŋ]

v. (strung–strung) 묶다, 매달다; n. 끈, 실; (악기의) 현[줄]
If you string something somewhere, you hang it up between two or more objects.

fancy ^{복습}
[fǽnsi]

a. 화려한, 고급스러운; v. 공상[상상]하다; 좋아하다; n. 공상; 기호, 선호
If you describe something as fancy, you mean that it is very expensive or of very high quality.

fill up

phrasal v. 가득 채우다, 가득 차다
When you fill up something, you make it completely full.

candle *
[kǽndl]

n. 양초, 등불
A candle is a stick of hard wax with a piece of string called a wick through the middle. You light the wick in order to give a steady flame that provides light.

light ***
[lait]

v. (lit/lighted–lit/lighted) 불을 붙이다, 빛을 비추다; 밝게 하다; n. 빛
If you light something such as a cigarette or fire, or if it lights, it starts burning.

fairyland
[fɛ́ərilæ̀nd]

n. 요정의 나라, 동화의 나라 같은 곳
If you describe a place as a fairyland, you mean that it has a delicate beauty.

swell *
[swel]

v. (swelled–swelled/swollen) 부풀다, 팽창하다; 넘실거리다, 넘치다
(swollen a. 부푼)
If the amount or size of something swells or if something swells it, it becomes larger than it was before.

desperate **
[déspərət]

a. 필사적인; 자포자기의, 절망적인 (desperately ad. 필사적으로)
If you are desperate for something or desperate to do something, you want or need it very much indeed.

shiny ^{복습}
[ʃáini]

a. 빛나는; 해가 비치는; 광택이 있는
Shiny things are bright and reflect light.

shimmer
[ʃímər]

vi. 희미하게 빛나다, 어른거리다; n. 반짝임 (shimmery a. 희미하게 빛나는)
If something shimmers, it shines with a faint, unsteady light or has an unclear, unsteady appearance.

high-heeled
[hái-híːld]

a. 굽 높은, 하이힐의
High-heeled shoes are women's shoes that have high heels.

wobble
[wabl]

v. 흔들흔들하다, 비틀대다; 동요하다; n. 흔들림
If something or someone wobbles, they make small movements from side to side, for example because they are unsteady.

back and forth ^{복습}

a. 앞뒤(좌우)로의; 여기저기의
If something moves back and forth, it moves in one direction and then in the opposite one, repeatedly.

sway *
[swei]

v. 흔들(리)다, 동요하다; 설득하다; n. 동요
When people or things sway, they lean or swing slowly from one side to the other.

treat ***
[triːt]

n. 맛있는 간식, 만족[즐거움]을 주는 것; 대접, 환대; vt. 다루다, 대우하다
If you give someone a treat, you buy or arrange something special for them which they will enjoy.

hand^{복습}
[hænd]

v. 건네주다, 넘겨주다; n. 손; 도움의 손길
If you hand something to someone, you pass it to them.

shake hands

idiom 악수하다
When you shake hands with someone, you take hold of their hand and move it up and down as a greeting or to show that you agree about something.

polite**
[pəláit]

a. 예의 바른, 공손한
Someone who is polite has good manners and behaves in a way that is socially correct and not rude to other people.

handful*
[hǽndfùl]

n. 한 움큼, 손에 그득, 한 줌
A handful of something is the amount of it that you can hold in your hand.

theme^{복습}
[θiːm]

n. 주제, 테마; a. 특정 분위기를 살린
A theme in a piece of writing, a talk, or a discussion is an important idea or subject that runs through it.

promise^{복습}
[prɑ́mis]

vt. 약속하다; n. 약속, 계약
If you promise that you will do something, you say to someone that you will definitely do it.

show up

phrasal v. 나타나다; 드러내 보이다
When someone shows up, they arrive or appear at the place you have arranged.

pat^{복습}
[pæt]

v. 톡톡 가볍게 치다, (애정을 담아) 쓰다듬다; n. 쓰다듬기
If you pat something or someone, you tap them lightly, usually with your hand held flat.

knock off^{복습}

phrasal v. 넘어뜨리다, 바닥에 떨어뜨리다; 때려눕히다
If you knock something off, you remove it and usually make it fall to the ground, by hitting it.

blond*
[bland]

a. 금발머리인; n. 금발머리의 여자
Blond hair can be very light brown or light yellow.

curl**
[kəːrl]

vt. 꼬다, 곱슬곱슬하게 하다; n. 컬, 곱슬머리
If you have curls, your hair is in the form of tight curves and spirals.

mean^{복습}
[miːn]

① a. 성질이 나쁜, 심술궂은; 비열한 ② vt. 의미하다, 뜻하다 ③ a. 평균의, 중간의
If you describe a behavior as mean, you are saying that it is very bad and evil.

extra^{복습}
[ékstrə]

a. 특별히, 각별히; a. 추가의, 여분의
You can use extra in front of adjectives and adverbs to emphasize the quality that they are describing.

one another^{복습}

pron. 서로 서로
One another refers to each other.

nervous^{복습}
[nə́ːrvəs]

a. 걱정하는, 불안해하는; 신경이 과민한
If someone is nervous, they are frightened or worried about something that is happening or might happen, and show this in their behavior.

112

screech *
[skriːtʃ]

v. 새된 소리를 지르다; 끼익 소리 나(게 하)다; n. 날카로운 외침
(screechy a. 날카로운 소리를 내는)
If a vehicle screeches somewhere or if its tires screech, its tires make an unpleasant high-pitched noise on the road.

bark ^{복습}
[baːrk]

v. (개가) 짖다; n. 나무껍질; (개 등이) 짖는[우는] 소리
When a dog barks, it makes a short, loud noise, once or several times.

sidewalk *
[sáidwɔ̀ːk]

n. (포장한) 보도, 인도
A sidewalk is a path with a hard surface by the side of a road.

jar **
[dʒaːr]

① n. 병, 단지 ② v. 덜컹덜컹 흔들리다; 삐걱거리다; n. 삐걱거리는 소리, 잡음
A jar is a glass container with a lid that is used for storing food.

land ^{복습}
[lænd]

v. 내려앉다, 상륙하다, 착륙하다; n. 육지, 국토, 나라
When someone or something lands, they come down to the ground after moving through the air or falling.

hardly ^{복습}
[háːrdli]

a. 거의 ~이 아니다; 거의 ~할 수 없다
You use hardly in expressions such as hardly ever, hardly any, and hardly anyone to mean almost never, almost none, or almost no-one.

lost **
[lɔːst]

a. 길을 잃은; 분실된
If you are lost or if you get lost, you do not know where you are or are unable to find your way.

tiny ^{복습}
[táini]

a. 몹시 작은
Something or someone that is tiny is extremely small.

turn around ^{복습}

phrasal v. 돌아서다, 몸을 돌리다; 회전하다
When you turn around, you move your head and shoulders or your whole body so that you face in the opposite direction.

Check Your Reading Speed

1분에 몇 단어를 읽는지 리딩 속도를 측정해보세요.

$$\frac{548 \text{ words}}{\text{reading time (} \quad \text{) sec}} \times 60 = (\quad) \text{ WPM}$$

Build Your Vocabulary

all the way ^{복습}

idiom 내내, 시종
If you have been doing something all the way, you are emphasizing the period of time during the whole journey.

run away ^{복습}

phrasal v. 도망치다, 탈주하다; 떠나다, 가출하다
When you run away, you escape from someone or a place.

run ***
[rʌn]

v. 경영하다; 뛰다, 달리다
If you run something such as a business or an activity, you are in charge of it or you organize it.

stick ^{복습}
[stik]

① v. (stuck–stuck) 내밀다; 찔러 넣다, 찌르다; 붙이다, 달라붙다; 고수하다
② n. 막대기, 지팡이
If something is sticking out from a surface or object, it extends up or away from it.

shuffle
[ʃʌfl]

v. ~을 섞다; 질질 끌다, 발을 끌며 걷다
If you shuffle things such as pieces of paper, you move them around so that they are in a different order.

jar ^{복습}
[dʒaːr]

① n. 병, 단지 ② v. 덜컹덜컹 흔들리다; 삐걱거리다; n. 삐걱거리는 소리, 잡음
A jar is a glass container with a lid that is used for storing food.

back and forth ^{복습}

a. 앞뒤(좌우)로의; 여기저기의
If something moves back and forth, it moves in one direction and then in the opposite one, repeatedly.

free up

phrasal v. 해방하다, 풀어주다; 해소하다
If you are freed up, you are able to do something else.

offer ***
[ɔ́ːfər]

v. 제공하다; 제의[제안]하다; n. 제공
If you offer something to someone, you ask them if they would like to have it or use it.

end up ^{복습}

phrasal v. (구어) 마침내는 (~으로) 되다; 끝나다
If you end up doing something or end up in a particular state, you do that thing or get into that state even though you did not originally intend to.

bend ^{복습}
[bend]

v. 구부리다, 돌리다; 구부러지다, 휘다; n. 커브, 굽음
When you bend a part of your body such as your arm or leg, or when it bends, you change its position so that it is no longer straight.

slide ^{복습}
[slaid]

v. (slid-slid) 미끄러지다, 미끄러지듯 움직이다
When something slides somewhere or when you slide it there, it moves there smoothly over or against something.

on purpose

idiom 고의로, 일부러
If you are doing something on purpose, you intend to do it deliberately.

amuse *
[əmjúːz]

vt. 즐겁게 하다, 재미나게 하다
If something amuses you, it makes you want to laugh or smile.

wipe ^{복습}
[waip]

vt. 닦다, 닦아 내다; n. 닦기
If you wipe something, you rub its surface to remove dirt or liquid from it.

pleasure **
[pléʒər]

n. 기쁨, 즐거움
If something gives you pleasure, you get a feeling of happiness, satisfaction, or enjoyment from it.

shake hands ^{복습}

idiom 악수하다
When you shake hands with someone, you take hold of their hand and move it up and down as a greeting or to show that you agree about something.

notice ^{복습}
[nóutis]

vt. 알아차리다, 주의하다; n. 주의, 주목
If you notice something or someone, you become aware of them.

shrug ^{복습}
[ʃrʌg]

v. (어깨를) 으쓱하다; n. (양 손바닥을 내보이면서 어깨를) 으쓱하기
If you shrug, you raise your shoulders to show that you are not interested in something or that you do not know or care about something.

witch ^{복습}
[witʃ]

n. 마녀
In fairy stories, a witch is a woman, usually an old woman, who has evil magic powers.

bless *
[bles]

vt. 축복하다, 은총을 내리다
When someone such as a priest blesses people or things, he asks for God's favor and protection for them.

nod ^{복습}
[nɔd]

v. 끄덕이다, 끄덕여 표시하다; n. 끄덕임 (동의 · 인사 · 신호 · 명령)
If you nod, you move your head downward and upward to show agreement, understanding, or approval.

throat ^{복습}
[θrout]

n. 목(구멍) (clear one's throat idiom 목을 가다듬다)
Your throat is the back of your mouth and the top part of the tubes that go down into your stomach and your lungs.

candlelight
[kǽndllàit]

n. 촛불
Candlelight is the light that a candle produces.

appreciate **
[əprí:ʃieit]

vt. 고맙게 생각하다; 평가하다, 감상하다
If you appreciate something that someone has done for you or is going to do for you, you are grateful for it.

complicated **
[kámplikèitid]

a. 복잡한, 뒤얽힌
If you say that something is complicated, you mean it has so many parts or aspects that it is difficult to understand or deal with.

task[**]
[tæsk]

n. 일, 과업, 과제
A task is an activity or piece of work which you have to do, usually as part of a larger project.

pray[복습]
[prei]

v. 기도하다, 기원하다, 빌다
When people pray, they speak to God in order to give thanks or to ask for his help.

whisper[복습]
[hwíspə:r]

v. 속삭이다
When you whisper, you say something very quietly.

croak[복습]
[krouk]

v. (까마귀가) 깍깍 울다; 쉰 목소리를 내다
When a frog or bird croaks, it makes a harsh, low sound.

fix[복습]
[fiks]

vt. (식사 등을) 준비하다; 고치다; 고정시키다
If you fix some food or a drink for someone, you make it or prepare it for them.

sneeze[복습]
[sni:z]

vi. 재채기하다; n. 재채기
When you sneeze, you suddenly take in your breath and then blow it down your nose noisily without being able to stop yourself, for example because you have a cold.

far-off
[fá:r-ɔ́:f]

a. 먼, 멀리 떨어진
If you describe something as far-off, you mean that it is a long distance from you or from a particular place.

rumble[복습]
[rʌmbl]

n. 우르르 하는 소리; 소음; v. 우르르 울리(게 하)다; (차 등이) 덜거덕거리며 가다
A rumble is a low continuous noise.

thunder[복습]
[θʌ́ndər]

n. 천둥; v. 천둥이 치다; 우르릉거리다
Thunder is the loud noise that you hear from the sky after a flash of lightning, especially during a storm.

stomach[복습]
[stʌ́mək]

n. 위; 복부, 배
Your stomach is the organ inside your body where food is digested before it moves into the intestines.

growl[복습]
[graul]

v. 으르렁거리다; n. 으르렁거리는 소리
When a dog or other animal growls, it makes a low noise in its throat, usually because it is angry.

predict[*]
[pridíkt]

v. 예상하다, 예언하다
If you predict an event, you say that it will happen.

wet[복습]
[wet]

a. 젖은, 축축한
If something is wet, it is covered in water, rain, sweat, tears, or another liquid.

pour[복습]
[pɔ:r]

v. 쏟아지다, 따르다, 붓다; 흐르듯이 이동하다, 쇄도하다
When it rains very heavily, you can say that it is pouring.

1. Who helped Miss Franny into the house?
   A. Amanda
   B. Opal
   C. Gloria
   D. Winn-Dixie

2. What did Opal forget to do?
   A. To get the sandwiches out of the rain
   B. To help Gloria into the house
   C. To protect Winn-Dixie from the thunder
   D. To look around the garden before going inside

3. Gloria said that you can't hold onto something that
   _____.
   A. wants to go
   B. is lost
   C. you never owned
   D. you cannot see anymore

4. What was the last thing Opal saw before she looked for Winn-Dixie?
   A. Gloria smiling
   B. Sweetie Pie holding dog signs
   C. Dunlap's bald head
   D. Miss Franny waving

5. What is NOT true about Winn-Dixie?
   A. He had a fear of thunderstorms.
   B. He snored.
   C. He liked to be alone.
   D. He didn't mind going to church.

6. Opal couldn't believe that the preacher _____.
   A. loved Winn-Dixie as much as she did
   B. left Opal's mother
   C. let Winn-Dixie run away
   D. started to cry

7. What did Opal's mother forget to take with her?
   A. Opal
   B. the preacher
   C. her wedding ring
   D. her favorite picture

Check Your Reading Speed

1분에 몇 단어를 읽는지 리딩 속도를 측정해보세요.

$$\frac{685 \text{ words}}{\text{reading time ( ) sec}} \times 60 = (\quad) \text{ WPM}$$

Build Your Vocabulary

yell^{복습}
[jel]

v. 소리치다, 고함치다; n. 고함소리, 부르짖음
If you yell, you shout loudly, usually because you are excited, angry, or in pain.

tear^{복습}
[tɛər]

① v. 찢다, 찢어지다; 부리나케 가다; n. 찢음 ② n. 눈물
If you tear off something, you remove it quickly by pulling violently.

grab^{복습}
[græb]

v. 부여잡다, 움켜쥐다; n. 부여잡기
If you grab something, you take it or pick it up suddenly and roughly.

platter
[plǽtər]

n. (타원형의 얕은) 큰 접시
A platter is a large, flat plate that is used for serving food.

teeter
[tíːtər]

v. 건들건들 움직이다; 시소를 타다; n. 상하 움직임 (teetery a. 불안정한)
If someone or something teeters, they shake in an unsteady way, and seem to be about to lose their balance and fall over.

knock over^{복습}

phrasal v. 뒤집어엎다; 때려눕히다
If you knock something over, you push or hit it and making it fall or turn on its side.

hold on to^{복습}

phrasal v. 지키다, 고수하다; 보유하다
If you hold on to something or someone, you keep them not to lose.

tight^{복습}
[tait]

ad. 단단히, 꽉; a. 단단한, 팽팽한, 빈틈없는
If you hold someone or something tight, you hold them firmly and securely.

melt^{**}
[melt]

v. 녹(이)다, 용해하다; (감정 등이) 누그러지다; n. 용해
When a solid substance melts or when you melt it, it changes to a liquid, usually because it has been heated.

candle^{복습}
[kǽndl]

n. 양초, 등불
A candle is a stick of hard wax with a piece of string called a wick through the middle. You light the wick in order to give a steady flame that provides light.

jar^{복습}
[dʒaːr]

① n. 병, 단지 ② v. 덜컹덜컹 흔들리다; 삐걱거리다; n. 삐걱거리는 소리, 잡음
A jar is a glass container with a lid that is used for storing food.

holler^{복습}
[hάlər]

v. 고함지르다; 큰 소리로 부르다; n. 외침, 큰 소리
If you holler, you shout loudly.

downpour
[dáunpɔːr]

n. 억수 (같은 비), 호우
A downpour is a sudden and unexpected heavy fall of rain.

120

preacher^{복습}
[priːtʃər]

n. 목사, 설교자, 전도자
A preacher is a person, usually a member of the clergy, who preaches sermons as part of a church service.

squawk^{복습}
[skwɔːk]

v. (오리 등이) 꽥꽥 울다; 불평하다; n. 꽥꽥거리는 소리
When a bird squawks, it makes a loud harsh noise.

thunder^{복습}
[θʌndər]

n. 천둥; v. 천둥이 치다; 우르릉거리다
Thunder is the loud noise that you hear from the sky after a flash of lightning, especially during a storm.

boom[*]
[buːm]

v. 쿵 하고 울리다, 번창하다, 호황을 맞다; n. 쿵 울리는 소리, 인기, 붐
When something such as someone's voice, a cannon, or a big drum booms, it makes a loud, deep sound that lasts for several seconds.

crack^{복습}
[kræk]

v. 날카로운 소리가 나(게 하)다; 금이 가다, 깨다, 부수다;
n. 갑작스런 날카로운 소리; 갈라진 금
If something cracks, or if you crack it, it makes a sharp sound like the sound of a piece of wood breaking.

wave^{복습}
[weiv]

v. 흔들다, 신호하다; 파도치다; n. 파도, 물결
If you wave or wave your hand, you move your hand from side to side in the air, usually in order to say hello or goodbye to someone.

wad
[wad]

n. 다발, 뭉치, 작은 덩어리
A wad of something such as paper or cloth is a tight bundle or ball of it.

protect^{복습}
[prətékt]

v. 보호하다, 막다, 지키다
To protect someone or something means to prevent them from being harmed or damaged.

underneath^{복습}
[ʌndərníːθ]

prep. ~의 아래에; ~의 지배하에; ~에 숨어서
If one thing is underneath another, it is directly under it, and may be covered or hidden by it.

flashlight[*]
[flǽʃlàit]

n. 손전등, 회중 전등
A flashlight is a small electric light which gets its power from batteries and which you can carry in your hand.

bush^{**}
[buʃ]

n. 관목, 덤불, 우거진 것
A bush is a large plant which is smaller than a tree and has a lot of branches.

fault^{**}
[fɔːlt]

n. 과실, 잘못; 결점
If a bad or undesirable situation is your fault, you caused it or are responsible for it.

porch^{복습}
[pɔːrtʃ]

n. (본 건물 입구에 달린 지붕이 있는) 현관, 포치
A porch is a sheltered area at the entrance to a building, which has a roof and sometimes has walls.

shine^{***}
[ʃain]

v. (shone/shined–shone/shined) 비추다; 빛나다
If you shine a torch or other light somewhere, you point it there, so that you can see something when it is dark.

hand^{복습}
[hænd]

v. 건네주다, 넘겨주다; n. 손; 도움의 손길
If you hand something to someone, you pass it to them.

stare^{복습}
[stɛər]

v. 응시하다, 뚫어지게 보다
If you stare at someone or something, you look at them for a long time.

reach^{복습}
[riːtʃ]

v. (손 · 팔을 ~쪽으로) 뻗다, 내밀다; 도착하다, 도달하다; n. 뻗침, 범위
If you reach somewhere, you move your arm and hand to take or touch something.

whisper^{복습}
[hwíspər]

v. 속삭이다
When you whisper, you say something very quietly.

squeeze^{복습}
[skwiːz]

vt. 꽉 쥐다[죄다]; 비집고 들어가다; n. 압착, 짜냄; 꽉 끌어안음
If you squeeze something, you press it firmly, usually with your hands.

step off

phrasal v. (탈것에서) 내리다
When you step off from a vehicle or something, you descend from it.

lost^{복습}
[lɔːst]

a. 길을 잃은; 분실된
If you are lost or if you get lost, you do not know where you are or are unable to find your way.

turn around^{복습}

phrasal v. 돌아서다, 몸을 돌리다; 회전하다
When you turn around, you move your head and shoulders or your whole body so that you face in the opposite direction.

bald^{복습}
[bɔːld]

a. (머리 등이) 벗어진, 대머리의; vi. 머리가 벗어지다
Someone who is bald has little or no hair on the top of their head.

glow^{***}
[glou]

v. 빛나다, 빛을 내다; n. 빛, 밝음
If something glows, it looks bright because it is reflecting light.

1분에 몇 단어를 읽는지 리딩 속도를 측정해보세요.

$$\frac{953 \text{ words}}{\text{reading time (} \qquad \text{) sec}} \times 60 = (\qquad) \text{ WPM}$$

Build Your Vocabulary

preacher
[priːtʃər]

n. 목사, 설교자, 전도자
A preacher is a person, usually a member of the clergy, who preaches sermons as part of a church service.

whistle
[hwisl]

v. 휘파람 불다; n. 휘파람; 호각
When you whistle or when you whistle a tune, you make a series of musical notes by forcing your breath out between your lips, or your teeth.

show up
[쇼업]

phrasal v. 나타나다; 드러내 보이다
When someone shows up, they arrive or appear at the place you have arranged.

memorial
[məmɔ́ːriəl]

a. (죽은 사람을) 기념하기 위한, 추도[추모]의; n. 기념비(적인 것)
A memorial event, object, or prize is in honor of someone who has died, so that they will be remembered.

trailer
[tréilər]

n. 트레일러하우스, (자동차가 끌고 다니는) 이동식 주택
A trailer is a container on wheels which is pulled by a car or other vehicle and which is used for transporting large or heavy items.

all the way

idiom 내내, 시종
If you have been doing something all the way, you are emphasizing the period of time during the whole journey.

railroad
[réilròud]

n. 철로, 선로
A railroad is a route between two places along which trains travel on steel rails.

track
[træk]

n. 철도 선로; 지나간 자취; v. 추적하다, ~의 뒤를 쫓다
Railway tracks are the rails that a train travels along.

rush
[rʌʃ]

v. 돌진하다, 급히 움직이다, 서두르다
If you rush somewhere, you go there quickly.

glow
[glou]

v. 빛을 내다, 빛나다; n. 빛, 밝음
If something glows, it produces a dull, steady light.

mean
[miːn]

① a. 비열한, 성질이 나쁜, 심술궂은 ② vt. 의미하다, 뜻하다 ③ a. 평균의, 중간의
If you describe a behavior as mean, you are saying that it is very bad and evil.

stare
[stɛər]

v. 응시하다, 뚫어지게 보다
If you stare at someone or something, you look at them for a long time.

run over

phrasal v. (사람·동물을) 치다

If you run someone or something over, you knock them down and often pass over their body or part of it.

neighborhood*
[néibərhùd]

n. (도시의) 지역[구역]; 이웃 사람들

A neighborhood is one of the parts of a town where people live.

pathological
[pæθəládʒikəl]

a. 병적인, 걷잡을 수 없는

You describe a person or their behavior as pathological when they behave in an extreme and unacceptable way, and have very powerful feelings which they cannot control.

thunderstorm^{복습}
[θʌ́ndərstɔ́ːrm]

n. 폭풍우

A thunderstorm is a storm in which there is thunder and lightning and a lot of heavy rain.

snore^{복습}
[snɔːr]

v. 코를 골다

When someone who is asleep snores, they make a loud noise each time they breathe.

squish^{복습}
[skwiʃ]

v. 찌부러뜨리다, 으깨다

If something soft squishes or is squished, it is crushed out of shape when it is pressed.

stand^{복습}
[stænd]

vi. 참다, 견디다; 서다, 일어서다; n. 가판대, 좌판; 관람석

If you cannot stand something, you cannot bear it or tolerate it.

couch^{복습}
[kautʃ]

n. 소파, 긴 의자

A couch is a long, comfortable seat for two or three people.

mind^{복습}
[maind]

v. 상관하다, 언짢아하다; 주의하다; n. 마음, 정신

If you do not mind something, you are not annoyed or bothered by it.

keep on^{복습}

phrasal v. 계속하다

When you keep on doing something, you continue or persist doing it.

memorize^{복습}
[méməràiz]

vt. 기억하다, 암기하다

If you memorize something, you learn it so that you can remember it exactly.

hold on to^{복습}

phrasal v. 지키다, 고수하다; 보유하다

If you hold on to something or someone, you keep them not to lose.

quit^{복습}
[kwit]

v. 그만두다; (술·담배 등을) 끊다

If you quit an activity or quit doing something, you stop doing it.

give up^{복습}

phrasal v. 포기하다, 단념하다

If you give up, you decide that you cannot do something and stop trying to do it.

rub^{복습}
[rʌb]

v. 비비다, 문지르다; 스치다; n. 문지르기

If you rub a part of your body, you move your hand or fingers backward and forward over it while pressing firmly.

argue***
[áːrgjuː]

v. 논쟁하다, 주장하다
If one person argues with another, they speak angrily to each other about something that they disagree about.

let up

phrasal v. (비 · 눈 등이) 멎다, 약해지다; (추위 · 더위가) 누그러지다
If something has let up, it became less strong.

drizzle
[drizl]

n. 이슬비, 가랑비; vi. 이슬비[가랑비]가 내리다
Drizzle is light rain falling in fine drops.

head^{복습}
[hed]

v. 특정 방향으로 가다; 앞서다; n. 한발 앞선 출발, 우위
If you are headed for a particular place, you are going toward that place.

turtle^{복습}
[təːrtl]

n. [동물] 거북, 바다거북
A turtle is a large reptile which has a thick shell covering its body and which lives in the sea most of the time.

shell^{복습}
[ʃel]

n. 껍데기; 조가비; v. 껍데기를 벗기다
The shell of an animal such as a tortoise, snail, or crab is the hard protective covering that it has around its body or on its back.

bet^{복습}
[bet]

v. ~임이 틀림없다; 걸다, 내기를 하다; n. 내기, 건 돈
You use expressions such as 'I bet', 'I'll bet', and 'you can bet' to indicate that you are sure something is true.

run off^{복습}

phrasal v. 서둘러 떠나다; 달아나다, 꽁무니를 빼다
When you run off, you depart in haste.

spread^{복습}
[spred]

v. (spread–spread) 뻗다, 펼치다, 퍼지다; 뿌리다; n. 퍼짐, 폭, 넓이
If you spread your arms, hands, fingers, or legs, you stretch them out until they are far apart.

snuffle^{복습}
[snʌfl]

v. 훌쩍이다, 코를 킁킁거리다; n. 코를 킁킁거리는 소리; 콧소리
(snuffly a. 코를 훌쩍이는)
If you snuffle, you breathe noisily because you have a cold or you are crying.

wrap^{복습}
[ræp]

v. 감싸다; 포장하다; n. 싸개, 덮개
If someone wraps their arms, fingers, or legs around something, they put them firmly around it.

waist**
[weist]

n. 허리
Your waist is the middle part of your body where it narrows slightly above your hips.

rock^{복습}
[rɑk]

① v. 흔들다, 진동하다 ② n. 바위, 암석
When something rocks or when you rock it, it shakes violently.

back and forth^{복습}

a. 앞뒤(좌우)로의; 여기저기의
If something moves back and forth, it moves in one direction and then in the opposite one, repeatedly.

nerve**
[nəːrv]

n. 대담성, 용기; 신경
If you refer to someone's nerves, you mean their ability to cope with problems such as stress, worry, and danger.

whisper ^{복습}
[hwíspəːr]

v. 속삭이다
When you whisper, you say something very quietly.

pray ^{복습}
[prei]

v. 기도하다, 기원하다, 빌다
When people pray, they speak to God in order to give thanks or to ask for his help.

realize **
[ríːəlaiz]

vt. 깨닫다; 실현하다
If you realize that something is true, you become aware of that fact or understand it.

tight ^{복습}
[tait]

ad. 단단히, 꽉; a. 단단한, 팽팽한, 빈틈없는
If you hold someone or something tight, you hold them firmly and securely.

Chapters Twenty-Five & Twenty-Six

1. What is NOT true when Opal returned to Gloria's house?
   A. Winn-Dixie was there.
   B. Amanda was smiling.
   C. Otis was playing his guitar.
   D. Gloria and Sweetie Pie were sitting on the floor.

2. How did Gloria know that Winn-Dixie was in the house?
   A. He barked.
   B. He sneezed.
   C. He snored.
   D. He came into the kitchen.

3. Where was Winn-Dixie hiding during the storm?
   A. Under Gloria's chair.
   B. In Gloria's closet.
   C. Under Gloria's bed.
   D. In Gloria's bathroom.

4. What did Opal say underneath Gloria's mistake tree?
   A. She said she wouldn't think about her mother as often as she did in the summer.
   B. She said she wouldn't have another party.
   C. She said she would never know anything else about her mother.
   D. She said she would cut the bottles from Gloria's mistake tree.

5. What did Opal look for in the garden?
   A. Winn-Dixie
   B. Her tree
   C. Dunlap
   D. Wet candles

6. How did Dunlap surprise Opal?
   A. He said he was sorry.
   B. He beat Opal in a race.
   C. He taught Otis a song.
   D. He helped Opal stand up.

7. Who did everyone sing for at the end of the book?
   A. Gloria
   B. Otis
   C. Winn-Dixie
   D. Opal

1분에 몇 단어를 읽는지 리딩 속도를 측정해보세요.

$$\frac{959 \text{ words}}{\text{reading time ( ) sec}} \times 60 = (\quad) \text{ WPM}$$

Build Your Vocabulary

clap ^{복습}
[klæp]

v. 박수를 치다
When you clap, you hit your hands together to show appreciation or attract attention.

wonder ^{복습}
[wʌ́ndər]

v. 호기심을 가지다, 이상하게 여기다; n. 경탄할 만한 것, 경이
If you wonder about something, you think about it because it interests you and you want to know more about it.

sidewalk ^{복습}
[sáidwɔ̀:k]

n. (포장한) 보도, 인도
A sidewalk is a path with a hard surface by the side of a road.

lap ^{복습}
[læp]

① n. 무릎; (트랙의) 한 바퀴 ② v. (파도가) 찰싹거리다; (할짝할짝) 핥다
If you have something on your lap, it is on top of your legs and near to your body.

cane ^{복습}
[kein]

n. 지팡이
A cane is a long thin stick with a curved or round top which you can use to support yourself when you are walking.

poke ^{복습}
[pouk]

v. 찌르다, 쑤시다; 쑥 내밀다; 들이대다; n. 찌름, 쑤심
If you poke someone or something, you quickly push them with your finger or with a sharp object.

snuffle ^{복습}
[snʌfl]

n. 코를 킁킁거리는 소리; 콧소리; v. 코를 킁킁거리다, 훌쩍이다
If a person or an animal snuffles, they breathe in noisily through their nose, for example because they have a cold.

sigh ^{복습}
[sai]

n. 한숨, 탄식; v. 한숨 쉬다
When you sigh, you let out a deep breath, as a way of expressing feelings such as disappointment, tiredness, or pleasure.

plumb
[plʌm]

a. 완전히; 바로, 정확히
You use plumb to intensify the degree or extent of the situation.

wear (someone) out ^{복습}

phrasal v. 지치게 하다; 해지다, 낡아서 떨어지다
When you are worn out, you are completely tired.

underneath ^{복습}
[ʌ̀ndərníːθ]

prep. ~의 아래에; ~의 지배하에; ~에 숨어서
If one thing is underneath another, it is directly under it, and may be covered or hidden by it.

yawn ^{복습}
[jɔːn]

vi. 하품하다; n. 하품
If you yawn, you open your mouth very wide and breathe in more air than usual, often when you are tired or when you are not interested in something.

holler^{복습}
[hálər]

v. 고함지르다; 큰 소리로 부르다; n. 외침, 큰 소리
If you holler, you shout loudly.

squawk^{복습}
[skwɔːk]

v. (오리 등이) 꽥꽥 울다; 불평하다; n. 꽥꽥거리는 소리
When a bird squawks, it makes a loud harsh noise.

wag^{복습}
[wæg]

v. (꼬리 등을) 흔들다, 흔들리다; n. 흔들기
When a dog wags its tail, it repeatedly waves its tail from side to side.

tail^{복습}
[teil]

n. (동물의) 꼬리
The tail of an animal, bird, or fish is the part extending beyond the end of its body.

sneeze^{복습}
[sniːz]

vi. 재채기하다; n. 재채기
When you sneeze, you suddenly take in your breath and then blow it down your nose noisily without being able to stop yourself, for example because you have a cold.

wrap^{복습}
[ræp]

v. 감싸다; 포장하다; n. 싸개, 덮개
If someone wraps their arms, fingers, or legs around something, they put them firmly around it.

convince^{복습}
[kənvíns]

vt. 설득하다; 확신시키다, 납득시키다
If someone or something convinces you to do something, they persuade you to do it.

scary^{복습}
[skέəri]

a. 무서운, 두려운
Something that is scary is rather frightening.

witch^{복습}
[witʃ]

n. 마녀
In fairy stories, a witch is a woman, usually an old woman, who has evil magic powers.

spell^{복습}
[spel]

n. 주문(呪文), 주술; 마력, 마법; v. (낱말을) 맞춤법에 따라 쓰다
A spell is a situation in which events are controlled by a magical power.

potion
[póuʃən]

n. (특별한 효력·마력이 있는) 마시는 약
A potion is a drink that contains medicine, poison, or something that is supposed to have magic powers.

bald^{복습}
[bɔːld]

a. (머리 등이) 벗어진, 대머리의; vi. 머리가 벗어지다
Someone who is bald has little or no hair on the top of their head.

turn into

phrasal v. ~이 되게 하다, ~으로 바꿔 놓다
When something is turned into other thing, it changes into something different.

toad*
[toud]

n. [동물] 두꺼비
A toad is a creature which is similar to a frog but which has a drier skin and spends less time in water.

grin^{복습}
[grin]

v. (이를 드러내고) 싱긋 웃다, 활짝 웃다; n. 싱긋 웃음
When you grin, you smile broadly.

exist^{복습}
[igzíst]

v. 존재하다, 실재하다, 현존하다
If something exists, it is present in the world as a real thing.

myth[*]
[miθ]

n. 신화, 미신
A myth is a well-known story which was made up in the past to explain natural events or to justify religious beliefs or social customs.

witchy
[wítʃi]

a. 마녀의, 마녀 같은, 마녀적인; 마법에 의한
A witchy person looks or behaves like a witch. Witchy things are associated with witches.

pick up^{복습}

phrasal v. 알아채다; 줍다, 들다; 되찾다, 회복하다
When you pick something up, you identify or recognize it.

hum^{복습}
[hʌm]

v. 콧노래를 부르다; (벌 · 기계 등이) 윙윙거리다; n. 윙윙(소리)
When you hum a tune, you sing it with your lips closed.

gift^{***}
[gift]

n. 천부적인 재능, 선물
If someone has a gift for doing something, they have a natural ability for doing it.

light^{복습}
[lait]

v. (lit/lighted–lit/lighted) 밝게 하다; 불을 붙이다, 빛을 비추다; n. 빛
If a person's eyes or face light up, or something lights them up, they become bright with excitement or happiness.

burglar^{복습}
[bə́:rglər]

n. 강도, 밤도둑
A burglar is a thief who enters a house or other building by force.

go on^{복습}

phrasal v. 앞으로 가다, 나아가다; 계속하다; 자자, 어서
When you go on something, you behave or act on it ahead of others.

squeeze^{복습}
[skwi:z]

vt. 비집고 들어가다; 꽉 쥐다[죄다]; n. 압착, 짜냄; 꽉 끌어안음
If you squeeze a person or thing somewhere or if they squeeze there, they manage to get through or into a small space.

nod^{복습}
[nɔd]

v. 끄덕이다, 끄덕여 표시하다; n. (동의 · 인사 · 신호 · 명령의) 끄덕임
If you nod, you move your head downward and upward to show agreement, understanding, or approval.

creep^{복습}
[kri:p]

vi. 살금살금 걷다, 기다; n. 포복
If something creeps somewhere, it moves very slowly.

dust^{복습}
[dʌst]

n. 먼지, 가루, 티끌; v. 먼지를 털다
Dust is the very small pieces of dirt which you find inside buildings, for example on furniture, floors, or lights.

storm^{복습}
[stɔ:rm]

n. 폭풍우; vi. 돌진하다; 격노하다
A storm is very bad weather, with heavy rain, strong winds, and often thunder and lightning.

settle^{복습}
[setl]

v. (편하게) 앉다, 자리를 잡다; (논쟁 등을) 해결하다, 끝내다; 안정되다, 진정되다
If you settle yourself somewhere or settle somewhere, you sit down or make yourself comfortable.

fall asleep

phrasal v. 잠들다, 곯아떨어지다
When you fall asleep, you start sleeping.

tight^{복습}
[tait]

ad. 단단히, 꽉; a. 단단한, 팽팽한, 빈틈없는
If you hold someone or something tight, you hold them firmly and securely.

132

wheeze
[hwiːz]

v. 씨근거리다, 숨을 헐떡이다; n. 씨근거리는 소리, 숨을 헐떡이는 소리
If someone wheezes, they breathe with difficulty and make a whistling sound.

whistle^{복습}
[hwisl]

v. 휘파람 불다; n. 휘파람; 호각
When you whistle or when you whistle a tune, you make a series of musical notes by forcing your breath out between your lips, or your teeth.

tear^{복습}
[tɛər]

① v. (tore–torn) 찢다, 찢어지다; 부리나케 가다; n. 찢음 ② n. 눈물
If you tear paper, cloth, or another material, or if it tears, you destroy it by pulling it into two pieces.

hymn[*]
[him]

n. (교회의) 찬송가, 찬미가
A hymn is a religious song that Christians sing in church.

lie^{복습}
[lai]

vi. (lay–lain) 눕다, 누워 있다; 놓여 있다, 위치하다; 거짓말하다; n. 거짓말
If you are lying somewhere, you are in a horizontal position and are not standing or sitting.

swell^{복습}
[swel]

v. 넘실거리다, 넘치다; 부풀다, 팽창하다
If you swell with a feeling, you are suddenly full of that feeling.

pure^{복습}
[pjuər]

a. 순전한, 완전한; 순수한, 맑은
Pure means complete and total.

snore^{복습}
[snɔːr]

v. 코를 골다
When someone who is asleep snores, they make a loud noise each time they breathe.

Check Your Reading Speed

1분에 몇 단어를 읽는지 리딩 속도를 측정해보세요.

$$\frac{820 \text{ words}}{\text{reading time ( ) sec}} \times 60 = (\quad) \text{ WPM}$$

Build Your Vocabulary

breeze
[bri:z]

n. 산들바람, 미풍; vi. 산들산들 불다
A breeze is a gentle wind.

hang^{복습}
[hæŋ]

v. 매달리다; 걸다, 달아매다; 교수형에 처하다
If something hangs in a high place or position, or if you hang it there, it is attached there so it does not touch the ground.

empty^{복습}
[émpti]

a. 빈, 공허한; vt. 비우다
If you feel empty, you feel unhappy and have no energy, usually because you are very tired or have just experienced something upsetting.

all the way^{복습}

idiom 내내, 시종
If you have been doing something all the way, you are emphasizing the period of time during the whole journey.

promise^{복습}
[prámis]

vt. 약속하다; n. 약속, 계약
If you promise that you will do something, you say to someone that you will definitely do it.

underneath^{복습}
[ʌndərní:θ]

prep. ~의 아래에; ~의 지배하에; ~에 숨어서
If one thing is underneath another, it is directly under it, and may be covered or hidden by it.

stare^{복습}
[stɛər]

v. 응시하다, 뚫어지게 보다
If you stare at someone or something, you look at them for a long time.

constellation^{복습}
[kànstəléiʃən]

n. [천문] 별자리, 성좌
A constellation is a group of stars which form a pattern and have a name.

planet^{**}
[plǽnit]

n. 행성
A planet is a large, round object in space that moves around a star.

crawl^{**}
[krɔ:l]

vi. 기어가다, 느릿느릿 가다; 우글거리다; n. 서행; 기어감
When you crawl, you move forward on your hands and knees.

leaf^{복습}
[li:f]

n. (pl. leaves) 잎, 한 장
The leaves of a tree or plant are the parts that are flat, thin, and usually green.

134

branch ^{복습}
[bræntʃ]

n. 가지; 지점; 분파; v. 가지를 내다
The branches of a tree are the parts that grow out from its trunk and have leaves, flowers, or fruit growing on them.

pray ^{복습}
[prei]

v. 기도하다, 기원하다, 빌다
When people pray, they speak to God in order to give thanks or to ask for his help.

bald ^{복습}
[bɔːld]

a. (머리 등이) 벗어진, 대머리의; vi. 머리가 벗어지다
Someone who is bald has little or no hair on the top of their head.

witch ^{복습}
[witʃ]

n. 마녀
In fairy stories, a witch is a woman, usually an old woman, who has evil magic powers.

tease ^{복습}
[tiːz]

v. 놀리다, 괴롭히다; 졸라대다; n. 골리기
To tease someone means to laugh at them or make jokes about them in order to embarrass, annoy, or upset them.

hold out ^{복습}

phrasal v. (손 혹은 손에 든 것을) 내밀다, 내뻗다
If you hold out your hand, you move your hand away from your body, for example to shake hands.

race ^{**}
[reis]

① v. 경주하다; 질주하다, 달리다; n. 경주 ② n. 인종, 민족
If you race, you take part in a race.

warn ^{***}
[wɔːrn]

v. 경고하다; ~에게 통지하다
If you warn someone about something such as a possible danger or problem, you tell them about it so that they are aware of it.

beat ^{복습}
[biːt]

v. 이기다, 패배시키다; 치다, 두드리다; n. [음악] 박자, 고동
If you beat someone in a competition or election, you defeat them.

porch ^{복습}
[pɔːrtʃ]

n. (본 건물 입구에 달린 지붕이 있는) 현관, 포치
A porch is a sheltered area at the entrance to a building, which has a roof and sometimes has walls.

trip ^{복습}
[trip]

v. 걸려 넘어지다; 경쾌한 걸음걸이로 걷다; n. 여행
If you trip when you are walking, you knock your foot against something and fall or nearly fall.

lap ^{복습}
[læp]

① n. 무릎; (트랙의) 한 바퀴 ② v. (파도가) 찰싹거리다; (할짝할짝) 핥다
If you have something on your lap, it is on top of your legs and near to your body.

(would you) care for ^{복습}

idiom ~하시겠어요?; ~을 좋아하다
People use 'would you care for' to ask someone if they would like something to eat or drink.

pass ^{***}
[pæs]

v. 건네주다, 지나가다, 통과하다; n. 통행, 통과
If you pass something to someone, you take it in your hand and give it to them.

bowl ^{복습}
[boul]

n. 사발, 그릇, 공기
A bowl is a round container with a wide uncovered top.

unwrap ^{복습}
[ʌnrǽp]

v. (포장 등을) 풀다
When you unwrap something, you take off the paper, plastic, or other covering that is around it.

jar ^{복습}
[dʒɑːr]

① n. 병, 단지 ② v. 덜컹덜컹 흔들리다; 삐걱거리다; n. 삐걱거리는 소리, 잡음
A jar is a glass container with a lid that is used for storing food.

lean ^{복습}
[liːn]

① v. 기울다, 몸을 구부리다; 기대다, 의지하다 ② a. 야윈, 마른
When you lean in a particular direction, you bend your body in that direction.

pinch ^{복습}
[pintʃ]

v. 여위게 하다, 초췌하게 하다; 꼬집다; n. 꼬집기 (pinch-faced a. 파리한 얼굴의)
If someone's face is pinched, it looks thin and pale, usually because they are ill or old.

crack ^{복습}
[kræk]

v. 날카로운 소리가 나다; 금이 가다, 깨다; n. 갑작스런 날카로운 소리; 갈라진 금
If something cracks, or if you crack it, it makes a sharp sound like the sound of a piece of wood breaking.

knuckle ^{복습}
[nʌkl]

n. 손가락 관절[마디]; v. 손가락 마디로 치다
Your knuckles are the rounded pieces of bone that form lumps on your hands where your fingers join your hands, and where your fingers bend.

echo *
[ékou]

v. (남의 말·의견을) 그대로 되풀이하다; 울려 퍼지다, 메아리치다; n. 메아리
If you echo someone's words, you repeat them or express agreement with their attitude or opinion.

sit up ^{복습}

phrasal v. 일어나 앉다
If you sit up, you move yourself into a sitting position, for example, from lying down.

strum
[strʌm]

v. (현악기를) 가볍게 퉁기다, 연주하다; n. 가볍게 타기
If you strum a stringed instrument such as a guitar, you play it by moving your fingers backward and forward across the strings.

flavor ^{복습}
[fléivər]

n. 맛, 풍미, 향
The flavor of a food or drink is its taste.

bloom **
[bluːm]

v. 꽃이 피다, 개화하다; 번영시키다; n. 꽃
When a flower blooms, it opens.

136

수고하셨습니다!

드디어 끝까지 다 읽으셨군요! 축하드립니다! 여러분은 이 책을 통해 총 22,123개의 단어를 읽으셨고, 800개 이상의 어휘와 표현들을 익히셨습니다. 이 책에 나온 어휘는 다른 원서를 읽을 때에도 빈번히 만날 수 있는 필수 어휘들입니다. 이 책을 읽었던 경험은 비슷한 수준의 다른 원서들을 읽을 때 큰 도움이 될 것입니다. 이제 자신의 상황에 맞게 원서를 반복해서 읽거나, 오디오북을 들어 볼 수 있습니다. 혹은 비슷한 수준의 다른 원서를 찾아 읽는 것도 좋습니다. 일단 원서를 완독한 뒤에 어떻게 계속 영어 공부를 이어갈 수 있을지, 도움말을 꼼꼼히 살펴보고 각자 상황에 맞게 적용해 보세요!

리딩(Reading)을 확실하게 다지고 싶다면? 반복해서 읽어 보세요!

리딩 실력을 탄탄하게 다지고 싶다면, 같은 원서를 2~3번 반복해서 읽을 것을 권합니다. 같은 책을 여러 번 읽으면 지루할 것 같지만, 꼭 그렇지도 않습니다. 반복해서 읽을 때 처음과 주안점을 다르게 두면, 전혀 다른 느낌으로 재미있게 읽을 수 있습니다.

처음 원서를 읽을 때는 생소한 단어들과 스토리로 인해 읽으면서 곧바로 이해하기가 매우 힘들 수 있습니다. 전체 맥락을 잡고 읽어도 약간 버거운 느낌이지요. 하지만 반복해서 읽기 시작하면 달라집니다. 일단 내용을 파악한 상황이기 때문에 문장 구조나 어휘의 활용에 더 집중하게 되고, 조금 더 깊이 있게 읽을 수 있습니다. 좋은 표현과 문장을 수집하고 메모할 만한 여유도 생기게 되지요. 어휘도 많이 익숙해졌기 때문에 리딩 속도에도 탄력이 붙습니다. 처음 읽을 때는 '내용'에서 재미를 느꼈다면, 반복해서 읽을 때에는 '영어'에서 재미를 느끼게 되는 것입니다. 따라서 리딩 실력을 더욱 확고하게 다지고자 한다면, 같은 책을 2~3회 정도 반복해서 읽을 것을 권해 드립니다.

리스닝(Listening) 실력을 늘리고 싶다면?
귀를 통해서 읽어 보세요!

많은 영어 학습자들이 '리스닝이 안 돼서 문제'라고 한탄합니다. 그리고 리스닝 실력을 늘리는 방법으로 무슨 뜻인지 몰라도 반복해서 듣는 '무작정 듣기'를 선택합니다. 하지만 뜻도 모르면서 무작정 듣는 일에는 엄청난 인내력이 필요합니다. 그래서 대부분 며칠 시도하다가 포기해 버리고 말지요.

따라서 모르는 내용을 무작정 듣는 것보다는 어느 정도 알고 있는 내용을 반복해서 듣는 것이 더 효과적인 듣기 방법입니다. 그리고 이런 방식의 듣기에 활용할 수 있는 가장 좋은 교재가 오디오북입니다.

리스닝 실력을 향상하고 싶다면, 이 책에서 제공하는 오디오북을 이용해서 듣는 연습을 해 보세요. 활용법은 간단합니다. 일단 책을 한 번 완독했다면, 오디오북을 통해 다시 들어 보는 것입니다. 휴대 기기에 넣어 시간이 날 때 틈틈이 듣는 것도 좋고, 책상에 앉아 눈으로는 텍스트를 보며 귀로 읽는 것도 좋습니다. 이미 읽었던 내용이라 이해하기가 훨씬 수월하고, 애매했던 발음들도 자연스럽게 교정할 수 있습니다. 또 성우의 목소리 연기를 듣다 보면 내용이 더욱 생동감 있게 다가와 이해도가 높아지는 효과도 거둘 수 있습니다.

반대로 듣기에 자신 있는 사람이라면, 책을 읽기 전에 처음부터 오디오북을 먼저 듣는 것도 좋은 방법입니다. 귀를 통해 책을 쭉 읽어보고, 이후에 다시 눈으로 책을 읽으면서 잘 들리지 않았던 부분들을 보충하는 것이지요.

중요한 것은 내용을 따라가면서, 내용에 푹 빠져서 반복해 들어야 한다는 것입니다. 이렇게 연습을 반복해서 눈으로 읽지 않은 책이라도 '귀를 통해' 읽을 수 있을 정도가 되면, 리스닝으로 고생하는 일은 거의 없을 것입니다.

왼쪽의 QR 코드를 인식하여 정식 오디오북을 들어 보세요!
더불어 롱테일북스 홈페이지(www.longtailbooks.co.kr)에서도
오디오북 MP3 파일을 다운로드 받을 수 있습니다.

스피킹(Speaking)이 고민이라면? 소리 내어 읽어 보세요!

스피킹 역시 많은 학습자들이 고민하는 부분입니다. 스피킹이 고민이라면, 원서를 큰 소리로 읽는 낭독 훈련(Voice Reading)을 해 보세요!
'소리 내어 읽는 것이 말하기에 정말로 도움이 될까?'라고 의아한 생각이 들 수도 있습니다. 하지만 인간의 두뇌 입장에서 봤을 때, 성대 구조를 활용해서 '발화'한다는 점에서는 소리 내어 읽기와 말하기에 큰 차이가 없다고 합니다. 소리 내어 읽는 것은 '타인의 생각'을 전달하고, 직접 말하는 것은 '자신의 생각'을 전달한다는 차이가 있을 뿐, 머릿속에서 문장을 처리하고 조음기관(혀와 성대 등)을 움직여 의미를 만든다는 점에서 같은 과정인 것이지요. 따라서 소리 내어 읽는 연습을 꾸준히 하는 것은 스피킹 연습에 큰 도움이 됩니다.
소리 내어 읽기를 하는 방법은 간단합니다. 일단 오디오북을 들으면서 성우의 목소리를 최대한 따라 하며 같이 읽어 보세요. 발음뿐 아니라 억양, 어조, 느낌까지 완벽히 따라 한다고 생각하면서 소리 내어 읽습니다. 따라 읽는 것이 조금 익숙해지면, 옆의 누군가에게 이 책을 읽어 준다는 생각으로 소리 내어 계속 읽어 나갑니다. 한 번 눈과 귀로 읽었던 책이기 때문에 보다 수월하게 진행할 수 있고, 자연스럽게 어휘와 표현을 복습하는 효과도 거두게 됩니다. 또 이렇게 소리 내어 읽은 것을 녹음해서 들어 보면 스스로에게도 좋은 피드백이 됩니다.
최근 말하기가 강조되면서 소리 내어 읽기가 크게 각광을 받고 있기는 하지만, 그렇다고 소리 내어 읽기가 무조건 좋은 것만은 아닙니다. 책을 소리 내어 읽다 보면, 무의식적으로 속으로 발음을 하는 습관을 가지게 되어 리딩 속도 자체는 오히려 크게 떨어지는 현상이 발생할 수 있습니다. 따라서 빠른 리딩 속도가 중요한 수험생이나 상위권 학습자들에게는 소리 내어 읽기가 적절하지 않은 방법입니다. 효과가 좋다는 말만 믿고 무턱대고 따라 하기보다는 자신의 필요에 맞게 우선순위를 정하고 원서를 활용하는 것이 좋습니다.

라이팅(Writing)까지 욕심이 난다면? 요약하는 연습을 해 보세요!

원서를 라이팅 연습에 직접적으로 활용하는 데에는 한계가 있지만, 적절히 활용하면 원서도 유용한 라이팅 자료가 될 수 있습니다.

특히 책을 읽고 그 내용을 요약하는 연습은 큰 도움이 됩니다. 요약 훈련의 방식도 간단합니다. 원서를 읽고 그날 읽은 분량만큼 혹은 책을 다 읽고 전체 내용을 기반으로, 책 내용을 한번 요약하고 나의 느낌을 영어로 적어보는 것입니다.

이때 그 책에 나왔던 단어와 표현을 최대한 활용하여 요약하는 것이 중요합니다. 영어 표현력은 결국 얼마나 다양한 어휘로 많은 표현을 해 보았느냐가 좌우하게 됩니다. 이런 면에서 내가 읽은 책을, 그 책에 나온 문장과 어휘로 다시 표현해 보는 것은 매우 효율적인 방법입니다. 책에 나온 어휘와 표현을 단순히 읽고 무슨 말인지 아는 정도가 아니라, 실제로 직접 활용해서 쓸 수 있을 만큼 확실하게 익히게 되는 것이지요. 여기에 첨삭까지 받을 수 있는 방법이 있다면 금상첨화입니다.

이러한 '표현하기' 연습은 스피킹 훈련에도 그대로 적용될 수 있습니다. 책을 읽고 그 내용을 3분 안에 다른 사람에게 영어로 말하는 연습을 해 보세요. 순발력과 표현력을 기르는 좋은 훈련이 될 것입니다.

꾸준히 원서를 읽고 싶다면? 뉴베리 수상작을 계속 읽어 보세요!

뉴베리 상이 세계 최고 권위의 아동 문학상인 만큼, 그 수상작들은 확실히 완성도를 검증받은 작품이라고 할 수 있습니다. 특히 '쉬운 어휘로 쓰인 깊이 있는 문장'으로 이루어졌다는 점이 영어 학습자들에게 큰 호응을 얻고 있습니다. 이렇게 '검증된 원서'를 꾸준히 읽는 것은 영어 실력 향상에 큰 도움이 됩니다.

아래에 수준별로 제시된 뉴베리 수상작 목록을 보며 적절한 책들을 찾아 계속 읽어 보세요. 꼭 뉴베리 수상작이 아니더라도 마음에 드는 작가의 다른 책을 읽어 보는 것 또한 아주 좋은 방법입니다.

• 영어 초보자도 쉽게 읽을 만한 아주 쉬운 수준. 소리 내어 읽기에도 아주 적합.
Sarah, Plain and Tall*(Medal, 8,331단어), The Hundred Penny Box (Honor, 5,878단어), The Hundred Dresses*(Honor, 7,329단어), My Father's Dragon (Honor, 7,682단어), 26 Fairmount Avenue (Honor, 6,737단어)

- 중 · 고등학생 정도 영어 학습자라면 쉽게 읽을 수 있는 수준. 소리 내어 읽기에도 비교적 적합한 편.

Because of Winn-Dixie* (Honor, 22,123단어), What Jamie Saw (Honor, 17,203단어), Charlotte's Web (Honor, 31,938단어), Dear Mr. Henshaw (Medal, 18,145단어), Missing May (Medal, 17,509단어)

- 대학생 정도 영어 학습자라면 무난한 수준. 소리 내어 읽기에 적합하지 않음.

Number The Stars* (Medal, 27,197단어), A Single Shard (Medal, 33,726단어), The Tale of Despereaux* (Medal, 32,375단어), Hatchet* (Medal, 42,328단어), Bridge to Terabithia (Medal, 32,888단어), A Fine White Dust (Honor, 19,022단어), Jennifer, Hecate, Macbeth, William McKinley and Me, Elizabeth (Honor, 23,266단어)

- 원서 완독 경험을 가진 학습자에게 적절한 수준. 소리 내어 읽기에 적합하지 않음.

The Giver* (Medal, 43,617단어), From the Mixed-Up Files of Mrs. Basil E. Frankweiler (Medal, 30,906단어), The View from Saturday (Medal, 42,685단어), Holes* (Medal, 47,079단어), Criss Cross (Medal, 48,221단어), Walk Two Moons (Medal, 59,400단어), The Graveyard Book (Medal, 67,380단어)

뉴베리 수상작과 뉴베리 수상 작가의 좋은 작품을 엄선한 「뉴베리 컬렉션」에도 위 목록에 있는 도서 중 상당수가 포함될 예정입니다.

★ 「뉴베리 컬렉션」으로 이미 출간된 도서

어떤 책들이 출간되었는지 확인하려면, 지금 인터넷서점에서
뉴베리 컬렉션을 검색해 보세요.

뉴베리 수상작을 동영상 강의로 만나 보세요!

영어원서 전문 동영상 강의 사이트 영서당(yseodang.com)에서는 뉴베리 컬렉션 『Holes』, 『Because of Winn-Dixie』, 『The Miraculous Journey of Edward Tulane』, 『Wayside School』 시리즈 등의 동영상 강의를 제공하고 있습니다. 뉴베리 수상작이라는 최고의 영어 교재와 EBS 출신 인기 강사가 만난 명강의! 지금 사이트를 방문해서 무료 샘플 강의를 들어 보세요!

'스피드 리딩 카페'를 통해 원서 읽기 습관을 길러 보세요!

일상에서 영어를 한마디도 쓰지 않는 비영어권 국가에서 살고 있는 우리가 영어 환경에 가장 쉽고, 편하고, 부담 없이 노출되는 방법은 바로 '영어원서 읽기'입니다. 언제 어디서든 원서를 붙잡고 읽기만 하면 곧바로 영어를 접하는 환경이 만들어지기 때문이지요. 하루에 20분씩만 꾸준히 읽는다면, 1년에 무려 120시간 동안 영어에 노출될 수 있습니다. 이러한 이유 때문에 영어 교육 전문가들이 영어 원서 읽기를 추천하는 것이지요.

하지만 원서 읽기가 좋다는 것을 알아도 막상 꾸준히 읽는 것은 쉽지 않습니다. 그럴 때에는 13만 명 이상의 회원을 보유한 국내 최대 원서 읽기 동호회 〈스피드 리딩 카페〉(cafe.naver.com/readingtc)를 방문해 보세요.

원서별로 정리된 무료 PDF 단어장과 수준별 추천 원서 목록 등 유용한 자료는 물론, 뉴베리 수상작을 포함한 다양한 원서의 리뷰를 무료로 확인할 수 있습니다. 특히 함께 모여서 원서를 읽는 '북클럽'은 중간에 포기하지 않고 원서를 끝까지 읽는 습관을 기르는 데 큰 도움이 될 것입니다.

Answer Key

Chapters One & Two

1. B   I walked into the produce section of the Winn-Dixie grocery store to pick out my two tomatoes and I almost bumped right into the store manager. He was standing there all red-faced, screaming and waving his arms around. "Who let a dog in here?" he kept on shouting. "Who let a dirty dog in here?"

2. A   He skidded to a stop and smiled right at me. I had never before in my life seen a dog smile, but that is what he did.

3. C   He was big, but skinny; you could see his ribs. And there were bald patches all over him, places where he didn't have any fur at all. Mostly, he looked like a big piece of old brown carpet that had been left out in the rain.

4. B   But he calls me by my second name, Opal, because that was his mother's name.

5. D   My daddy is a good preacher and a nice man, but sometimes it's hard for me to think about him as my daddy because he spends so much time preaching or thinking about preaching or getting ready to preach.

6. A   When we got to the Friendly Corners Trailer Park, I told Winn-Dixie that he had to behave right and be quiet, because this was an all adult trailer park and the only reason I got to live in it was because the preacher was a preacher and I was a good, quiet kid.

7. D   I stared at the preacher really hard. Sometimes he reminded me of a turtle hiding inside its shell, in there thinking about things and not ever sticking his head out into the world.

Chapters Three & Four

1. C   But I don't have a mama. I mean, I have one, but I don't know where she is. She left when I was three years old.

2. B   "I don't even have any friends, because I had to leave them all behind when we

144

moved here from Watley."

3. D   "I want to know more about her. But I'm afraid to ask the preacher; I'm afraid he'll get mad at me."

4. C   "I've been talking to him and he agreed with me that, since I'm ten years old, you should tell me ten things about my mama. Just ten things, that's all."

5. A   "Two," he said. "She had red hair and freckles." "Just like me," I said. "Just like you." The preacher nodded.

6. C   "Five," he said. "She couldn't cook. She burned everything, including water."

7. A   I wanted to know those ten things inside and out. That way, if my mama ever came back, I could recognize her, and I would be able to grab her and hold on to her tight and not let her get away from me again.

Chapters Five & Six

1. A   Winn-Dixie couldn't stand to be left alone; we found that out real quick.

2. C   The building used to be a Pick- It-Quick store, and when you walk in the front door, the first thing you see is the Pick-It-Quick motto.

3. B   And he wasn't but two or three words into his sermon when there was a terrible howl outside.

4. A   Winn-Dixie stood up there in front of the whole church, wagging his tail and holding the mouse real careful in his mouth, holding on to him tight but not squishing him.

5. D   I prayed for my mama. . . . And then I talked to God about how I was lonely in Naomi because I didn't know that many kids, only the ones from church. . . . And finally I prayed for the mouse, like the preacher suggested.

6. D   But I showed him how he could stand up on his hind legs and look in the window and see me in there, selecting my books; and he was okay, as long as he could see me.

7. A   But the thing was, the first time Miss Franny Block saw Winn-Dixie standing up on his hind legs like that, looking in the window, she didn't think he was a dog. She thought he was a bear.

Chapters Seven & Eight

1. B   "And I was a little girl who loved to read. So I told him, I said, 'Daddy, I would most certainly love to have a library for my birthday; a small little library would

be wonderful.' "

2. B   "He went. But this is what I will never forget. He took the book with him.

3. A   "No, I never saw him again. Well, the men in town used to tease me about it. They used to say, 'Miss Franny, we saw that bear of yours out in the woods today. . . .' "

4. D   "I finished Johnny Tremain and I enjoyed it very much. I would like something even more difficult to read now, because I am an advanced reader."

5. D   I said, "I don't get a big enough allowance to afford something this fancy. But I love this collar and leash, and so does my dog, and I was thinking that maybe you could set me up on an installment plan."

6. A   "Or I could work for you," I said. "I could come in and sweep the floors and dust the shelves and take out the trash. I could do that."

7. C   "I'm going to be six years old in September. I got to stop sucking on my knuckle once I'm six," said Sweetie Pie. "I'm having a party. Do you want to come to my party? The theme is pink."

Chapters Nine & Ten

1. B   Neither one of them had any hair on his head, because their mama shaved their heads every week during the summer because of the one time Dunlap got fleas in his hair from their cat, Sadie.

2. A   "You better go get your dog out of there," Dunlap said. "The witch will eat that dog," Stevie said.

3. D   "This dog sure likes peanut butter," she said. "You can always trust a dog that likes peanut butter."

4. A   "I can't see nothing but the general shape of things, so I got to rely on my heart."

5. B   What Gloria Dump picked for me to grow was a tree. Or she said it was a tree. To me, it looked more like a plant. She had me dig a hole for it and put it in the ground and pat the dirt around it tight, like it was a baby and I was tucking it into bed.

6. C   That night when the preacher was tucking me into bed, I told him how I got a job at Gertrude's Pets, and I told him all about making friends with Miss Franny Block and getting invited to Sweetie Pie's party, and I told him about meeting Gloria Dump.

7. A   Winn-Dixie looked at the preacher. He didn't smile at him, but he opened his mouth wide like he was laughing, like the preacher had just told him the funniest joke in the world, and this is what amazed me the most: the preacher laughed back.

Chapters Eleven & Twelve

1. D   But what woke me up wasn't the thunder and lightning. It was Winn-Dixie, whining and butting his head against my bedroom door.

2. B   I stood up and opened the door and Winn-Dixie flew through it like something big and ugly and mean was chasing him.

3. B   He said, "Opal, I believe Winn-Dixie has a pathological fear of thunderstorms."

4. C   I looked around to see where it was coming from, and that's when I noticed that all the animals were out of their cages. . . . He was playing a guitar and he had on skinny pointy-toed cowboy boots and he was tapping them while he was playing the music. . . . Just then, Gertrude caught sight of Winn-Dixie. "Dog," she croaked, and flew over and landed on his head.

5. C   "I have been in jail," Otis said. He looked up at me real quick and then looked back down at his boots.

6. B   I waved at the woman on the porch and she waved back, and I watched Sweetie Pie run off to tell her mama about Otis being a magic man.

7. D   I had a feeling that these were the kind of stories my mama would like, the kind that would make her laugh out loud, the way the preacher said she liked to laugh.

Chapters Thirteen & Fourteen

1. D   But my favorite place to be that summer was in Gloria Dump's yard. And I figured it was Winn-Dixie's favorite place to be, too, because when we got up to the last block before her house, Winn-Dixie would break away from my bike and start to run for all he was worth, heading for Gloria Dump's backyard and his spoonful of peanut butter.

2. D   "Otis is not retarded," I said. "And my daddy knows that he was in jail." That was a lie.

3. A   "Why don't you play with them boys?" Gloria asked me. "Because they're ignorant," I told her.

4. C   "Look at this tree," Gloria said. I looked up. There were bottles hanging from just about every branch.

5. A   "Mmmm-hmmm," said Gloria. "More than that." "But you're the nicest person I know," I told her.

6. B   "There's whiskey bottles on there," I told her. "And beer bottles." "Child," said Gloria Dump, "I know that. I'm the one who put 'em there. I'm the one who drank what was in 'em."

7. A   But in the meantime, you got to remember, you can't always judge people by the things they done. You got to judge them by what they are doing now.

Chapters Fifteen & Sixteen

1. D   Sometimes, when Miss Franny was telling a story, she would have a fit. They were small fits and they didn't last long. But what happened was she would forget what she was saying. She would just stop and start to shake like a little leaf.

2. A   I wanted to comfort Gloria Dump. And I decided that the best way to do that would be to read her a book, read it to her loud enough to keep the ghosts away.

3. B   "I know about the Civil War," I told her. "That was the war between the South and the North over slavery." "Slavery, yes," said Miss Franny. "It was also about states' rights and money. It was a terrible war. . . ."

4. A   ". . . Littmus told his mama that he could not stand by and let the South get beat, and so he went to fight, too." . . . "Anyway, Littmus went and enlisted. He lied about his age. . . ."

5. D   "You cannot imagine. Littmus was hungry all the time. And he was covered with all manner of vermin: fleas and lice. And in the winter, he was so cold he thought for sure he would freeze to death. . . . And he got shot at quite a bit. And he was nothing more than a child." "Did he get killed?" I asked Miss Franny. "Good grief," said Amanda. She rolled her eyes. "Now, Opal," Miss Franny said, "I wouldn't be standing in this room telling this story if he was killed.

6. A   He walked. And when he got home, there was no home there." "Where was it?" I asked her. I didn't care if Amanda thought I was stupid. I wanted to know. "Why," Miss Franny shouted so loud that Winn-Dixie and Amanda Wilkinson and me all jumped, "the Yankees burned it! Yes ma'am. Burned it to the ground."

7. C   "What about his sisters?" Amanda asked. She moved around the desk and came and sat on the floor. She looked up at Miss Franny. "What happened to them?" "Dead. Dead of typhoid fever."

Chapters Seventeen & Eighteen

1. B   When he finally finished crying, he had the strangest sensation. He felt like he wanted something sweet. He wanted a piece of candy.

2. C   "Planning what?" I asked. "Why, planning the candy factory." "Did he build it?" I asked. "Of course he did. It's still standing out on Fairville Road."

3. C   "There's a secret ingredient in there," Miss Franny said. "I know it," I told her. "I can taste it. What is it?" "Sorrow," Miss Franny said. "Not everybody can taste it. Children, especially, seem to have a hard time knowing it's there."

4. D   "It makes me miss Carson," said Amanda. She sounded like she was going to cry. "I have to go."

5. B   "Sad," said the preacher. He rubbed his nose some more. "It makes me think of your mother."

6. B   "I think you should apologize," said the preacher. "Me?" I said. "Yes," he said. "You. You tell Stevie you're sorry if you said anything that hurt his feelings. I'm sure he just wants to be your friend."

7. A   "Do you know something about her and somebody named Carson?" "Carson was her brother. He drowned last year."

Chapters Nineteen & Twenty

1. C   He nodded his head. "It tastes good, but it also tastes a little bit like being in jail."

2. D   "I wouldn't stop playing my guitar. Used to be I played it on the street and sometimes people would give me money. . . . Anyway, the police came. And they told me to stop it. . . . They tried to put handcuffs on me." He sighed. "I didn't like that. I wouldn't have been able to play my guitar with them things on." "And then what happened?" I asked him. "I hit them," he whispered.

3. A   I swept the floor real slow that day. I wanted to keep Otis company. I didn't want him to be lonely. Sometimes it seemed like everybody in the world was lonely.

4. D   Sweetie Pie came in and I gave her a Littmus Lozenge, and she spit it right out; she said that it tasted bad. She said that it tasted like not having a dog.

5. B   I couldn't stand to think about sad things that couldn't be helped any more, so I said, "Do you want to hear some more Gone with the Wind?"

6. D   "You got to invite them Dewberry boys." "Dunlap and Stevie?" "Hmmm-mmm, ain't gonna be no party unless you invite them." "I have to?" "Yes," said Gloria Dump. "You promise me." "I promise," I said. I didn't like the idea. But I promised.

7. C   The last person I asked was Otis. I told him all about the party and that he was invited and he said, "No, thank you." "Why not?" I asked. "I don't like parties," said Otis.

Chapters Twenty-One & Twenty-Two

1. D   And the afternoon before, we worked in Gloria's kitchen and made egg-salad sandwiches. . . . The last thing we did was decorate the yard all up. I strung pink and orange and yellow crêpe paper in the trees to make it look fancy. We also filled up paper bags with sand and put candles in them, and right before it was time for the party to start, I went around and lit all the candles.

2. C   Miss Franny Block was the first person to arrive. She was wearing a pretty green dress that was all shiny and shimmery.

3. B   Sweetie Pie had a whole handful of pictures of dogs that she had cut out of magazines.

4. A   And sure enough, standing there on the sidewalk was Otis. He had his guitar on his back and Gertrude on his shoulder, and in his hands he was holding the biggest jar of pickles I had ever seen in my life.

5. A   ". . . And we got a preacher, who can bless this party for us." Gloria Dump looked over at the preacher. He nodded his head at Gloria and cleared his throat and said, "Dear God, thank you for warm summer nights and candlelight and good food. . . . We pray in Christ's name. Amen."

6. B   "Opal," said Gloria, "when are them boys getting here?" "I don't know," I said. I shrugged. "I told them what time we were starting." What I didn't tell her was that they probably weren't coming, because they were afraid to go to a party at a witch's house.

7. D   The preacher looked up at the sky. And just then, the rain came pouring down.

Chapters Twenty-Three & Twenty-Four

1. A   . . . and when I ran back outside, I saw that Amanda had hold of Miss Franny Block and was helping her into the house.

2. C   "Where's Winn-Dixie?" I shouted. "I forgot about him. I was just thinking about the party and I forgot about Winn-Dixie. I forgot about protecting him from the thunder."

3. A   "There ain't no way you can hold on to something that wants to go, you understand? You can only love what you got while you got it."

4. C   I turned around and looked back, and the last thing I saw was the porch light shining on Dunlap Dewberry's bald head.

5. C   Number one was that he had a pathological fear of thunderstorms. . . . Number four was that he snored. . . . Number eight was he couldn't stand to be left alone.

. . . Number ten was he didn't mind going to church.

6. D   "I tried," he said. "I tried." Then he did something I couldn't believe. He started to cry.

7. A   When I told you your mama took everything with her, I forgot one thing, one very important thing that she left behind." "What?" I asked. "You," he said. "Thank God your mama left me you."

Chapters Twenty-Five & Twenty-Six

1. D   We walked up Gloria's sidewalk and around the back, through her yard and into her kitchen, and what we saw was Otis playing his guitar, and Miss Franny and Gloria sitting there smiling and singing, and Gloria holding Sweetie Pie in her lap. Amanda and Dunlap and Stevie were sitting on the kitchen floor, clapping along and having the best possible time. Even Amanda was smiling. . . . She took her cane and poked at something under her chair. "Come on out of there," she said.

2. B   ". . . We got Otis to play them and we started singing them, teaching the words to these children." "And then somebody sneezed," Sweetie Pie shouted.

3. C   "That dog of yours was all hid underneath my bed, squeezed under there like the world was about to end.

4. A   ". . . He misses you and I miss you, but my heart doesn't feel empty any more. It's full all the way up. I'll still think about you, I promise. But probably not as much as I did this summer."

5. B   And then I remembered my own tree, the one Gloria had helped me plant. I hadn't looked at it for a long time. I went crawling around on my hands and knees, searching for it.

6. D   And then he surprised me. He did something I never in a million years thought a Dewberry boy would do. He held out his hand to help me up.

7. C   "Let's sing," said Sweetie Pie, opening her eyes and sitting up straight. "Let's sing for the dog."

BECAUSE OF WINN-DIXIE

1판 1쇄   2012년 11월 12일
2판 2쇄   2025년 1월 20일

지은이   Kate DiCamillo
기획   이수영
책임편집   김보경 차소향
콘텐츠제작및감수   롱테일 교육 연구소
저작권   명채린
마케팅   두잉글 사업본부

펴낸이   이수영
펴낸곳   롱테일북스
출판등록   제2015-000191호
주소   04033 서울특별시 마포구 양화로 113, 3층(서교동, 순흥빌딩)
전자메일   help@ltinc.net

이 도서는 대한민국에서 제작되었습니다.

ISBN   979-11-91343-97-7   14740